NATURAL
CAT CARE

NATURAL CAT CARE

DR. BRUCE FOGLE

DORLING KINDERSLEY
LONDON · NEW YORK · SYDNEY · MOSCOW
www.dk.com

A DORLING KINDERSLEY BOOK
www.dk.com

Project Editor TRACIE LEE DAVIS
Art Editor ANNA BENJAMIN
Managing Editor FRANCIS RITTER
Managing Art Editor DEREK COOMBES
DTP Designer SONIA CHARBONNIER
Picture Researcher ANGELA ANDERSON
Production GAVIN BRADSHAW, WENDY PENN

First published in Great Britain in 1999
by Dorling Kindersley Limited,
9 Henrietta Street, London WC2E 8PS

2 4 6 8 10 9 7 5 3 1

A CIP catalogue record for this book
is available from the British Library.

ISBN 0-7513-0611-8

Reproduced by Bright Arts, Hong Kong
Printed and bound in China by
L. Rex Printing Co., Ltd

CONTENTS

INTRODUCTION

WHILE TECHNOLOGICAL ADVANCES in cat care accelerate faster than ever before and cats are consequently living longer, in Europe, North America, and Australasia interest in "natural" forms of cat care paradoxically has never been greater. Cat owners are concerned about the side effects caused by some forms of modern veterinary medicine. As they learn more about complementary health care for themselves, they question whether less invasive therapies might also be applied to their cats.

LIFE-STYLE CHANGES

The combination of the cat becoming an indoor companion and the success of modern veterinary medicine has reduced accidents, almost eliminated some parasitic and infectious diseases, and created remedies for conditions that in the past were untreatable. At the same time, we have unwittingly created new feline health problems, some so unique that in its evolution the cat has developed no natural defences to control them.

BREEDING FOR THE FUTURE
We have only intervened in cat breeding relatively recently, and their conformation remains virtually perfect. Creating hairless breeds such as this Sphynx threatens their genetic integrity.

CONVENTIONAL vs. COMPLEMENTARY

As pet owners pursue more personalized approaches to their own well-being, there is a rapidly maturing interest and understanding of complementary forms of therapy, treatments that attempt to stimulate the body's self-healing and self-regulating mechanisms. Conventional and complementary forms of veterinary medicine have the same objective, to enhance a cat's ability to heal itself, but traditionally the two approaches have been different. Conventional or orthodox vets tends to treat a specific problem, while complementary vets consider illness to be a disruption of physical and mental well-being and will often treat the whole body rather than target a specific part of it.

AN OPEN MIND

In this book I have used American veterinarian Carvel Tiekert's definition of medicine. He says it is "anything that works". In human medicine, the placebo effect, improvements induced by non-physical means, is a potent component of natural repair. About 40 per cent of patients respond to any new form of therapy, regardless of what it is. Drs Brenda Bonnett and Carol Poland at the Ontario Veterinary College, University of Guelph, in Canada, in a study of different treatments for canine arthritis, observed that around 40 per cent of veterinarians

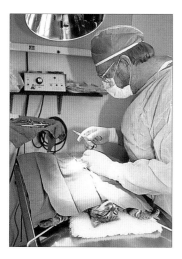

CONVENTIONAL
SUCCESS
Sophisticated medical procedures save the lives of countless cats. Use these facilities to create the best circumstances for your cat's body to repair itself. Always consider the quality of your pet's life when deciding what therapy is best.

and dog owners felt their dogs improved on placebo capsules containing wheat and rice flour that they believed to be painkillers. The dog owners and the vets wanted the new treatments to work. We should bear this in mind when considering the value of any complementary therapy for our cats.

CHANGING ATTITUDES TO MEDICINE

Fifty years ago, we thought that wonder drugs would answer all health problems, and new medicines have indeed saved the lives of countless cats. However, we now know of the problems of side effects, growing resistance to antibiotics, and, regrettably, that in trying to prevent one problem, we may unwittingly increase the risk of another. Informed cat owners shrewdly want to use the advanced technologies to control diseases and to provide critical care and surgery.

COMPLEMENTARY THERAPIES
Eliminating as many stresses as possible helps your cat's body to repair itself. Only use therapies that your cat accepts without fear or anxiety.

Simultaneously, the same people question the indiscriminate application of modern medicine, especially for chronic conditions. "What are the alternatives?" is just about the most common question that cat owners ask me.

HOW TO USE THIS BOOK

In this book I'll discuss alternative therapies, but before making any decisions about how your cat should be treated, remember, a cat is a cat. It is not a furry person. What works for a highly sociable species like us (or dogs) may not be appropriate for your cat. For any therapy ask, "Will this stress my cat? Does it work? Is it safe?" Don't use alternatives just because they fit your personal or spiritual values. Do what is in your cat's genuine best interest. Understand the nature of illness and how your cat responds to it. Help your pet to avoid illness and be in the best condition to confront it when it occurs. The cat's inherent capacity for self-repair is awesome. Use the best of all forms of medicine to enhance the cat's own natural healing.

NATURAL DEVELOPMENT

Cats often seem mysterious to us because they are, in
many ways, so different to other "domesticated"
species. The cat is essentially an independent, self-
domesticated animal. Its African ancestors chose to live
close to human habitation, and our ancestors
discovered that early handling produced cats that were
content to live among us.

Like us, the cat retains a lifelong enjoyment of playful
activities and with our help it can live into old age,
reaching its maximum genetic life potential. To care for
a cat as naturally as possible, it is important to
understand its emotional as well as physical needs.

The Scottish wildcat is strikingly similar to the domestic cat but is only a distant relative.

EARLY CAT DEVELOPMENT

NATURAL DEVELOPMENT

NATURAL TRAINING

NATURAL NUTRITION

NATURAL HEALTH CARE

HEALTH DISORDERS

UNTIL VERY RECENTLY, the domestic cat was valued primarily for its abilities as a vermin exterminator. Today, in North America and many regions of Europe, the cat is our most popular pet. We intervene in its breeding, choosing for shape, colour, and temperament, but so long as we understand its needs and do not undo what nature has done so well, this African emigrant has a bright future.

THE NUCLEAR FAMILY
To be relaxed and at ease with people as an adult, a kitten must spend part of each day with humans from roughly the third to the eighth week of life. Experience of other animals at this early age reduces naturally fearful behaviour towards them.

NATURAL SELF-INTEREST

Although we consider today's pet cat as a domesticated animal, its evolution from wild feline to family companion is closer to that of the mouse and rat than to the dog or any other "domesticated" species. Cats chose to live near to humans for the same reasons that rodents did. Our lifestyle created rich pickings for them, an ideal environment for food, shelter, and security. While all other domesticated species are, like us, sociable by nature, the cat walks alone, thinking primarily of itself and its own comforts. Curiously, it is the cat's solitary nature and preoccupation with self that makes it such an attractive, but also misunderstood, species.

AFRICAN ORIGINS

The African wildcat is the most recent major species to have chosen to live in close proximity to humans. Between the Tigris and Euphrates rivers, in what is now Iraq, but also in Egypt, permanent human settlements and their associated granaries and silos attracted large concentrations of rodents. Two species of small, wild cats lived in these arid regions, the inaptly named jungle cat, *Felis chaus*, which lived near rivers, and the African wildcat, *Felis silvestris lybica*, a small but successful local predator. With a less fearful nature than other feline species, and perhaps favoured by a minor genetic mutation augmenting this natural inclination, the African wildcat followed its prey into human settlements. There it found a ready resource of food and ample security from larger predators. This hunter not only killed rodents, it was equally proficient at killing snakes, two good reasons for people to encourage this attractive intruder to live with them.

A NEW ALLIANCE

In the cat's new environment subtle human pressures dictated survival. The innate beauty of the cat was as obvious to our ancestors 6,000 years ago as it is to us today. Placidity was also a benefit, and people soon discovered that if kittens were exposed to people at an early age they looked upon people as mother-substitutes and care-givers. The sensuous beauty of the cat – nocturnal, quiet, fecund, self-sufficient – invited myth and legend. In Egypt, cats were worshipped as messengers of the gods.

Trade in cats developed, and the African wildcat arrived in Europe. The cats that spread from Europe to the Americas and Australasia were the descendants of the African wildcat.

Like us, the African wildcat has been successful in populating even the remotest parts of the world. Only the high Arctic, Antarctica, and some small islands have not been colonized by its descendants.

THE MATRIARCHAL SOCIETY

From its home in North Africa, the lone hunter spread into mainland Asia, reaching all major islands such as Java and Japan by AD 600. In its new circumstances as a traded commodity, unique pressures came to bear on natural selection. Cats that accepted others of their own kind were more likely to survive transport to new parts of the world. This revealed a previously unknown genetic potential. When food was abundant and a cat did not have to defend a large hunting territory, it had the potential to form a matriarchal society of blood-related females, a cat colony content to live together, to feed together, even to care for one another's young.

CHANGING COATS

Once cats started living near people, coat colours began to depart from their African origins. In the cat's new circumstances, its coat, which was its natural camouflage, was no longer a life-saving asset. Other natural colours, black being the first, had far greater survival possibilities in this new niche.

Although all coat colours that are found today potentially exist in nature, it is only with the development of selective breeding that coats have diversified from the original stripes. As cats migrated to the colder north, coats became denser, sometimes longer, and more vividly coloured. Cats that migrated south to the warmth of tropical Asia developed shorter, sparser coats in muted shades.

FILLING A VOID

Prior to the domestic cat arriving in Europe, indigenous small carnivores such as weasels were used as natural vermin killers. When cats first arrived in Greece they were called *gale*, the Greek word for polecats, while in the Roman world, the cat was called *felis*, a Latin word used to describe yellowish-coated carnivores, including weasels. Eventually *felis* came to be used only to describe the domestic cat, and its wild relatives. Today *Felis domesticus*, the domestic cat, is the world's most successful natural rodent killer.

NEAR YET FAR
Although in looks, size, and hunting habits, the European wildcat (Felis silvestris) is very similar to the domestic cat, its temperament is different in one dramatic detail. Virtually all attempts to tame this cat have failed. It retains an inherent fear of people.

PHYSICAL PERFECTION

Unlike virtually all other domesticated species, especially the dog, that have diverged from their wild roots, the cat has remained true to its origins throughout its evolution as a domesticated species. Although its size has changed slightly and, in common with other domesticated animals, its brain size is almost one third smaller than that of its wild cousins, the pet cat looks almost identical to its wild African forbears. The cat remains physically perfect. Both as a lone hunter and as a strikingly beautiful resident in our homes, the cat, as it evolved in nature, cannot be improved upon.

There is, however, a cloud in this picture. When I began in clinical practice, genetic disesases that were common in dogs, such as hip dysplasia, progressive retinal atrophy, and heart disease, were unheard of in cats. This is no longer the case: I now diagnose these genetic diseases in breeds of cat, too. Selective breeding of cats for a certain coat colour or texture, carried out within a small population, increases the risk, and the incidence, of inherited medical problems. We must be careful and responsible, and guard against doing to the cat what we have unfortunately done to the dog.

GENETIC DEVELOPMENT

Recent advances in our understanding of the genetic make-up of cats mean that, by splicing specific genes in and out, we can finely tune looks and even behaviour. While ethical controls will hopefully exist for human genetic manipulation, similar controls are equally necessary in feline genetics.

NATURAL DEVELOPMENT

NATURAL TRAINING

NATURAL NUTRITION

NATURAL HEALTH CARE

HEALTH DISORDERS

MATING, PREGNANCY, AND BIRTH

THE CAT HAS A UNIQUE FORM of reproduction that evolved to suit the needs of an independent hunter. Like most other species, the male is always ready to mate, but females only release their eggs after mating, an efficient method for avoiding waste of genetic material. Females come into season more frequently as daylight increases, giving birth at the time of year when food is most abundant.

IN SEASON

When a female cat comes into season she makes caterwauling noises and will claw forwards on the ground or carpet while dragging her slightly raised hindquarters. Owners are often concerned that their cat is in acute pain or discomfort. She is not. It is simply her natural way of displaying that she is in season.

CHOOSING A MATE

For most of the cat's evolutionary history it was a lone hunter in the arid regions of North Africa. After leaving its litter the only time it came into contact with other cats was in disputes over territory, or to mate. Social species such as humans or dogs always have potential mates available. In these circumstances females can afford to manufacture eggs, release them, then choose a mate to fertilize them. But in the isolated circumstances of the cat's development a different scheme evolved. Cats are induced to ovulate by the physical act of mating. Eggs are released after the female has successfully mated, usually several times.

Like other animals, the female cat leaves scent markers in her urine as odour clues to her fertility. When she comes into season she also uses her voice, uttering a guttural noise that carries a great distance, signalling males of her receptivity. The approaching

VACCINATIONS DURING PREGNANCY

Kittens inherit protection against infectious diseases in the first breast milk they consume after birth. The higher the mother's level of protective antibodies, the greater the level of inherited protection, which usually lasts from six to 20 weeks. Never vaccinate pregnant cats to increase this level of inherited protection. They should be vaccinated before they are pregnant. Live panleucopenia (enteritis) vaccine can damage the developing brain of kittens in the womb.

Never vaccinate other cats in the household of a pregnant female. Vaccine virus can be shed by vaccinated cats and affect the pregnant individual.

THE VALUE OF MANY FATHERS

In the more sociable circumstances of the modern domestic cat, a variation in mating rituals has evolved. Females are serially mated by several males who seldom fight with each other but, at least to the human eye, seem to patiently sit and wait their turn. Unplanned breeding of pedigree females by

"It is not unusual for cats to take their kittens from the whelping box provided by the owner to a secluded den such as a closet."

male behaves in a circumspect manner and only after she approaches him does he mount her. At the same time, he grasps her neck with his teeth to prevent her from turning and biting. Although courtship may last hours, mating itself is over in seconds. As the male withdraws from the female, barbs on his penis stimulate the lining of her vagina, inducing hormonal changes that lead to her releasing eggs to be fertilized.

both pedigree and non-pedigree males can produce mixed litters of pure-bred and cross-bred kittens from both sires. There are logical, evolutionary reasons for the mother to mate with several sires. The genetic variability of her offspring is potentially increased, and the possibility of several fathers also reduces the risk of infanticide, which occurs in other branches of the cat family such as the lion.

NATURAL BIRTH

As birth approaches, the female retires to her secluded birthing den, where she gives birth quietly and efficiently. Often, within two days of birth, she moves her litter to a new den free from the odours of birth that may attract predators. In the home environment it is not unusual for cats to take their kittens from the whelping box provided by the owner to a secluded den such as a closet or behind heavy curtains or furniture. It is natural for the mother to eat the placenta and to consume all the kittens' urine and faeces. This is her way of hiding evidence that defenceless kittens have arrived.

QUIET BIRTH
The cat's small size puts it at risk from predators, so during birth the mother remains quiet. Afterwards, she consumes all evidence of the birth.

AN ACTIVE PREGNANCY
The female remains physically active throughout her pregnancy, which lasts two months. Only after a month does she show the first evidence of pregnancy, an increasing vividness to the colour of her nipples. Weight gain becomes evident soon after.

HOW YOU CAN HELP

In the wild, cats seldom reach puberty until they are over one year old. In these natural circumstances puberty coincides with emotional maturity. In the security of our homes, where food is always available, puberty occurs at an earlier age, usually by seven months. Some breeds, such as the Siamese, are sexually precocious, reaching puberty as early as four months of age, before their adult teeth have fully developed. At this age they are physically capable of mating, but you should not let them do so. They make poor mothers and create lines of poor mothers.

Nature and nurture are equally important to good motherhood. Most cats have natural common sense and will reduce their physical activity when they feel the need to. You can help your cat by making sure it has no unnecessary drugs throughout pregnancy but especially during the first trimester when major development is occurring in the foetuses. Do not give herbal tonics designed for human use – they can be toxic to cats. Provide nourishing food (*see pages 42-43*), and, most importantly, when your cat is pregnant do not fuss over it. Its natural inclination is simply to get on with life, and that includes independently giving birth and caring for the newborn kittens.

Dr Eugenia Natoli at the University of Catania in Italy was the first biologist to report how several mother cats raise their kittens together, sharing the responsibilities of feeding, washing, protecting, and playing with the young. This is an evolving social behaviour in cats and is at the root of why a female may let you help, both at birth and later. A dependent cat looks upon you as "mother". You feed it, comfort it, and offer security. Under these circumstances, most modern domestic cats willingly allow you, as "mother", to care for her litter too.

CHECKLIST

- Do not even think of breeding from your cat unless you know you can find homes for the resulting litter.

- Ensure your breeding female has emotional as well as physical maturity.

- Coming into season is "natural" but not for a female that spends her life indoors, unable to induce ovulation by mating.

- Good nourishment is necessary for the development of kittens. Offer a balanced diet to the mother while she is pregnant and during her period of milk production.

- Feral toms are excellent breeders but are the likeliest carriers of feline immunodeficiency virus (FIV) and feline leukemia virus (FeLV).

NATURAL DEVELOPMENT

NATURAL TRAINING

NATURAL NUTRITION

NATURAL HEALTH CARE

HEALTH DISORDERS

14

EARLY LEARNING

A KITTEN FIRST LEARNS to live within the social structure of its litter. When food is scarce, that structure breaks down and by 20 weeks of age the litter disperses. If food is plentiful, kittens continue to live in harmony with mother and siblings. Social learning is concentrated before seven weeks of age, so routine contact with people before that time is essential for a future harmonious life with us.

NOURISHMENT AND LEARNING

A well-balanced diet is important both for the mother and her kittens to ensure proper early learning as well as physical development. Poorly fed mothers produce kittens that are slower to learn to crawl, suck, walk, run, play, and climb. Kittens of undernourished mothers have a tendency to become poor mothers themselves, producing kittens with learning deficits and emotional abnormalities.

THE EARLY ENVIRONMENT

It is surprising how influential the womb environment is to the emotional and physical development of kittens. Studies of other animals, especially rats, suggest that if a mother is stressed during pregnancy, her young are likely to have a more fearful nature, to have reduced learning ability, and suffer from extremes of behaviour.

Despite living in the social structure of the litter, from the beginning of its emotional development a kitten will think first and foremost of itself. In the 1970s, American behaviourist Jay Rosenblatt showed that by the third day of life, 80 per cent of kittens developed a preference for a single nipple position. If one of the 20 per cent without teat preference latched on to that nipple, the "owner" pushed it aside. This is the start of the cat's magnificent self-sufficiency.

NATURAL BRAIN DEVELOPMENT

The cat's brain is already well developed at birth and continues to develop at an astonishing rate for the next three months. When it is born, a kitten is only three per cent of its adult weight, yet its brain is already 20 per cent of adult weight.

MATERNAL CARE
The mother provides food, warmth, and security for her kittens. Later in life, a mature cat looks upon us as a mother-substitute. We provide protection, shelter, and a constant supply of food upon demand.

LEARNING PERSONAL HYGIENE

One of the reasons why cats have become more popular pets than dogs in recent years may be because of their fastidious natural cleanliness. Kittens are well equipped from an early age to clean themselves. This behaviour is not learned but is already "hard-wired" into the kitten's brain. From approximately three weeks of age, kittens start to take over personal hygiene from their mothers. Barbed tongues are ideal for coat cleaning, while face washing follows a stereotypical pattern of applying saliva to the forepaw then rubbing it over the head. In the same way that we might scratch our heads when indecisive, cats will often revert to natural grooming when they are puzzled or frightened.

At Temple University in Philadelphia, Pennsylvania in the early 1980s, Dr Eileen Karsh showed that early and routine handling, from three to seven weeks of age, produced adult cats that head- and flank-rubbed, chirped, and purred when human visitors approached. Routine handling also helps kittens grow faster and possibly bigger. If social contact with people does not begin until after seven weeks, kittens develop into more withdrawn adults. Equally important, Karsh showed that calm mothers, at ease with people, teach their kittens to be equally at ease in the presence of such potentially intimidating predators as we are.

SOCIAL TIMING

Until recently, early learning was divided into "critical periods", important timeslots in the emotional development of kittens. Kittens develop their social manners between three and seven weeks of age. If, during this time, a kitten frequently meets a member of another species, whether it is a dog, rat, horse, or human, it will develop a social rapport with that species and not look upon it as predator or prey. That is at the very heart of a contented relationship with cats. If a cat does not learn, at this early stage in life, how to live in harmony with us or other animals, natural fears are likely to develop.

However, while it is certainly true that the period between three and seven weeks is critical for a cat's social development, a new study by John Bradshaw at Southampton University in England has shown that, if the conditions are right, some cats over seven weeks old can still be conditioned to live harmoniously and fearlessly with us. It is likely to be difficult, but some older cats do retain the ability to learn new social lessons.

RELATIONSHIPS WITH US

If you want a kitten to mature into a cat that is relaxed in our society, the last thing to do is leave it to nature. If you let the mother raise her litter on her own, the kittens do not learn to control their natural fear of large animals. Some people feel that by involving ourselves in the cat's natural life we are interfering with nature. This simply is not true. We enhance a cat's life by understanding the importance of early learning and ensuring it is socialized to the environment it will live in during its adult life.

HOW KITTENS LEARN

Kittens learn by watching what mother and littermates do, by trial and error experience, and, important to a good relationship with us, through training. Between three and 10 weeks of age a kitten will learn reasonably well by observing mother, but trial and error experience is at the root of its mental development. A kitten's natural inquisitiveness is profound early in life and this is when it learns what tastes good, what bites back, what is dangerous, and what is fun.

At this young age, cats are also receptive to training. I used food, a natural reward, to train my kitten Millie to miaow when she heard her name and to come on command (*see pages 32-34*). Another natural reward is touch, but this is only useful for dependent cats. If, through early learning, your kitten comes to depend upon you for security, food, and warmth, it will probably, for its lifetime, think of you as its "mother". It will enjoy contact with you as it enjoyed the comfort of grooming by its real mother. Touch becomes a powerful reward in this case, although it can also lead to curious emotional conflicts, so-called "petting-aggression". Our "mother" role is the essence of the social relationship we have with cats. Individuals that are independent – because they have been socialized later in life, or because their mothers taught them fearful behaviour – will have a more restricted relationship with you. These cats will consider you simply as a useful resource.

CHECKLIST

- Kittens benefit from being raised by a mother that is emotionally competent. Never breed from young females who have not reached emotional maturity.

- Allow kittens to continue to suckle to 12 weeks of age, for proper social development.

- Handle kittens frequently, especially from three to seven weeks of age, and expose them to mild sensory stimulation.

- Think of how the kitten will live as an adult. Introduce different species early in life.

- Do not be surprised if your cat occasionally lashes out while you pet it. This response is known as "petting-aggression". Touch is a natural part of dependency but unnatural in the evolution of an adult lone hunter.

HARMONIOUS LIVING
If you routinely introduce a kitten to another species during its socializing period between three and seven weeks of age, it accepts that species as non-threatening, or non-edible.

NATURAL DEVELOPMENT

NATURAL TRAINING

NATURAL NUTRITION

NATURAL HEALTH CARE

HEALTH DISORDERS

NATURAL PLAY

THE WAY CATS PLAY is changing. Unlike dogs, they are not naturally playful as adults. Historically, cats went through an early play period then settled down to the serious business of capturing prey. Today, as a result of altered early experience and selective breeding, most cats maintain a lifelong interest in play. This inclination has blossomed under the unique circumstances of living with us.

SHAPING NATURAL PLAY ACTIVITIES

Play activities that kittens feel are perfectly natural, like pouncing and biting, most of us find quite unacceptable when applied to us. Intervene constructively. Channel your kitten's need to play into creative activities. If you already have a cat, do not let a new kitten jump on it playfully. Your resident will simply hate it. Introduce your mature cat to the new kitten while the newcomer is fast asleep. Let the older cat set the tone of their meetings. Play may develop but control the situation so that it evolves at the right pace.

CHECKLIST

Play is essential for natural development:

- It stimulates physical dexterity and mental flexibility.
- It improves co-ordination.
- It permits experimentation under safe conditions.
- It teaches problem solving.
- It teaches a kitten how to carry out sequences of events.
- It can become a lifelong activity in cats.

EARLY PLAYFUL ACTIVITY

Kittens start to play with each other and with objects at about three weeks of age, when their senses and co-ordination are on the way to full development, which is reached by 12 weeks. Play begins when kittens make flamboyant rushes at each other. By four weeks of age, kittens are wrestling, grasping with the forepaws, and kicking vigorously with the hindlegs. By five weeks the pounce has been perfected, and by six weeks littermates are leaping and chasing each other with incredible dexterity. Kitten play is naturally very rough, so much so that some owners are concerned about the severity of the kittens' activity.

SOCIAL PLAY

Kittens play in two different ways — with other cats and with other things. Playing with objects exercises what will become a cat's hunting skills, while social play with littermates, with mother, or with other members of the cat colony teaches social graces. Some of the manoeuvres that are used in social play are also used in object play. Social play between kittens includes sparring, hugging, licking, or simply and quite endearingly lying belly-up waiting for something to happen. Social play begins to increase during the kittens' sixth week, when mother becomes less tolerant and starts to reduce her time with her litter. A mother swats and growls at her kittens if their play annoys her. Other adult cats rarely show similar anger when kittens play with them. Increased social play among kittens at this time has a natural logic. As the mother

spends more time away from the nest, social play acts like glue, keeping the litter together until the mother's return.

Social play continues until about 14 weeks of age, while the kittens are maturing. At this age, it enters a natural decline. Play evolves into stand-offs. Play between female kittens continues a little longer but females become less tolerant of males. By 18 weeks of age, social play between male and female siblings occurs at 10 per cent of its previous level. Play between males becomes even more rare, and social relationships naturally begin to disintegrate, a necessary stage for the dispersal of the litter.

OBJECT PLAY

Playing with objects also begins at about three weeks of age. Some play manoeuvres — activities such as leaps and pounces — are similar to those used in social play. Other play actions are used only with objects, movements such as pats, bats, pokes, scoops, and tosses. Kittens also grasp, mouth, and chew objects. All of these play activities appear to be geared towards a kitten learning to be a proficient hunter. However, repeated experiments have shown that neither the quantity nor quality of object play is related to hunting proficiency later in life. Playful activity certainly teaches kittens about their environment. Hunting, it seems, has to be learned from mother.

NATURAL DEVELOPMENT

NATURAL TRAINING

NATURAL NUTRITION

NATURAL HEALTH CARE

HEALTH DISORDERS

ENHANCING
NATURAL PLAY
We can control and direct natural play activity constructively by providing kittens with toys that are practical and exciting. Simple "fishing lines" stimulate batting, poking, and grasping activities, which are used in the wild to catch insects and birds.

EDUCATIONAL PLAY

Active play is good schooling. Play with other members of the litter creates social bonds that under the right circumstances may become permanent. Under genetic and hormonal influences, male play activity becomes fiercer and fiercer, leading to the decline and often the end of play activity between the sexes. This natural conclusion can be avoided through neutering early, before sexual maturity. Under these circumstances, the neutered male's play activity is very similar to the neutered female's play activity. Male individuals are likely to continue playing with each other well into adulthood with the same intensity and frequency that two adult female siblings naturally play with each other.

During play, kittens learn manual dexterity by grasping with their forepaws. They also learn naturally how to inhibit their biting and how to play with sheathed claws in order to control these sharp weapons. If, for example, a kitten bites or claws its mother too hard, she reprimands it by nipping back. If the kitten claws or bites a littermate too severely and hurts it, the hurt kitten bites back or squeals in pain and stops playing. In these natural ways kittens learn the limits of what is permissible.

LESSONS AND PLAY

Both sociable play and playing with objects naturally decline but do not disappear completely. You can entice a cat of almost any age to play. Kittens that continue to live together into adulthood continue social play. This could be "neoteny", the perpetuation of juvenile characteristics into adulthood, or it could be a natural way in which cats in social groups continue to "bond" with each other. In the absence of another cat, cats treat us as cat substitutes and carry out their playful leaps and pounces on us, or our dogs.

In normal play, sexual, predatory, and aggressive behaviours occur out of context. Of these activities, the kitten's predatory play is most sophisticated and consists of three hunting manoeuvres; the "mouse pounce", the "bird swat", and the "fish scoop". Small items and rustling sounds provoke the mouse pounce. Light items dangled from string induce bird swats, and table tennis balls are ideal for kittens to fish scoop. These toys teach mental and physical dexterity, and improve the kitten's co-ordination. They can also stimulate play activities in your adult cat.

LACK OF
PLAYMATES
Kittens need both social and object play activities. In the absence of other animals, a kitten may develop the habit of stalking your ankles, carrying out glorious hit-and-run attacks. In the absence of objects to play with, cats find climbing curtains and walking on mantelpieces delightful alternatives (*see page 32*).

SLEEPING PATTERNS
Kittens play actively then settle into sleep, huddling together for warmth and security. Female siblings raised together are more likely to continue this behaviour into adulthood than males or male/female groups. Independent individuals almost always sleep alone.

NATURAL GROOMING

CATS ARE MAGNIFICENT natural groomers, typically spending from eight to 15 per cent of their waking hours tidying themselves. This is water-wasteful; by grooming so much, cats lose as much moisture per day through saliva as they lose in urine. However, the advantage of constant grooming is profound. It not only cleans the skin but also makes the cat a more successful predator.

CHECKLIST

The following suggestions will help you to overcome your cat's natural reluctance to be groomed by you.

- Start young. Introduce grooming to a kitten while it is still with its mother.

- Be brief. Start with short sessions, working up to longer sessions.

- Learn the limits. Watch your cat's body language. Tail-lashing means your cat has had enough.

- Reward your cat. Give rewards for good behaviour. They are well deserved.

MORE THAN CLEAN SKIN

The cat may appear to be a fastidious eater, but killing and eating small mammals is a messy business. Fur becomes contaminated with debris from the last meal. If it is left unattended, this leads to smells that draw unwelcome attention from predators, but efficient grooming removes dirt and smell from a cat's coat. Grooming also regulates body temperature. When properly maintained, there is an insulating layer of air in the cat's coat that protects it from overheating and, on very hot days, the evaporation of saliva left by licking has a cooling effect on the body.

PARASITE CONTROL

In clinical practice, I see fewer cats with bacterial skin problems than dogs. This apparent natural resistance to skin infections may be because grooming removes bacteria or because saliva actively prevents bacterial growth. Whatever the reason, grooming is necessary for healthy skin condition.

However, I see more cats than dogs with fleas. Cats seem either less able to control fleas or are more attractive to them. In many parts of the world, including where I practise, dog fleas (*Ctenocephalides canis*) are rare. When dogs have fleas they have cat fleas (*Ctenocephalides felis*), so it may be that cats appear to be more troubled by fleas simply because fleas prefer them. Dr Bob Eckstein in North Carolina investigated the efficiency of grooming on cat flea populations, simply by preventing cats from grooming themselves for three weeks by making them wear cone-shaped "Elizabethan" collars. Self-grooming certainly helps. Cats wearing Elizabethan collars had twice as many fleas as those that wore normal collars.

GOOD LICKS
Licking is both cleansing and relaxing. Cats sweat only through the pads of their feet, so licking is another way to rid the body of excess liquid.

FIRST LICKS

Grooming is an instinctive behaviour in cats. They do not need to watch their mothers to learn how to groom. By six weeks of age, kittens groom themselves as proficiently as adult cats. Grooming follows a set ritual. It begins with the head, proceeds along the back and sides, and ends at the base of the tail. Thorough bathing extends over the anogenital region, across the belly, down the legs, and between the toes of the feet. Cats are ambidextrous, using both forepaws with equal efficiency to wash both sides of the face and neck. Dr Eckstein found that grooming appears to be controlled by a biological clock. A certain amount of grooming is necessary each day. Cats unable to groom for three days spent the first 12 hours afterwards catching up on missed grooming.

GROOMING EACH OTHER

Mother is responsible for all of a kitten's grooming needs for the first weeks of life and, under the right circumstances, this can evolve into mutual grooming. This behaviour occurs almost entirely between related females that live together in a matriarchal colony, mother and her own descendants or her sister's descendants. Unrelated cats that grow up from kittenhood in the same household and have socially bonded with each other may also continue to groom each

other into adult life. Cats permit us to groom and stroke them because we are, in essence, mother substitutes. Some cats lick and "groom" their owners; this is not grooming but rather a comforting behaviour akin to suckling. Often, these cats were taken from their mothers before 12 weeks of age, when comfort suckling ends. In these unnatural circumstances, a cat treads with its paws on its owner (to stimulate milk release), then licks away for as long as its owner will allow.

HAIR LENGTH AND HAIRBALLS

The cat's tongue is the best cleaning device for cats with short coats, but long-haired cats need our help. Hair adheres to the barbs on the tongue and is swallowed. When a long-haired cat moults, the swallowed hair forms a ball in its stomach. Cats usually regurgitate hairballs, but occasionally one enters the intestines and causes a blockage. Laxatives are necessary to expel them (*see page 135*). Quite simply, long-haired cats cannot groom themselves properly. Use a wide-toothed comb and a bristle brush twice weekly to remove dead hair and prevent mats from forming.

GROOMING PROBLEMS

Efficient grooming is a natural sign of good mental and physical health. If a cat stops grooming itself, that is a powerful sign that something is wrong physically. If this happens, contact your vet. Your cat may be hiding a significant medical problem. Conversely, excess grooming can be a sign of emotional rather than physical problems. Cats will certainly groom excessively because of skin wounds, infections, or parasites, but they will also groom in excess when anxious. This is a "displacement" behaviour, somewhat similar to our twisting our hair or pulling our ear lobes when we are anxious or tense.

BATHING A CAT

Dry shampoos are available and mimic natural dust baths, but occasionally (for example, when toxic matter has got on to the cat's coat) a wet bath is inevitable. Give your cat something like a rope to grasp with its forepaws while you wash it. This gives it a greater sense of security and protects you while you carry out this unwelcome activity.

PRODUCTIVE NIBBLES
Nibbling relieves itches and removes irritants from the coat. Cats also nibble their nails, as well as use scratching posts, to keep them sharp.

NATURAL DEVELOPMENT

NATURAL TRAINING

NATURAL NUTRITION

NATURAL HEALTH CARE

HEALTH DISORDERS

NATURAL AGEING

ONE OF BIOLOGY'S GREAT PUZZLES is why animals age. One answer could be that early in evolution, because most creatures died from violence or disease before the ageing process developed, the genes responsible for ageing were not weeded out by natural selection. Whatever the reason, more cats reach their genetic potential than ever before – becoming geriatrics, with all the associated needs.

CHECKLIST

- Feed smaller meals more frequently.
- Provide a litter tray on each floor for easy access.
- Keep your eye on your cat's weight. It will be healthier if it keeps trim.
- Provide warmth and comfort for sleeping and resting.
- Change the diet according to your cat's medical needs.
- Offer mental stimulation with toys and activities.
- Gently groom as often as possible. It helps blood circulation in the skin.

A NEW PHENOMENON

In the competitive wild, a cat's life expectancy depends upon finding food and avoiding injury, illness, or predators. In the benign circumstances of living with us there are, with the exception of automobile accidents and the infectious diseases that have increased because of cat crowding, fewer threats to life (*see pages 108-109*). As a consequence, for the first time in their evolutionary history, cats are naturally living very long lives, well over twice as long as cats in the wild. Evolution did not plan for this, which is why, for example, female cats do not have a menopause. Under natural circumstances most cats die young. In the "unnatural" security of our homes, unneutered elderly females continue to cycle, although their heat periods become more erratic and the incidence of womb infection in late life is very high (*see pages 142-143*).

NATURAL PHYSICAL CHANGES

Professor Jacob Mosier at Kansas State University studied the physical changes of ageing and found some of the most significant modifications in the brain. In its prime, a cat depends on swift mental and physical reflexes for survival. Messages travel along the nervous system at approximately 6,000 m (6,560 yds) per second. In the

elderly cat these messages slow down to about 1,300 m (1,420 yds) per second. Other changes also affect brain function. Blood vessels in the brain lose their elasticity; the brain's surrounding membrane, the meninges, becomes hard and brittle; and the lungs become less efficient. The brain does not receive as much oxygen and this affects memory and learning. At the same time tiny haemorrhages may occur in brain tissue. Elderly cats are prone to mild, and occasionally severe, strokes. A consequence is that elderly cats can become irritable when disturbed, and sometimes appear to "lose" their minds.

WHAT CONTROLS AGEING

Ageing is ultimately controlled by a genetic biological clock, located in the part of the brain called the hypothalamus, which in turn controls the body's hormone system. Some breeds, such as the Siamese, have ageing clocks set to last longer than others. Professor Ben Hart at the University of California has studied behaviour changes due to ageing. He found that cats experience similar changes to those we go through, including the changes that in humans are called senile dementia. He found that loss of brain function was natural in most 16-year-old cats. Signs of old age involve increased irritability, increased hissing and spitting, sleeping changes, loss of litter-box hygiene, and disorientation.

NATURAL AGEING VERSUS ILLNESS

With natural ageing, cats slow down. In the absence of good mental stimulation, the elderly cat becomes dull and lethargic. Its appetite may change. These changes also occur when a cat is not well, so it is important to differentiate between natural ageing changes and illness. Conversely, if a cat develops an overactive thyroid, it becomes more active and has more energy (*see pages 150-151*). Don't assume that changes in your elderly cat's behaviour are just the changes of growing older. Any change is significant. Elderly cats benefit from twice-yearly medical examinations.

APPETITE CHANGES
As a cat grows older, food it previously enjoyed may lose its attraction. Changes in eating habits can also be a sign of illness and should be discussed with your vet.

NATURAL DEVELOPMENT

NATURAL TRAINING

NATURAL NUTRITION

NATURAL HEALTH CARE

HEALTH DISORDERS

NATURAL SIGNS OF AGEING

Professor Hart discovered that by 16 years of age, about 20 per cent of cats passed urine or faeces outside as well as inside the litter tray for no medical or acquired behavioural reason. Twenty-five per cent of cats this age change their sleep-wake cycles, sleeping more in the day but less at night, when they are more restless and demanding of their owners. A majority of cats this age, 60 per cent, were more irritable with their family, with strangers, even with the family dog, hissing or spitting with little or no provocation. Finally, over 70 per cent of 16-year-old cats become disoriented, forgetting how to use the cat flap, getting stuck in corners, or simply staring into space. Seemingly pointless and plaintive miaowing also increases.

At a hormonal level, elderly cats have more trouble turning off their stress response. Even when relaxed, elderly cats secrete more stress-related hormones. Technically, the ultimate cause of death is an excess of these hormones, called glucocorticoids. Training your cat to relax is extremely difficult but could control its stress response and, at least in theory, could prolong life (see page 98).

As ageing progresses, the chemical factory in the brain and nervous system produces fewer chemicals called neuroendocrines. Specifically, production of the brain chemical called dopamine drops. This is the brain's master chemical. If dopamine production can be maintained, a cat will probably live longer.

HOW TO INFLUENCE AGEING

You can actively slow down natural ageing by providing your cat with routine mental and gentle physical stimulation. Massaging your cat does more than help loosen up stiff joints. It improves the circulation of blood to all parts of the body (see pages 80-81). With natural ageing, the brain shrinks, until it is 25 per cent lighter than at maturity.

Excellent studies in the 1980s showed that with mental stimulation the brain can regain some of its lost weight. It does not produce more cells but instead the cells already there grow more connections with other cells. In its prime, each brain cell might have connections with 10,000 other brain cells. These are lost through natural ageing. With mental stimulation alone, a single brain cell might develop lost connections with up to 2,000 other cells. You may be able to alter the natural decay of memory by providing your cat with mental activities. Offer mental stimulation with appropriate toys. Touch and hand-feed when it is possible to do so. With the right genes and a stimulating environment, many cats have the capacity to survive for over two decades.

Another way to improve your cat's later years is to feed nourishing, healthy food. Until recently, veterinary nutritionists thought it was wise to reduce the protein level in diets for older cats, reducing the work of the kidneys. More recent evidence shows that, unless your cat has kidney problems, good quality protein probably helps the ageing process rather than hinders it. Feed your cat a well-balanced diet that contains the increased levels of vitamins and antioxidants that older cats naturally need (see pages 42-43). Finally, do not expect too much. Go with the flow, and respect the fact that your cat ages faster than you would like.

A NATURAL DIGNITY
Many cats, as they mature, prefer their own company. Do not force yourself on your cat. Remember, the culture it comes from is radically different from that of the dog. Pamper it if it wants, but also respect its desire to march to its own tune.

COMPARING CAT YEARS TO HUMAN YEARS

Until recently, one cat year was said to equal seven human years. This was based on the then natural life expectancy of cats and people of 10 and 70 years respectively. Today, life expectancy of both has increased, but much more for cats than people. A more accurate comparison today is one cat year for five human years.

NATURAL DEVELOPMENT

NATURAL TRAINING

NATURAL NUTRITION

NATURAL HEALTH CARE

HEALTH DISORDERS

NATURAL TRAINING

The cat is naturally independent but, through our intervention, it learns to rely upon us for the comforts of life, food, warmth, and protection. It looks upon its owner as a mother-substitute. When training your feline companion, try to think like a cat. Understand its inherent desire to hunt, mark its domain, and defend its territory from other cats.

The urban outdoors is fraught with dangers, especially traffic, but life indoors is tedious, driving some cats to create their own mental stimulation. Prevent behavioural problems by anticipating your cat's needs. Teach it how to cope with life with us.

Kittens have an insatiable curiosity and greatly benefit from toys and activity.

24

YOU AND YOUR CAT

THE CAT DID NOT EVOLVE over millions of years in order to live with us. Its origins were as a lone hunter. In that sense our modern relationship is "unnatural". However, evolutionary development has led the kitten to begin life dependent on its mother for food and security. Selective breeding perpetuates this juvenile dependency in cats, and is the basis of the relationship they have with us today.

SEEK TO UNDERSTAND

Do not be selfish in your relationship with your cat. Imposing what you feel is best may be in direct conflict with what your cat wants from life. Take special care when introducing another cat into your home. You might want your cat to have a feline companion, but it may be more content with a human one.

CHANGING RELATIONS

Scientists tell us that the cat's first relationship with us was "commensal" – it used us as a food and habitat source without adversely affecting our lives. Eventually this led to the cat's domestication, but even within this more intimate relationship the cat retained its independence. Historically, our relationship with the cat was practical or utilitarian. It found its own food and moved on when it chose to do so. Its relationship with us was that of the accidental helper, our best vermin exterminator. This changed radically in the latter part of this century. Today, we live with cats primarily for social

EMOTIONAL SUPPORT
Many cats seem to comfort their owners when they are not well. While some behaviourists say that the cat is simply seeking out a warm body, many cat owners believe that their cat is reciprocating the care it receives when it is not well.

and psychological reasons. We enjoy their company. We feel better when they are near us. And we grieve when they leave us. Over the past 20 years studies have revealed how and why cats make us feel this way.

Dr Warwick Anderson at Monash University, Australia, discovered that cat owners have less risk of heart disease than non-pet owners. Dr Ericka Friedmann in the United States observed that cat owners who did have a major heart attack were more likely to survive the following year than people who did not go home to pets. Dr Aaron Katcher at the University of Pennsylvania showed that when people stroke their cats, their own blood pressure drops. By the mid 1980s, the World Health Organization (WHO) reported that, "Companion animals that are properly cared for bring immense benefits to their owners and to society and are a danger to no one".

There have been fewer reports on how we affect the health of cats, but if you are a responsible owner, you act as your cat's mother, train it, protect it, and nurse it. You are its lifelong "care-giver". To be an effective care-giver, you need to understand the needs of your cat. If you do not, the relationship is strained and your cat is stressed. Excess stress throws the body out of equilibrium or balance (homeostasis). When homeostasis is affected, the risk of

BENEFICIAL CATS

Outwardly, our relationship with cats seems straightforward. We are the care-givers and they are the care-receivers. But in a subtle, even subliminal way, the relationship can be reversed. We become co-dependent upon each other. When you stroke your own cat, your body experiences the same positive physiological changes that occurred when you touched mother as an infant. This experience, together with the need to be needed, might explain why, when cats are introduced into nursing homes, residents become more animated, talk more, and want to share the satisfaction of touching and feeding the cat.

illness increases. Most types of complementary medicine recognize that you are an important element of your cat's physical and emotional balance. Physically, cats respond to excess stress in exactly the same way as we do. Their hormonal biofeedback system is overworked. Excess stress, including the stress of an unhealthy relationship, inhibits the immune system, leading to potential medical problems (*see pages 152-153*).

Enhancing Good Relations

Good relations vary considerably, according to how old your cat was when it was introduced to living with people. Cats raised with us from early kittenhood are likely to enjoy a dependent relationship in which you are mother.

Cats raised by their own mothers, in the absence of human contact, may not want an intimate association with humankind. These cats want the security of your home and the largesse of your kitchen but not necessarily your constant affection. Cats not socialized to people early in life may be friendly with one individual and may even accept touch from that person, but are likely to retain their independence. These cats are not usually suitable individuals for any physical complementary therapy.

If your cat thinks of you and your family as its family, emotional changes in your family can affect your cat's physical well-being. Family tension can lead to emotional conflict for the cat, a situation that on occasion can lead to apparent loss of toilet training or even to self-mutilation. There is now convincing evidence that medical problems such as bladder inflammation (cystitis), stomach irritation (gastritis), and itchy skin conditions (dermatitis) can be initiated by changes a cat experiences in its relationships with its human family.

Influences on a Cat's Emotions

Obvious changes in circumstances, like the introduction of a new dog, cat, or person into the family, radically alters relationships.

However, moving the furniture around can be enough to stress a cat, and even changing the brand of litter may alter its behaviour. Your cat depends upon a stable relationship with you for its own emotional well-being. Do not put a harness on a cat and take it outdoors just because you think it is natural for cats to visit the real world. Cats that have never been outdoors may find the experience overwhelmingly frightening. Never use a complementary therapy on your cat without first considering how it feels about what you are doing. The therapy may be more stressful than the problem you are trying to address. The best way to understand what is in your cat's interest is to try to think like a cat.

Checklist

- Avoid tension in your family relationships. Aim for stability.
- Recognize your cat's emotional limitations. Do not expect too much.
- Understand normal cat behaviour. Cats are superb at hiding signs of stress.
- Do not use your pet as an emotional crutch.
- Never neglect your cat's needs. Benign neglect is as harmful as active neglect.

At Risk

The modern environment is fraught with danger for our cats. Whether or not to let your cat outdoors is a difficult decision. Cats derive great enjoyment outdoors, but outdoor cats have a shorter life expectancy than indoor ones.

Natural Development

Natural Training

Natural Nutrition

Natural Health Care

Health Disorders

26

THINKING LIKE A CAT

CATS AND PEOPLE ARE VERY DIFFERENT, so thinking like your cat takes imagination. A cat's natural world is more three-dimensional than ours, and far less sociable. We are gregarious creatures that wither emotionally if denied companionship, but most cats are happy to be alone. Understanding your cat's needs, and its independent nature, will help you to train it successfully.

DISEASE RISKS
Kitten kindergarten (*see page 27*) is an ideal way to introduce cats to an array of new experiences. However, your cat risks exposure to infectious diseases, especially viral diseases such as FIV, FIP and FeLV. Discuss these risks with your vet. Risks vary from one locality to another, depending upon the incidence of infectious disease.

MEETING OTHER SPECIES
Kittens between three and seven weeks of age willingly play with their littermates but also with other kittens, cats, and other species. This is the best time to socialize kittens to dogs. If you have a dog, you should ask your cat breeder to introduce the kitten daily to his or her own dog. This will help ease the kitten's move into your home.

PAVLOV'S LESSONS
You might not realize it, but your cat will respond to training. Does it gallop into the kitchen when it hears the sound of a can opener or the rustle of the cat-food box? If it does, it has learned that a certain sound is usually followed by a reward, food. Early this century, the Russian physiologist Ivan Pavlov studied this behaviour in dogs and found that by pairing the sound of a bell with food he could train a dog to salivate when the bell rang. Pavlov's observations explained how a biological response like salivating can be stimulated, but they did not explain how an animal learns to perform a complex behaviour such as understanding to come to you when you call its name.

REWARDS AND DISCIPLINE
The American psychologist B.F. Skinner explained how, by using rewards, an animal is trained to perform a desired behaviour, such as coming when called. He defined rewards as positive reinforcement, and discipline as either negative reinforcement or punishment.

The two forms of discipline are subtly different. A negative reinforcer is something a cat finds mildly unpleasant but, as a result of its use, the cat does what you want. Someone grabbing your cat and bringing it to you is a negative reinforcer. Unfortunately, negative reinforcers are of little use in training your cat because, unlike dogs, cats have little desire to please.

The aim of training a cat is to prevent what we consider destructive behaviour, and to instill lessons that will ensure the cat's safety. Punishment, though harsh-sounding,

will achieve the required results, but it should never harm a cat. A punishment is used to stop a cat in the act of doing what it should not be doing. For instance, a squirt from a water pistol as your cat climbs the curtains is an excellent, mild punishment.

Cats respond to rewards and discipline because both are components of life in the natural world. Food is their main reward, which they gain after patiently stalking prey. Discipline is usually administered by their mother, either with a sound or a swipe of her paw. Early in life, kittens learn to interpret the meanings of different sounds, from the calming purr, through the demanding miaow, to the menacing hiss and spit. They have little difficulty learning to understand our sounds too, from rewarding murmurs to disciplinary shouts. If you associate a mild punishment such as a squirt of water with a firm "No!", eventually use of words alone will discipline your cat.

CAT TRANSPORT

It is simple to train your cat to enjoy the comforts of its travel basket because cats naturally enjoy the security of enclosed spaces. Leave the cat carrier open, in a warm place, and with an enticing food treat inside. Your cat will learn to retreat to it naturally and treat it as a personal den; and it will feel less frightened and insecure when you use the basket to take it to the vet's for its annual check-ups. Avoid using a body harness when taking your cat outdoors. A collar and lead are less threatening.

SOCIAL THINKING

Cats are not social creatures in the way that people and dogs are. In the wild they tend to live and hunt alone, although colonies of related females exist (*see page 11*). Littermates form relationships with each other early in life, but it is not natural for these individuals, in adulthood, to play willingly with unrelated cats. Cats do not naturally want to live with or play with other cats they have not met during the first two months of life, and it is unwise for us to expect them to do so. Instinctively, a cat thinks of an unrelated cat as an intruder on its territory and will want to expel it.

It is difficult not to apply our own social needs to the rest of our family members, including our cats. We are lonely without companionship and feel our cats suffer if they are denied feline social support. The ideal solution is to have two kittens from the same litter, but if you wish to integrate strange cats in your home you will need to control their meetings and to reward calm behaviour. The younger the cats, the more open their minds will be to experience.

KITTEN KINDERGARTEN

In the 1960s, Dr Ian Dunbar, a British veterinarian in California, developed the concept of puppy pre-school – weekly classes where owners were taught how to mould the social development and behaviour of young dogs. In the mid 1990s, Dr Kersti Seksel, a veterinarian in Sydney, Australia extended the idea to kittens, with the "kitten kindergarten". Dr Seksel was concerned that the cat's increasingly common indoor lifestyle denied it natural outlets for normal cat behaviour. Through her understanding of how cats think, she developed a two-week programme that, in essence, trains owners in ways they can enrich their cat's environment and extend the cat's social activity from its litter to other cats and other species. Having been taught to appreciate how the cat's mind works, owners learn to think like cats when devising activities at home.

Kitten kindergarten consists of two classes and is open to kittens between six and 14 weeks old. It is only appropriate in areas where the incidence of feline transmissible disease is low (*see box, page 26*). Owners are shown how a mother cat carries and grooms her young, and they learn to use variations of these methods when restraining and grooming their cats. Dr Seksel explains the importance of play and teaches owners how to use play to develop their cats' mental and physical abilities. They also learn how to turn the cat carrier into a space that their cat likes, rather than a mobile prison that signifies a visit to the vet, and are shown how to introduce their cat to other species.

Owners are also taught to think like cats, to understand, for example, that it is pointless to discipline a cat if you find it has knocked something off the mantelpiece. Discipline is only useful when the cat is caught in the act. Cats do not understand cause and effect in the way that we do. You can be conditional with your children and say, "If you do that once more, I'll be angry with you," but you cannot expect your kitten to understand that type of statement. If you can transport yourself into your cat's way of thinking, then training is both possible and surprisingly simple, because you will never be asking your cat to do more than it naturally can.

CHECKLIST

- Understand what a cat wants in life and use those wants positively.
- Remember that young cats learn faster than mature individuals.
- Offer food and touch as potent rewards.
- Associate food and touch with the less potent reward of words.
- Eventually use words alone as rewards.
- Use discipline only when necessary.
- Use discipline theatrically, not for retribution.

LEARNED HELPLESSNESS

For the first weeks of life, a kitten depends on its mother's milk for survival. In the following weeks it needs its mother's hunting ability to fill its stomach. Because we know how to use can openers and open cardboard boxes, we assume the role of mother as food providers. Cats learn to depend on us for food.

NATURAL DEVELOPMENT

NATURAL TRAINING

NATURAL NUTRITION

NATURAL HEALTH CARE

HEALTH DISORDERS

EARLY TRAINING

ALTHOUGH THERE ARE FEW cat-owning homes today
without a litter tray, this accessory is a recent invention.
Fortunately, because of the cat's natural cleanliness and
desire to bury its waste, and because its mind is open to
our suggestions when it is young, we can use its natural
instinct to our advantage. With a little early help from
us, all cats are easily house-trained.

HEALTH DANGERS TO US

While all mammals
carry the disease
toxoplasmosis, cats
can transmit this
condition to other
species, including us,
via their faeces. Only
cats that eat wildlife
contract and pass
on toxoplasmosis.
If you are pregnant,
and your cat goes
outdoors, and
especially if it preys
on birds and mice,
wear protective
gloves when handling
the litter tray (see
page 138).

A RECEPTIVE MIND

The cat is an extraordinarily fast learner
and is intuitively clean. Early in life, all its
toileting needs are met by its mother. For
the first three weeks of her kittens' lives,
she stimulates them to urinate and defecate
by licking their anogenital regions and
consuming all waste. This is a practical
evolutionary behaviour. The mother protects
her young from potential predators by
removing signs of their presence. From
about three weeks of age, and with its
mother's guidance, a kitten intuitively
chooses a toileting site with a "diggable"
surface, and returns to this site each time it
needs to empty its bladder or bowels.

NATURAL HYGIENE

Virtually all cats are naturally "house-
trained" when they come to live with us. In
contrast to a puppy, there is rarely a need to
spend weeks or months training a cat to
eliminate in a specific area. It is important,
however, to provide both a location and a
form of litter that is as natural as possible.
With the exception of the most dominant
cats, which vary their toileting sites as a

TOILETING PROBLEMS

Your cat may refuse to use its litter tray for social
reasons. You may not be cleaning it often enough
or, conversely, you may be cleaning it too often.
Loss of toilet training can be a sign of medical
problems. Cats that defecate just outside their
litter tray sometimes do so because they feel pain
when defecating. This can be caused by blocked
anal glands and is simply corrected (see page 139).
Cats that urinate on unusual surfaces, such as in
the sink or bathtub, often do so because of the
burning sensation caused by cystitis. The cause
must be determined by your veterinarian and
eliminated (see pages 140-141).

means of marking territory, all others prefer
to use a single site for toileting. Both kittens
and adults routinely bury their waste in
order to leave as little evidence as possible of
their presence, thereby reducing the risk of
attack from predators. Unneutered toms are
the cats most likely to use their urine and
unburied faeces as territory markers.

THE CAT'S PREFERENCES

In North Africa, where the domestic cat
evolved, earth and sand were excellent for
burying waste. They still are, especially earth
that we have already broken up to make
digging easier – that is why cats enjoy
burying their droppings in fresh flowerbeds.
This natural preference extends into your
home. Some cats discover, with glee, the
earth in your potted plants. The feel under-
foot is very important to cats; generally
speaking, the finer the feel, the more attractive
the substance. Sand appeals to most cats,
which is why outdoor sandpits for children
are likely to be contaminated with cat faeces.

The amount of digging a cat does varies
between individuals. Some are content to
give their litter a cursory paw before and
after eliminating, while others carry out
complex engineering works, meticulously
creating excavations beforehand, then
sculpting pyramids afterwards.

LITTER TRAYS
*The choice of open or
covered tray is yours, but
remember to introduce your
kitten to your preferred
receptacle as early as
possible. Cats that are
familiar with open trays
may be apprehensive about
using an enclosed model.*

OUR PREFERENCES

While each cat has its own personal litter preference, so do we. Fortunately, our requirements coincide with theirs. Both of us want absorbent substances that control odour, although deodorizing agents that smell good to us may not smell good to a cat.

Because of their origins, cats naturally prefer sand but this is not an ideal material, in our opinion, because it is not absorbent. Urine runs to the bottom of a sand container and leads to odour build-up. Earth is absorbent but can be cumbersome and messy. Commercial cat litter is a relatively recent product. Gravel-like clay litter was first commercially packaged about 50 years ago. Manufacturers dried and ground natural clay to small, gravel-sized, absorbent pellets. Dust and odour-controlling agents were added. More recently, clay litters, ground to a finer degree, have been marketed. These clump when wet, which makes it easier to remove waste, and more economical because the remaining clean litter is topped up. It can stick to long hair and be pulled out of the litter tray, however.

The choice of litter material is yours. Whatever you choose, remember that early learning is potent. Introduce a kitten to your choice of litter as soon as possible, and that litter is likely to become your cat's favourite.

LITTER ETIQUETTE

Kittens are inquisitive and likely to taste any new type of cat litter. Some vets feel that kittens are more likely to taste clumping litters than other varieties. Remember that the whole concept of commercially produced cat litter is unnatural. Supervise your kitten when introducing it to any form of litter until it understands what the litter box is for. Remember too that a masking odour you find pleasant might be deeply offensive to a cat. Lemon and pine appeal to us but not to all cats. When you introduce a new cat into your home, when possible set up two litter trays with different forms of litter, both of which are acceptable to you. Given this opportunity, your cat can show you which one it naturally prefers.

Always place litter trays in secluded but easily accessible locations. Cats do not like to toilet in busy thoroughfares. In natural circumstances, different cats seldom use the same latrine site. If you are a multiple-cat household, set up two or more litter trays.

When your vet needs a urine sample from your cat, empty its litter tray of its normal absorbent cat litter and refill it with non-absorbent litter. If this is not available, use thoroughly washed, very fine gravel or even Styrofoam beads. Collect the urine straight away, and place in a clean container.

CHECKLIST

- Provide litter that your cat finds acceptable.
- Encourage your outdoor cat to toilet on your own property. Provide a tray outside.
- Provide two or more trays in multiple-cat households.
- Place litter trays in quiet locations.
- Clean litter trays at least every other day.

NATURAL DEVELOPMENT

NATURAL TRAINING

NATURAL NUTRITION

NATURAL HEALTH CARE

HEALTH DISORDERS

TYPES OF LITTER

WOOD-BASED
Wood-based, pelleted litter expands as it absorbs moisture. It can be composted, buried, or dried out and burned. It has a tendency to be trailed out of the litter box.

EARTH OR SAND
These natural substances are a cat's favourite materials for toileting. Because they are bulky and non-biodegradable, they are not suitable for urban use.

CLAY
Clay is the most popular type of litter, absorbing urine and moisture from faeces. Clumps are easily removed. Do not flush down the toilet: it sediments in drains.

NON-ABSORBENT
Sometimes made of pelleted corncob coated in paraffin wax, this litter is used in a tray with a urine collecting unit below. Faeces is removed and the litter washed and reused.

PREPARING FOR LIFE INDOORS

FOR A NATURAL LONE HUNTER there is perhaps nothing more "unnatural" than a life indoors, deprived of the physical and sensory challenges of the outdoor world, but this is the reality of life for most loved, urban cats. In fact, most come to enjoy the hedonistic existence of living indoors. By understanding a cat's needs it is simple to prepare our homes for permanent indoor feline residents.

REWARD GOOD BEHAVIOUR

Use of positive reinforcement in training is similar for cats and dogs. The moment your cat behaves as you want it to, give a food reward. For example, train your hungry cat to come to its name by showing it a food treat and speaking its name as it approaches you.

POUNCE GAMES

Wrap string or wool round a table-tennis ball. When batted, the cat's claws cause the ball to go in unexpected directions. Take care that your cat does not eat the wool or string.

NATURAL DEMANDS

Your cat's physical and emotional needs vary during its life. Kittens thrive on frequent, highly energetic, and often vigorous play. Older indoor cats enjoy play but the style of play changes. They tend to play for shorter periods and at a more considered pace than kittens, often utilizing the innate stalking and hunting skills that they have never exercised on real prey. If you fail to provide entertainment for your cat, then, left to its own ingenuity, it is adept at creating its own amusement. What your cat sees as exciting projects — climbing the curtains, scratching furniture, knocking food off shelves — can be annoying and expensive to you.

Use ingenuity and forward planning to prevent feline boredom and its associated problems. Think about how your cat would be occupied if it were outdoors, patrolling its territory and hunting for food, and try to ensure that energy is directed in a creative and stimulating way. Give your cat its own furniture, customized games, and training.

THE VALUE OF NEUTERING

The need to find a mate is basic in all animals and is hormonally controlled. Mature male cats produce sex hormone year round. Outdoor females release their hormone in the spring but indoor females may have heat cycles throughout the year. If you keep a cat indoors it is unnatural, and unfair, to allow it to produce sex hormone permanently, with the associated need to mark and patrol a territory and find a mate. Neutering before puberty eliminates this stress for indoor cats and allows for a more relaxed life.

WHAT CATS THINK OF US

Because our cats think of us as permanent providers — lifelong "mothers" — the most logical way to teach and train your cat is to use a feline mother's natural methods. She rewards good behaviour with food and disciplines bad behaviour with a vocal threat or social ostracism, but never with severe abuse. If you think of yourself as your cat's "mother", and understand that this confers lifelong kittenhood on your cat, you will realize how dependent your cat is on you. You supply its food and teach it right and wrong. Dr Ian Dunbar of the Center for Applied Animal Behavior in Berkeley, California says, "Anything you can teach a dog, apart from barking, you can teach a cat."

PERSONALITY TYPES

Genetics and early learning ultimately create different personality types (*see page 68*). Some cats, especially the long, lean oriental breeds, are naturally more confident, gregarious, and "interactive" with people than others. As a general rule, longhaired cats, like Persians, are more self-contained. The degree and type of play activity needed by a cat varies with its own personality and its early experience. Cats raised from birth in active human households need more play than cats that spend time outdoors. Lifelong indoor cats tend to retain kittenish behaviour.

THE IMPORTANCE OF PLAY

At first sight, playful activity might seem a waste of time and energy. It does not fill a cat's stomach, and some cats get so reckless when they play that they run the risk of injuring themselves. Yet play is very important for cats and especially so for those who will live their lives indoors. Play is not just a natural way to learn about the home environment, it is also a normal way to release the pent-up energy historically needed by cats for successfully stalking and capturing their food. Channel your cat's inherent predatory abilities into constructive games. Supply your cat with a variety of toys that will stimulate its natural inclinations to stalk, chase, grab, and bite.

HOW TO PLAY WITH YOUR CAT

Both young and adult cats enjoy grab-and-hold games. These are really "capture and release" activities but are played with suitable toys rather than helpless small animals. A fluffy object on the end of a string is ideal for grab-and-hold games. Dangle and move the object in front of your cat – the essential attraction to the cat is the movement, which should echo the movement of its natural prey. It will enjoy it more if you make it difficult: if you have stairs, dangle the toy on one side of the stair-rails while your cat moves up and down the stairs, reaching with its paw through the rail. This type of play provides the stimulation that an outdoor cat gets from climbing fences and grabbing at butterflies.

RELEASING CAT ENERGY

Outdoor life involves periods of quiet and solitude interspersed by episodes of stalking, chasing, or being chased. Indoor adult cats create their own variations of this naturally episodic behaviour. Some owners call their cat's actions "the mad half-hour", although the indoor cat's surge of activity seldom lasts anywhere near that long. A typical variation in this form of creative play is "the wall of death". Out of seeming somnolence, the housebound cat suddenly bursts into the

room, races around with such velocity that it may run off the floor and onto the walls as it circles the room, and, just as abruptly, it darts out of the room. If you follow it, you are likely to find your cat sitting inscrutably, as if nothing happened, calmly grooming itself. This is creative self-amusement, a normal activity of any indoor cat.

RESPONSIBLE OWNERSHIP

In the absence of real hunting opportunities, and in the absence of our channelling their behaviour into non-damaging play, indoor cats can behave in ways that their owners find unacceptable. As far as your cat is concerned, there is nothing wrong with climbing curtains and scratching furniture, but some owners of indoor cats find these natural inclinations so offensive they are willing to keep their pets only if the animal is surgically altered by amputating all the claws on its forepaws. If you live where it is not safe to let a cat outdoors but you still want the joyful companionship that comes from living with a cat, you have an obligation to supply your feline with its own scratching post and teach it to scratch that but not other objects. If you do not, you must accept that scratching furniture to leave visible territory markers is an ingrained, natural behaviour.

CAT GYMNASIUM
Consider investing in, or building, a cat gymnasium if you have two kittens and want to provide them with a play area that allows climbing and jumping, both natural kitten needs. Placing food treats on the platforms stimulates climbing to investigate.

NATURAL DEVELOPMENT

NATURAL TRAINING

NATURAL NUTRITION

NATURAL HEALTH CARE

HEALTH DISORDERS

NATURAL PROBLEMS INDOORS

LIFE LIVED INDOORS is a relatively new phenomenon for cats. It is only in recent times, with our inclination to live in urban high-rise buildings and to value the safety of our cats, that they have needed to learn to adapt to this new ecological niche. The cat's adaptability is magnificent, but its instinctive needs remain. If we provide for these needs, we can avoid most behaviour problems indoors.

A SEDENTARY EXISTENCE

Many cats are closet hedonists. Presented with the comforts of life indoors, they just eat, relax, and grow fat. Naturally slothful cats, for inexplicable reasons, have a higher incidence of urinary tract disorders. Reduce this indoor risk by encouraging your cat to take part in routine mental and physical activity.

IS IT REALLY A PROBLEM?

Cats naturally behave in cat-like ways. They lead three-dimensional lives, so they climb heights. They keep their weapons sharp and ready for use, so they manicure their nails. Some use both solid and liquid body waste to mark territory. Some eat plants. Some instinctively hunt anything small that moves, and if there is nothing small, they stalk larger things that move. All of these behaviours are perfectly normal. But when our indoor cats climb our curtains, scratch our furniture, urinate in our flower pots, eat our plants, or stalk our ankles, we define their behaviour as unacceptable. Cats need to do certain things. Our obligation is to train them to channel their behaviours in directions they enjoy and we find acceptable.

TRAINING PRINCIPLES

Training your indoor cat provides mental stimulation, even entertainment, for both of you. Rewards are the key to training and food treats are the best rewards, but take care you do not overfeed your cat. If it eats dry food, measure out its daily allotment

and set aside part of it for training. If it eats wet food, feed a little less to compensate for the extras it gets on training days.

Begin by training your cat to eat from your hand. At a mealtime, place a little food on the floor. After your cat eats it, rest your hand on the floor with food on your palm. Some cats take longer than others, but soon your cat will be eating from your hand. Once this is accomplished, train it to take food from between your thumb and forefinger. Your cat is now ready for active training.

BASIC TRAINING

It really does not matter what you want to teach your cat, the basic strategy for all "positive reinforcement" training is the same. You lure your cat into doing what you want it to, and, as it does so, you give the command and then you give the reward. For example, train your cat to come to its name by luring it with a food reward. Keep saying its name as it approaches you, and then give the reward. With practice, it will associate the behaviour with your voice and come to you each time you call its name.

DON'T JUST SAY "NO"

Reward training is quite easy and immensely satisfying but still there are times when your cat does something that cats inherently need to do, like scratch, climb, or stalk, and no amount of simple reward training will eliminate the instinct. Saying "No" will not be enough. To control your cat's instinctive behaviour, you need to train your cat to do what it wants to do, where you want it to. This is the basis for preventing or overcoming most common indoor problems.

SCRATCHING FURNITURE

Damage to your furniture can be prevented by providing a sturdy, stable, and preferably tall scratching post. Cats seem to prefer scratching posts covered with a vertical weave. Cut (non-looped) carpet or sisal are attractive surfaces. Experiment to discover what texture your cat likes to scratch most.

EATING PLANTS
An inventive approach to solving the problem of eating house plants is to place set mousetraps under paper around a plant. Feline foot pressure on the paper activates the traps to spring shut and throws the paper in the air. Provide alternative grass for eating.

CLIMBING CURTAINS
A water pistol or spray is a cheap, safe, and effective form of discipline for most cats. A quick squirt as the cat starts to climb the curtains is usually sufficient "punishment" to reduce and eventually extinguish the behaviour.

STALKING ANKLES

Actively play stalk-and-pounce games with your indoor cat. Provide well-designed toys to pounce on. Toy designers have created excellent battery-operated toys that stimulate cats to stalk, capture, and hold "prey". If your cat has already decided that your ankles are its favoured prey, arm yourself with the water pistol and squirt your friend when you see what it is planning.

EATING HOUSE PLANTS

Many cats enjoy eating vegetation. Unlike dogs, they do not eat it only when they feel unwell, or just to induce vomiting. They simply enjoy the taste of plants and grass. Provide your housebound cat with its own "cat grass", which you can purchase from pet shops or grow yourself from seed. Any fast-growing thin grass is suitable. If your cat is attracted to plants, put them out of reach or surround them with double-sided sticky tape. Tape is also the method of choice to prevent your cat jumping onto restricted places such as the kitchen work surface. It usually takes no more than three weeks before a cat decides that sticky surfaces are to be permanently avoided.

CHECKLIST
- Prevent problems by providing suitable outlets for natural cat activities.
- Channel normal activities towards these facilities.
- Don't just say "No" to bad behaviour.
- Train your cat using food rewards.
- Associate words with these rewards.
- Use only very mild "punishment" such as noise or water during retraining.
- Reward training works as well with cats as it does with dogs.

Position the scratching post near the middle of your cat's favourite room. This is only temporary. Once your cat is using it, move it slowly, inches per day, into a less obtrusive location. Eventually site the scratching post near your cat's favourite sleeping area. Catnip rubbed on the post, lavish verbal praise, and food rewards given when it is used all promote continuing use. If your cat has already been scratching furniture, temporarily cover the damaged area with aluminium foil, heavy plastic, or even double-sided sticky tape while retraining is undertaken.

CLIMBING CURTAINS

Provide your cat with its own gymnasium (*see page 31*). Be creative. The most attractive I have seen was built by one of my clients, who installed stepped ledges on a brick wall of his living room. His cat climbed and leapt up to the final ledge, near the ceiling, which contained soft bedding. From this vantage point it viewed its home with utter contentment. Use mild forms of punishment to retrain cats that climb where you do not want them to. As your cat starts to climb, make a loud noise, or squirt it with a water pistol. Soon it will associate climbing in that spot with something mildly unpleasant. Use rewards when it climbs where you want it to.

"Cats need to do certain things. Our obligation is to train them to channel their behaviours in directions they enjoy and we find acceptable."

AVOIDING THE LITTER TRAY

If your cat prefers to use flowerpots rather than its litter tray as its toilet, it is telling you it prefers the smell and feel of earth to cat litter. Reduce the attraction of earth by covering it with aluminium foil or rough pebbles. Also, reconsider the litter you are using. Switch to a finer, clumping litter that is closer in texture to earth. Whenever your cat chooses to avoid using its litter tray, keep in mind that it might feel pain when it urinates or defecates. Discuss what is happening with your vet before assuming it is simply a training problem.

SAFETY OUTDOORS

OUTDOORS IS THE CAT'S NATURAL HOME. It is filled with amazing smells, sounds, and activity, and is invigorating to a cat. It is also terribly dangerous. More pet cats die from road traffic accidents than from disease in the first years of life. We have a responsibility to our cats to ensure their outdoor safety, and to our neighbours to reduce any nuisance our cats may cause to their gardens or property.

CHECKLIST

If you want your cat to venture outdoors, plan ahead:

- Train it to miaow and come to you on command.

- Provide all necessary amenities in your garden.

- Introduce it to the outdoors when it is hungry and wants to return home for food.

- Do not force an outdoor life on a cat afraid of it.

- Prevent access to roads. Traffic kills more cats than any other cause.

- Vaccinate your cat against infectious and contagious cat diseases.

- Ensure your cat wears suitable, safe identification.

OUTDOOR EXPERIENCES

Outdoors may be the natural environment for cats but our outdoors is considerably different from the outdoors they evolved in. If you decide to let your cat outdoors, do so only after carefully preparing for the event. This involves training your cat to "speak" when it hears its name and to come when called. This basic training is important in case your cat is lost, trapped somewhere, or too frightened to return home. Just as you trained your cat to come when called (*see page 32*), teach your cat to miaow on command, by holding a food treat in front of it while it is hungry and repeating its name. During training, most cats will eventually miaow to demand the food

OUTDOOR RESTRICTIONS

In some localities, outdoor cats must be under the control of their owners. For a cat's own safety or to obey the law, think creatively when planning outdoor living for your cat. Balconies and patios can be "caged" attractively, using glass, wooden fencing, and linked wire for cover, especially if climbing vines are appropriately planted. Always explain to your neighbours what you are doing and why you are doing it. Get planning permission if necessary. Good garden security need not look like a gaol. Properly planned it enhances the environment.

reward. As soon as this happens, give the reward and plenty of verbal praise.

Once your cat responds with a miaow when its name is called, it should always be easier to locate. Most importantly, an injured or lost cat will lead us to its location when it miaows at the sound of its name being called. If there are many different voices in your family, you could train your cat to miaow at the sound of a vitamin-tablet container or box of food being shaken.

AN INVITING GARDEN
Provide elevated resting places in the sun, security in the shade, and places for your cat to hide. These amenities will ensure that your cat is less likely to wander far from your own garden.

IDENTIFICATION

Before letting your cat outdoors for the first time, make sure it is properly identified. Tiny microchip implants are safe, effective, and meet international standards. These are ideal for permanent identification. In addition, your cat should always wear a collar and identity tag with an emergency telephone number. The collar should have a fail-safe element to prevent strangulation in the form of an elastic section or breakaway clasp that pops under pressure if snagged. You should be able to slip one or two fingers under a well-fitted collar. If you travel with your cat, make sure to add a telephone number to its tag for the location you are visiting.

THE CAT-FRIENDLY GARDEN

To make your garden safe and interesting for your cat, cater for its natural behavioural needs. Use wooden posts stepped at various levels for flower-border edging. Your cat will enjoy using them to oversee the territory or simply as scratching posts. If, for good reason, you have not neutered your tomcat, place wooden posts at the corners of your property so that he has attractive territory markers to scent with his urine. Both brick and sea-smoothed pebble are pet-friendly surfaces for paths because they retain heat in warm weather, which invites feline lounging.

Bare soil is attractive to cats looking for a toilet site. Reduce the likelihood of your cat, or other cats, using your garden as a latrine by ensuring that planting is dense year round. Grassy or large-leafed plants provide a natural jungle for cats to weave through, and shade-providing shrubs provide cool sanctuary during the heat of the day. Use thorny plants like berberis where you do not want your cat to tread.

OUTDOOR TOILETS

Provide your cat with a toilet in a specific part of the garden, where you want it, by digging a small sand pit that you can reach easily for cleaning. Camouflage the toilet by surrounding it with long grasses and sift it

regularly. Never put cat waste on the compost heap as it is an ideal environment for parasites to thrive. Because feral cats might use it too, and pass toxoplasma in their faeces, it is a potential health hazard. Site your outdoor cat latrine away from where toddlers might play.

By planning toilet facilities carefully, and giving your cat opportunities to scratch boundary markers, to lounge on warm surfaces, to view the terrain from a raised platform, and wander through private thoroughfares, you create a safe and attractive environment and your cat is less likely to wander.

CAT FLAPS

After preparing your cat for outdoors you can introduce it to a cat flap. Cats are naturally willing to climb through small spaces but you may still need to show your cat how the flap works. Hold it fully open at first to allow ease of access, and reward successful use. Let the flap just touch your cat's body. Graduate to partial opening, stimulating your cat to use its body to keep the flap open. In only a short time it will use its head to open the flap without your help.

CAT FLAP
Install a cat flap suitable for your cat's size and the local weather conditions. Wherever possible, only install flaps into doors that lead to safe back gardens or enclosed terraces, patios, or balconies. Prevent your cat from gaining access to roads.

STIMULATING THE SENSES

CATNIP

No one knows exactly why cats are attracted to catnip (*Nepata cataria*). It is possible that the scent stimulates a sex-related interest. That may be why unneutered male cats find it so alluring, although juveniles and females may also enjoy this harmless and inviting plant.

NATURAL DEVELOPMENT

NATURAL TRAINING

NATURAL NUTRITION

NATURAL HEALTH CARE

HEALTH DISORDERS

NATURAL PROBLEMS OUTDOORS

OUR OUTDOORS HAS FAR more cats in it than nature intended. This population density leads to territorial aggression and spread of disease through bite wounds. Rodents and birds also live outdoors, and we want our cats to prey on one group but not the other – an impossible demand. As cat owners, we should control our cat's activities, including predation, on and off our property.

REDUCING OUTDOOR RISKS

- Train your cat to miaow and come on command.

- Because cats can slip their collars, they should carry two forms of ID.

- Use a safe collar with a break-away section.

- Use effective means to control infectious disease and parasites.

- Be considerate to the needs of your neighbours.

NATURAL BORN KILLERS

Cats are superb predators. Given the chance, they prey upon whatever is available. Indoor cats are restricted to batting at flies, the odd moth, and an occasional human ankle. Outdoor cats have real prey to catch. Some contentedly restrict themselves to moths, dragonflies, and butterflies. Others choose amphibia. Given the opportunity, most cats will prey upon small rodents, and wherever there are birds they will naturally stalk and kill them. On Stephen's Island, off the coast of New Zealand, a single cat was responsible for driving one species of bird, the Stephen's Island Wren, to extinction.

In some localities, preying upon birds may be simply a cause for annoyance, a natural cat habit that people find offensive. In other localities, where cats have been introduced as a new species, ground-nesting birds may never have evolved successful escape measures from such expert predators. From time to time, in different parts of

FINDING A LOST CAT

If you lose your cat, carry out an immediate search, helped by others if possible. Contact the police, local shelters, and your microchip or tag registry. Make sure your telephone answer machine is set to receive information when you are out. If this is not successful, contact local veterinary clinics to see if your cat has been taken there. Make a flyer with a photo of your cat, appropriate information, and reward offer, to post and send to everyone called. Keep a list of everyone you have contacted, and after your cat returns, call them with the good news.

different countries, legislation is proposed to control cats. Such legislation has been used in regions from Scandinavia to Australia.

There may be no genuine threat to bird populations in most regions, but we should understand that this is a social issue in many communities. Wherever you live, if your cat shows a liking for stalking and killing birds, reduce the risk of feathered predation by attaching a bell, or two, or three, to your cat's collar. It is also sensible to set any bird-feeding tables well out of reach of your cat.

SOCIAL ENCOUNTERS

Some outdoor problems are simply a result of so many urban cat owners allowing pets outdoors. In nature, individual cats spread themselves out thinly over a large hunting territory. They seldom come into contact with others and often use ritual rather than fighting to resolve territorial disputes. More cats in a given territory leads to more fights. Fights not only cause wounds. Certain cat viruses that were previously uncommon have taken advantage of the more frequent contact of outdoor domestic cats. These viruses spread via saliva transmitted in bites. Feline leukaemia virus (FeLV) and feline immune deficiency virus (FIV), which are both potentially fatal, are easily transmitted during cat fights (see page 118).

Many outdoor cats use our territorial markers – fences and hedges – as their own territory markers and only fight with intruders on their own turf. When cats meet at a demarcation point they will bare their teeth, and stare each other down. These displays of intent avoid injuries, as one cat will usually back down. However, unneutered cats need larger territories. They will invade your garden and fight with your cat, sometimes even following it indoors and spraying urine in your home to reinforce, for your cat, exactly who is territorial king. It is difficult to prevent another cat coming into your garden, but a magnetized cat flap that only opens when it is triggered by your own cat's collar will prevent strange cats invading your home.

GARDEN VANDALISM

Only the most dominant and territorial of all cats leave their faeces unburied in garden flowerbeds, or urinate on back doors and fence posts. If your neighbour is suffering from these problems, your cat is unlikely to be the culprit if it has been neutered. Explain to your neighbour that you had your cat neutered to avoid such behaviour. Neutering also reduces a cat's need for an extensive territory. If you neuter your cat, it is more likely to restrict itself to your own garden.

Faeces in your flowerbeds is usually left by unneutered feral toms. You can buy scented deterents that can be spread around the base of your plants, but a more long-term solution is to plant densely. Bare soil, particularly newly dug soil, is very inviting.

Ransacking the garbage is a more common pet-cat felony. Even the best-fed and mildest-mannered cat finds it difficult to resist slashing through a thin plastic rubbish bag to get at last night's chicken carcass. Keep your outdoor rubbish in bins that have secure lids, and if your cat is raiding your neighbour's bags, enhance good neighbourly relations by buying them cat-proof bins for their rubbish.

TOXIC SUBSTANCES

Do not use herbicides such as paraquat or pesticides like slug bait (metaldehyde) in your garden. Use natural alternatives. For example, control slugs by installing beer traps (ground level saucers filled with beer) or by encircling plants at risk with crushed, baked eggshells. Make sure your cat cannot gain access to your garage or garden shed if that is where you store such toxic substances as paint, paint remover, motor oil, and rodent poison. They cause skin irritation and burns, and your cat can be poisoned by licking toxic substances off its coat.

LETHAL TRAFFIC

More young cats die from traumatic injuries than from disease. Motor vehicles are the most common cause of serious cat injuries.

In cities, it has been estimated that half of all cats that venture outdoors will be involved in road traffic accidents, and half of those individuals will not survive. It is vitally important, whenever possible, to prevent your cat gaining access to any road.

Do not expect your cat to develop road sense. It won't. The glare of headlights at night will virtually paralyze a cat. If there is no alternative but to allow your cat outdoors, fit a reflective collar to reduce risk at night. Drivers might have a slight opportunity of seeing it near the road.

DANGER IN THE GARDEN

All cats, especially young ones, occasionally like to chew on plants. Avoid growing the following plants around your home.

POISONOUS PLANTS

Angels' trumpets *Brugmansia*

Autumn crocus *Colchicum autumnale*

Bleeding heart *Dicentra spectabilis*

Burning bush *Dictamnus*

Castor oil plant *Ricinus communis*

Chilean potato tree *Solanum crispum*

Dumb cane *Dieffenbachia*

Foxglove *Digitalis*

German primula *Primula obconica*

Golden rain *Laburnum*

Lily-of-the-valley *Convallaria*

Lords and ladies *Arum*

Monkshood *Aconitum*

Oleander *Nerium oleander*

Pokeweed *Phytolacca*

Rue *Ruta*

Wistaria *Wisteria*

Yew *Taxus*

CHILEAN POTATO TREE

MONKSHOOD

FOXGLOVE

NATURAL NUTRITION

Hunger is the cat's natural state, although it is not the only driving force of many of its activities. Hunting for the sake of the hunt is also a powerful instinct. If a cat has sufficient mental and physical stimulation, it will balance its energy consumption and expenditure, but many cats are insufficiently active and obesity has become a common problem. Your cat depends on you to provide it with the right quantities of the nutrients essential for maintaining a healthy body and efficient immune system. What it needs will vary according to its age, sex, size, body condition, level of activity, personality, and state of health.

The flesh and bones of a fish provide a natural, nutritional meal.

YOUR CAT'S NUTRITIONAL NEEDS

A CAT IS AN "OBLIGATE CARNIVORE" – it must eat meat to survive. Animal protein and fat contain essential amino acids and fatty acids that cats need and cannot gain in any other way. Indoor cats depend wholly upon us for their food. Choose your cat's nutrients according to its own needs, not according to any moral standpoint you may have concerning the eating of meat.

FOODS TO LIMIT

Never give any food or nutrient in excess. Avoid single-protein diets. For example, a diet restricted to tinned tuna may cause severe liver problems. Muscle-meat alone, without the naturally accompanying organs, bones, and fur is deficient in some essential nutrients and may lead to decalcification of the bones, chronic pain, and eventual death.

WHAT IS A NATURAL DIET?

It is not entirely true that cats are fussy eaters. When hungry, a cat is prepared to capture and consume a variety of foods, including insects, rodents, birds and their eggs, reptiles, amphibians, and even fish. A hungry cat will eat almost anything, and this naturally varied diet is ideal for providing the range of nutrients necessary for life.

In the wild, a hungry cat will capture, kill, and eat live prey once every one to two days. Well-fed cats actually kill more frequently than this, but they do not eat their prey. Muscle from prey provides protein and fat, while its bones and organs are a source of essential vitamins and minerals. Feathers and hair provide fibre. Live prey also provides most of the daily liquid that a cat needs. From an evolutionary viewpoint, the cat's natural metabolism has become lazy. While we (and dogs) can

EATING GRASS
Until recently, it was thought that fibre had little function in the cat's diet. Some cats eat grass to induce vomiting, but others appear to eat it for the simple reason that they enjoy it. Recent evidence suggests that some fibre in a cat's diet may enhance its immune system.

synthesize from vegetable matter all the essential substances we need, cats cannot. They depend upon eating other animals that contain essential substances that they cannot manufacture themselves. They also need a very large supply of protein. A whole mouse is probably the most natural cat diet there is.

NUTRITIONAL RISKS

Natural does not necessarily mean safe. A fresh mouse contains potentially harmful bacteria, as well as bones that can damage the intestines, and fur that might cause a hairball blockage. The mouse may have been poisoned with man-made chemicals.

Any diet you choose to feed your cat, no matter how "natural" or how "synthetic", is a compromise between potential benefits and possible risks. Feline nutrition is common sense, a combination of experience and new information. Do not approach it as a religion. Scientific methods can explain why some foods are so good for cats (and us). For example, certain strains of the bacteria *Lactobacillus acidophilus*, found in mother's milk, are beneficial in a kitten's diet because they enhance the immune system. These good bacteria protect the intestines from colonization by harmful bacteria. But also remember that, at any given time, it is thought that only about half the information disseminated by scientists is correct. Dietary guidelines change as scientists discover more about the particular needs of cats.

IN OUR HANDS

Cats have unique nutritional requirements, quite unlike our own. Indoor cats depend on us to make the right decisions. Do not apply directly to your cat what you know to be nutritionally right for us. For example, fibre from wholegrains may help prevent build-up of the carcinogens that cause colonic cancer in people, but wholegrains have never been a natural part of the cat's diet.

A vitamin C supplement may be beneficial for us because we are unable to manufacture vitamin C in our bodies, and it may enhance protection from the common cold virus. Cats manufacture their own vitamin C and do not suffer from common cold viruses so, unlike us, their diet does not need to be supplemented with foods rich in vitamin C.

Your cat's natural nutritional needs are those of the obligate carnivore. It shares some of our nutritional needs but its optimum levels of vitamins, minerals, essential fatty acids, protein, carbohydrate, fat, and fibre are quite different from ours.

BENEFICIAL BACTERIA

At birth, a kitten's intestines first become inhabited by good bacteria that have been passed on in its mother's milk. As the kitten grows, it receives new bacteria from the different foods it is given by its mother, or from food that it finds itself. Most of these bacterial "guests" are transient and die off within a few days, but some stay longer, creating a stable environment for digesting nutrients from the food that is eaten.

Inside each kitten's intestines there is a competitive and constantly changing ecosystem, with bacteria vying with each other for space and ultimately striking a balance among themselves. This creates the homeostatic balance necessary for optimum digestion of the nutrients needed by different parts of your cat's body. The good bacteria are also necessary for an efficient immune system that will protect your cat from harmful bacteria.

THE LEVIN ARCHIPELAGO

The changes that take place in the variety of intestinal bacteria were illustrated in a unique experiment carried out by the microbiologist Bruce Levin. For a year, he cultured and classified the bacteria on his toilet tissue. In scientific circles, the ebb and flow of bacterial life in Dr Levin's intestines came to be known as the Levin Archipelago, a living environment constantly altered by external events. For example, when another member of his family was treated with antibiotics, the bacteria in Levin's intestines were also affected.

TRUE CARNIVORES

Cats are highly adaptive, eating whatever animal protein is available. Their regular meals vary with where they live. Natural selection has adapted their abilities as hunters to be most successful with whatever is most abundant. Most natural prey will provide balanced nutrition for cats.

WHAT ALL CATS NEED

All cats need protein to provide amino acids, which are the building blocks of all body tissues. Protein also supplies enzymes, which support the body's chemical reactions. Some amino acids can be manufactured by cats, but others cannot. The amino acid taurine has to be acquired by eating meat. Taurine deficiency causes heart disease and blindness.

Cats also need fat, the most energy-dense nutrient, with more than twice as many calories per gram as protein. Fat transports fat-soluble vitamins around the body. Animal fat contains essential fatty acids that a cat cannot manufacture from vegetable fat. Carbohydrates are not a natural source of energy for cats, although they are broken down to glucose and stored as the energy source glycogen in muscle.

Vitamins and minerals are essential for energy conversion, enzyme activity, and bone growth. Water, the most mundane of all nutrients, is also the most important. It is an obvious essential for every living cell. A cat's body consists of 70 per cent water. It may lose 50 per cent of its muscle and fat and still survive, but no cat can survive a 15 per cent loss of its water weight.

CHECKLIST

Be wary of "experts" who say that:

- Malnutrition is common in felines.

- All commercial pet foods contain poisons.

- Their own brand of food or supplement is uniquely natural.

- There is a conspiracy to withhold information about food dangers to cats.

These statements are myths with no foundation.

CHANGING NUTRITION THROUGH LIFE

WHETHER YOUR CAT IS A vigorous kitten or a sedate senior citizen, its life-sustaining nourishment must come from animal tissue-based food. However, the amount of nutrients an individual cat needs will vary, depending upon its age, activity level, size, and even personality. Decide what to feed your cat after considering all of these factors, not just its chronological age.

CHECKLIST

- Food preferences are generally established early in life.

- Nutritional demands during illness are different from those in good health.

- Nutrient demands are highest during lactation, not during pregnancy.

- Stable weight is an excellent guide to homeostasis.

- Any sudden weight gain or loss is a sign of imbalance.

- Arbitrary diet changes as cats age are not necessary.

NOURISHMENT FROM MOTHER

Pregnant cats must be well nourished. Well-nourished mothers not only produce healthy litters, their kittens learn faster and have fewer emotional problems than kittens from malnourished mothers. Poorly nourished mothers that are fed low-protein diets during pregnancy, produce kittens that are slower to learn to crawl, suck, walk, and climb. Their kittens' eyes open later, and they do not control their posture as quickly as kittens from mothers that are well nourished during pregnancy. Most dramatic of all, kittens of poorly nourished mothers go on to become poor mothers themselves and the effects of malnourishment can be perpetuated for generations.

Appetite changes during pregnancy are normal, and morning sickness, although rare in cats, enables a mother to minimize her foetuses' exposure to toxins. This is also the reason why some cats develop food aversions during pregnancy. Be wary of giving drugs or herbs during early pregnancy because they may be harmful to the foetuses.

AGEING APPETITE

If your ageing cat is picky with its food, it is probably not being difficult on purpose. Gum disease, deteriorating teeth, diminished taste or smell, or underlying disease are common causes of finicky eating. Seek veterinary help, but also carry out a simple procedure when trying to encourage your elderly cat to eat: warm its food so that it is at "mouse temperature", about 35° C (95° F). Warmth releases aromas and enhances flavour.

FIRST MONTHS OF LIFE

An average kitten weighs little more than 100 g (4 oz) at birth, but by its first birthday it typically weighs 5 kg (11 lb). High levels of nutrients are needed to support this 50-fold increase in body mass. Cats' milk has almost twice the nutritional value of cows' or goats' milk. When a mother cannot provide enough milk for her kittens, you need to supplement her milk with specially formulated feline-milk replacer, which you can obtain from your veterinarian. The following home formula is fine in emergency situations:

FELINE MILK SUPPLEMENT

- 1 can condensed milk
- An equal quantity of water (1 can)
- 2 tbs live yoghurt
- 2 tbs mayonnaise
- 2 tsp glucose powder
- 25 g gelatin granules

Bring the water to the boil and whisk in the gelatin granules. Remove from the heat and add the condensed milk, then the yoghurt, mayonnaise, and glucose powder, whisking thoroughly. Allow to cool, then refrigerate. The mixture thickens in the fridge. Bring back to liquid consistency in the microwave or using a double boiler.

During growth, a kitten's diet should contain at least 30 per cent protein on a dry-matter basis. Dry-matter means "water removed from food". Dry-matter comparisons of one diet and another are difficult, but are the only valid way to compare the nutrient values of different foods (*see pages 48-49*). "Dry" cat foods have up to 10 per cent moisture, while "wet", or canned, foods, and fresh meat can contain more than 80 per cent.

Growing cats need extra levels of vitamins and minerals (*see pages 50-51*). After a kitten has finished growing and reached its full adult size, its nutrient needs will drop to "maintenance" levels. Encourage kittens to sample a range of foods. This will help prevent fussy eating later in life.

MAINTAINING NOT GAINING

A typical adult cat needs about two and a half times as much protein in its diet as we do. That is 26 per cent protein on a dry-matter basis (*see pages 46-47*). Otherwise, the adult cat's nutrient requirements as a percentage of the diet are the same as for growing cats. Many of the foods available for your cat, either commercially produced or home-prepared, contain more than enough nutrients, and are very tasty. If these nutrient-rich diets are fed freely, obesity is a possible outcome. By some estimates, between 30 and 40 per cent of cats are obese – that is 15 per cent or more above ideal body weight (*see pages 44-45*).

NATURAL AGEING CHANGES

There is no specific age at which cats become "old". In my veterinary practice, arbitrarily, I recommend to cat owners that we carry out a health check-up when a cat's age hits double figures. In 98 per cent of these preventative inspections I find no hidden problems, but in the remaining two per cent, blood tests reveal that the kidneys, or liver, or body hormones are out of balance.

Ageing is not an illness in itself, but loss of homeostasis can develop into clinical disease. Almost invariably, the most efficient way to restore homeostasis and good health is by altering the diet. Older cats do not always need drastic diet changes. The effects of natural ageing, or one of the specific health problems to which older cats are susceptible, may demand a subtle modification to the existing diet. As cats mature, most need less energy but more vitamins and minerals.

Later in life, older cats lose weight, not necessarily because they become less efficient at digesting their food, but more likely because of tooth or gum problems, diminished senses of smell and taste, and sometimes illness. Do not consider weight loss a natural consequence of ageing. If your elderly cat is either putting on or losing weight, make sure it has a clean bill of health before adjusting its diet.

ADJUSTING YOUR CAT'S DIET

Your cat's nutritional needs gradually change throughout its life. Switching from one source of nutrients to another should be carried out in an equally gradual way. Plan diet changes to occur over a five- to 10-day period. Cats do not like sudden changes, and nor does the living environment of micro-organisms in the cat's intestines. Begin by adding a little of the new food to your cat's existing diet. Gradually increase the proportion of new food over the following days. Any bowel problems or signs of going on hunger strike because of smell, taste, or texture will become obvious before these potential problems become serious.

Remember too that, like us, each cat has its own preferences for odours, textures, and flavours, but finicky eaters are made, not born. From early in life, offer your cat a variety of tasty foods, but do not let it dictate its diet. As time moves on, modify that diet according to your cat's unique demands. Provide more nutrients when they are obviously needed, for example, as the weather gets colder. Weigh your cat routinely. Steady weight is a simple sign of good health. Weight increases or losses mean that the natural balance has been upset. Almost certainly something is wrong and central to resolving the problem may be changing your cat's nutrition.

LACTOSE

Milk is the staple of life. Kittens produce special enzymes in their intestines to digest the lactose sugar in it, but with age these enzymes naturally diminish. This can lead to milk causing diarrhoea in older cats. Avoid this problem by giving lactose-free milk to adults.

HIGH ENERGY NEEDS
Try to vary your cat's diet according to its environment and energy demands. During youth, cats need energy to grow as well as to maintain themselves. Young cats need extra nutrients to fuel the demands of curiosity and activity.

NATURAL DEVELOPMENT

NATURAL TRAINING

NATURAL NUTRITION

NATURAL HEALTH CARE

HEALTH DISORDERS

ASSESSING BODY CONDITION

WHEN YOU LIVE WITH A CAT, it becomes so familiar that it is easy to miss changes in its body condition that are important indicators of its health. Weight gains and losses are always significant, but in small animals they often go unnoticed until the change is dramatic. Monitor your cat's weight routinely on an accurate scale. If its condition is changing, discuss this with your veterinarian.

SUBTLE CHANGES

After almost 30 years of clinical experience I still find it difficult, almost impossible, to see subtle changes in a cat's weight and body condition. It was only after I installed human-baby weigh-scales in the examining rooms at my veterinary clinic that I was able to detect small changes in weight and use them in assessing a cat's health. In actual weight, these changes begin imperceptibly. A cat might gain or lose only 225 g (½ lb) but this is five to 10 per cent of its body weight. It is like an average-sized person losing 5 kg (11 lb). And that is just the vague beginning of body condition changes. I see cats that are grossly overweight and when I mention their body condition to their owners, the typical answer is acknowledgement of the weight gain but a failure to understand just how dramatic the change has been.

FAT CATS

Obesity is overwhelmingly the most common nutritional problem in adult cats. Even young cats under a year of age can suffer from it. Obesity is increasing, quite simply because pet food manufacturers have been so successful in producing nutrient-rich, highly palatable foods. Cats enjoy them so much that they eat more than is necessary to maintain weight.

There is recent evidence that a diet high in fat early in life predisposes to later obesity. In simple terms, more calories are consumed daily than are used up. Surplus energy is efficiently stored in the form of fat. This is an excellent natural defence to sustain life when prey is in short supply but has little benefit to the well-fed cat. An indoor lifestyle may be an important factor. Quite simply, life indoors is tedious and dull. Just about the most exciting event is feeding time. Cats blackmail owners into feeding them more because eating is the most stimulating experience they have.

Obesity is of medical concern because fat cats are more likely than lean cats to become diabetic, have skin problems, or develop lameness. If your young feline is fat, get to the root of the problem. Make life more stimulating, physically and mentally. Look at its diet. Reducing dietary fat is one way to cut calories. Fat has about twice as many calories per gram as protein (*see pages 46-47*). Alternatively, rather than changing the food, you could try simply feeding less of your cat's usual diet. That way, you restrict calories but do not alter the nutritional balance of the food, nor upset your cat with unwelcome changes to its diet.

Portion control is very important if your cat is overweight. So too are frequent periods of activity. Cats naturally rest, then have bursts of energy. This exercise-and-rest cycle may increase a cat's resting metabolic rate, boosting energy consumption even when the cat is lazing between activities.

Remember, cats evolved to be most efficient and most healthy at their optimum weight. Extra weight puts extra strain on a cat's joints as well as on its heart and lungs. Obesity may also increase risks during anaesthesia and surgery.

BREED DIFFERENCES

Some cat breeds appear stockier than others. The "cobby" British shorthair has a naturally more rotund appearance while the modern Siamese is now quite elongated. Always assess body condition in comparison to the normal for that breed. For example, a Siamese may retain relatively slim shoulders but develop a dramatic abdominal fat flap between its hind legs. Naturally stocky breeds appear to have a greater tendency to gain weight than naturally more lean and active breeds.

THIN CATS

During or after illness, after pregnancy, or simply after going missing, cats have increased energy demands. By assessing your cat's body condition you can determine whether it needs more energy-dense food.

Fat is twice as energy-dense as protein. Feed as you would a pregnant or lactating cat (*see pages 48-49*). Remember, loss of body condition is a prime sign of illness. What may appear to be a limited weight loss, only a few hundred grams or a few ounces, is a considerable percentage of the natural weight of an animal as small as a cat. Use the assessment chart, right, to monitor these seemingly minimal but significant changes.

DEHYDRATION

A significant cause of weight loss during illness is dehydration. This may occur even when a cat continues drinking its normal amount of fluid. Some owners are surprised at how little water a cat normally drinks. Many cats get virtually all the water they need from the food they eat. The edible parts of a small rodent or bird consist of almost 80 per cent moisture, and most canned cat foods contain almost as much. Water absorbs water-soluble vitamins and is absorbed by fibre to add beneficial bulk to your cat's diet. A well-hydrated cat has taut skin. Assess dehydration by gently pinching the skin on your cat's neck. It should snap back into position. If it retracts slowly, or remains "tented", your cat is dehydrated.

CHANGING THE DIET

Always change a cat's diet gradually. A rapid shift, especially a drastic drop in protein, can result in fasting and hepatic lipidosis, a potentially fatal liver condition (*see pages 130-131*). Once you know what has caused the weight change, you can determine what to do about it. This involves an understanding of the different sources of calories, protein, fat, and carbohydrate, and how to balance the energy in calories that these sources supply with the energy demands of your cat's life.

ASSESSING YOUR CAT

Use this chart to assess your cat's body condition. Compare top and side views with the pictures below. If your cat is at either extreme, consult your vet for advice on the cause and treament of its condition.

BODY CONDITION	APPEARANCE
EMACIATED • Ribs showing, no fat cover • Severe abdominal tuck • Bones at base of tail raised with no tissue between skin and bone • No palpable abdominal fat	
THIN • Ribs easily felt with minimal fat cover • Waist obvious behind ribs • Bones at base of tail raised, and covered in minimal fat • Minimal abdominal fat	
IDEAL • Slight fat cover on ribs • Waist can be seen behind ribs • Bones at base of tail smooth, covered in thin layer of fat • Minimal abdominal fat	
OVERWEIGHT • Ribs not easily felt, with moderate fat cover • Waist hardly discernable • Bones at base of tail felt under moderate layer of fat • Moderate abdominal fat	
OBESE • Ribs not felt due to thick fat cover • No waist, abdomen distended • Bones at base of tail difficult to feel through fat • Extensive abdominal fat	

NATURAL DEVELOPMENT

NATURAL TRAINING

NATURAL NUTRITION

NATURAL HEALTH CARE

HEALTH DISORDERS

NATURAL DEVELOPMENT

NATURAL TRAINING

NATURAL NUTRITION

NATURAL HEALTH CARE

HEALTH DISORDERS

WHERE ENERGY COMES FROM

ENERGY COMES FROM THE PROTEIN, fat, and carbohydrate eaten by your cat. Protein, broken down into amino acids, is transported via the blood to help tissues grow and repair. Fat is broken down into fatty acids, essential for healthy cells and an efficient immune system. Carbohydrates convert to sugar and provide instant energy. The energy provided by food is calculated in kilocalories (kcals).

cannot: they need animal-derived protein to survive. Taurine, naturally found in chicken, clams, fish meal, squid, and other animals, is the most important amino acid that a cat cannot manufacture itself. Taurine deficiency can lead to blindness, heart failure, and reproductive problems. Cats need twice as much taurine in wet food as in dry food.

Fat provides energy and palatability to a cat's diet. Recent nutrition studies have shown that the type and amount of fat your cat eats affects not only its weight but also the sustained efficiency of its immune system (*see pages 50-51*). In the table below is a list of different animal-derived foods. You will see that energy comes in variable amounts from protein or fat.

CHECKLIST

- Never feed cats only on dog food. It is likely to be deficient in the levels of taurine a cat needs.

- Avoid raw meat. It may contain the parasite *Toxoplasma gondii*, the cause of toxoplasmosis.

- Never feed a cat a purely vegetarian diet. They cannot manufacture certain essential requirements from vegetarian sources.

- Cats need high-protein diets, at least 26 per cent protein on a dry-weight basis.

- Fat is a natural source of energy for cats.

SOURCES OF ENERGY

Cats need more protein than dogs do to grow, and to maintain and repair body tissues. Proteins are complex molecules made up of a variety of amino acids. While we, and dogs, can manufacture all the amino acids we need from vegetable-derived protein, cats

PROTEIN AND FAT SOURCES OF ENERGY

Meat from different sources varies in the amount of energy provided by its muscle or fat. This list details the energy content of different meats, and how much of that energy comes from protein or fat. For most cats, fat is an excellent energy source.

FOOD SOURCES (100 g)	ENERGY (kcals)	PROTEIN (g)	FAT (g)	CARBO-HYDRATE (g)
Chicken meat	121	20.5	4.3	0
Chicken meat with skin	230	17.6	17.7	0
Duck meat	122	19.7	5	0
Duck meat with skin	430	11.3	42.7	0
Lean beef	123	20	4.6	0
Lamb	162	21	9	0
Pork	147	20.7	7	0
Turkey without skin	107	22	2.2	0
Venison	198	35	6.4	0
Rabbit	124	22	4	0
Tripe	6	9.4	2.5	0
Cod	76	17.4	0.7	0
Herring	234	17	18.5	0
Egg	47	12.5	11	Trace
Cottage cheese	98	14	4	2.4
Low-fat plain yoghurt	56	5	0.8	7.5

Carbohydrates are not an important natural source of energy but, when cooked, they release available energy and a little protein and fat. The table below shows energy that can be gained from carbohydrate-rich foods.

THE IMPORTANCE OF FIBRE

Cats are intensely carnivorous but fibre is a natural part of their diet, eaten indirectly when they consume the feathers, fur, or viscera of small mammals. Fibre stimulates saliva and gastric-juice production. Soluble fibre slows down digestion while insoluble fibre stimulates "intestinal hurry". Water-soluble fibre increases the stickiness of food and keeps it in the stomach longer.

Fibre may even reduce the risk of bowel cancer and may be beneficial in preventing and treating obesity, inflammatory bowel disease, sugar diabetes, constipation, and excess fat in the bloodstream. Fermentable fibre creates substances in the intestines that may inhibit unpleasant bacteria.

The actual amount of fibre your cat needs varies with its age and lifestyle. Beet pulp, chicory, rice bran, and bran breakfast cereals are common sources of fermentable and non-fermentable fibre. Psyllium is an excellent form of soluble fibre.

SOURCES OF ENERGY
Rodents and birds are a cat's natural diet. The muscles contain an excellent balance of protein and fat, while bones and intestinal contents are a source of fibre and carbohydrate, both valuable for efficient digestion and good health.

DANGEROUS FOODS

Never use liver as an exclusive substitute for "muscle" meat. Small amounts of liver are tasty and nutritious, but the naturally high level of vitamin A in virtually all animal liver can be toxic to cats if consumed in large quantities over a long period. Even from the most hygienic sources, it is safest to assume that raw meat, eggs, or dairy products may be contaminated with Salmonella bacteria. Cook or pasteurize all animal-derived sources of energy before giving them to your cat.

CARBOHYDRATE SOURCES OF ENERGY

Use this chart if changing to a different source of carbohydrate energy. Remember, cats eat food that smells and tastes good.

Carbohydrates do neither and need to be masked by strong, attractive smells, textures, and tastes, which means meat.

FOOD SOURCES (100 g)	ENERGY (kcals)	PROTEIN (g)	FAT (g)	CARBO-HYDRATE (g)
White rice (uncooked)	383	7.3	3.6	86
Brown rice (uncooked)	357	6.7	2.8	81.3
Potato (boiled)	75	1.5	0.3	17.8
Yam (boiled)	133	1.7	0.3	33
White bread	235	8.4	1.9	49
Brown bread	218	8.5	2	44
Egg noodles (uncooked)	391	12	8.2	72

FOOD ADDICTIONS

Many cats will starve rather than eat something they find unappetizing. Some become addicted to single-ingredient foods. This can be quite dangerous if the chosen item is not nutritionally complete. Vary your cat's diet to prevent food faddism.

NATURAL DEVELOPMENT

NATURAL TRAINING

NATURAL NUTRITION

NATURAL HEALTH CARE

HEALTH DISORDERS

ADJUSTING ENERGY INTAKE

HOW MUCH ENERGY your cat needs depends upon its age, sex, activity level, metabolic rate, and probably a whole host of other factors. Each cat is individual. No particular quantity of a specific diet is correct for all cats. Adjust your cat's energy intake according to its personal needs. To do so, you need to know the kilocalorie (kcals) content of fresh foods and of commercial diets.

CHECKLIST

- Determine your cat's baseline energy needs.

- Increase energy consumption during pregnancy and lactation.

- Increase energy consumption during growth.

- To overcome obesity, do not just decrease your cat's energy consumption. Eliminate the social causes of the obesity.

- Ensure that all diets contain correct amounts of micronutrients (*see page 50*).

ENERGY DEMANDS

The energy requirements of cats can range from as little as 100 kcals per day for an inactive, indoor, lightweight cat to 2,000 kcals a day for a heavily lactating, massive mother. As a rough guideline, an indoor, inactive cat needs about 50 kcals of energy per kilo of body weight daily (25 kcals per pound of body weight). See the box below for guidelines to energy requirements for cats of different body weights.

CALCULATING ENERGY IN FOOD

If you feed your cat fresh food, you can use the table that appears on page 46 to calculate how many calories you are providing for your cat. Determining how many calories there are in commercial cat food is more difficult because few manufacturers give this information on the label.

As a guideline, a standard (400 g) can of cat food contains about 300 to 400 kcals. Nutritionists calculate energy on a dry-matter basis but, unfortunately, cat food labels do not give this information so it is

TACKLING FELINE OBESITY

Keep a record of exactly what your cat eats. This will make you more conscious of all the extras it receives. Feed low-fat, high-fibre foods. This lowers calories while maintaining bulk. Fibre or water added to food "dilutes" the calories in it. Feed and play with your cat frequently. This might accelerate its basic metabolic rate. Avoid crash diets: they upset your cat and only drive its metabolism to be more efficient and fat-storing in the future. You may need as much help sticking to a healthy feline diet as your cat does. If your cat becomes demanding and bullies you for food, discuss the problem with your veterinary staff. In these circumstances, they make fine counsellors.

difficult to compare the nutritional content of one cat food to another. To calculate the nutritional value of food, you first need to know its moisture content. Then you work out dry-matter content with a calculator.

Here's what you do. Read the Guaranteed Analysis on the label. It gives the moisture content, as well as protein, fat, and fibre levels in percentages.

A TYPICAL LABEL

- Crude protein ....8 %
- Crude fat.......................................6 %
- Fibre ....1 %
- Moisture ....78 %

ENERGY REQUIREMENTS FOR DIFFERENT BODY WEIGHTS

These are guideline kilocalorie requirements for mature cats with different lifestyles. Cats in cool climates use up more energy keeping warm and, if they go outdoors, will need slightly increased calories, particularly during cold or wet weather.

ADULT WEIGHT	2 KG	4 KG	6 KG	8 KG	10 KG
Inactive lifestyle	100–140	200–280	300–420	400–560	500–700
Active lifestyle	140–180	280–360	420–540	560–720	700–900
Pregnant female	200–280	400–560	600–840	800–1120	1,000–1,400

The dry-matter content is what remains when moisture is removed. In the example, if the food is 78 per cent moisture, it must be 22 per cent dry matter. Next comes more advanced but still simple arithmetic. Calculate the dry-matter nutrient content for protein, fat, and fibre using this formula.

FORMULA TO CALCULATE NUTRITION IN COMMERCIAL FOODS

- Dry-matter nutrient content =

$$\frac{\text{The label's nutrient percentage} \times 100}{\text{Dry-matter content percentage}}$$

Therefore:

- Crude protein = $\dfrac{8 \times 100}{22}$ ...... = 36.4 %

- Crude fat = $\dfrac{6 \times 100}{22}$ ...... = 22.7 %

- Crude fibre = $\dfrac{1.0 \times 100}{22}$ .... = 4.5 %

By doing these simple calculations you can accurately compare one type of commercial cat food with another. This is important when you are switching from one source of nutrients to another in order to adjust your cat's energy intake.

WHEN TO ADJUST ENERGY INTAKE

Almost everywhere in the world where cats are fed by us, obesity is a problem. Living indoors, neutering, and access to tasty food are all implicated. If your vet's advice is that your cat needs to lose weight, it is important to take it seriously. An overweight cat is risking its health (*see page 44*). If you suspect you are overfeeding your cat, use the table on page 48 to assess your cat's correct intake, and adjust its diet accordingly.

There are certain occasions when you may need to increase a cat's energy intake. Cats may lose weight when they have been ill, or lost for some time. Assess your cat's body condition to see if it is underweight (*see page 45*). Always consult a vet if there is no apparent reason for weight loss.

When a cat is lactating, and when kittens are growing, there are special dietary needs.

CONVALESCING CATS
Energy needs increase during convalescence. At the same time, a cat's desire to eat may be impaired. Warm energy-dense food in order to stimulate your cat's interest. Unless your vet advises otherwise, you will need to increase dietary fat as well as protein.

LACTATING MOTHERS

Energy requirements increase by about 50 per cent during pregnancy, then soar during lactation. Cat's milk contains about 40 per cent more energy than cow's or goat's milk. To produce such energy-dense milk requires a considerable increase in energy consumption (*see table below*). Even after her kittens have reduced their milk consumption, a cat's energy demands remain 50 per cent above her usual needs until she replaces the body weight she lost on behalf of her kittens.

GROWING KITTENS

Until a kitten reaches half its adult size, it needs about two and a half times the amount of energy needed simply for body maintenance. Calculate the calories needed according to its weight, then increase this by two and a half times until the kitten is 18 weeks old, then by 50 per cent until it is mature. At this stage, its energy needs drop to normal for the first time.

GERIATRIC DIETS

Older cats have varying needs. Most thrive on their adult maintenance diet supplemented with vitamins and minerals. Overweight elderlies should be slimmed very gradually, while underweight seniors or those recovering from illness benefit from an increase in energy food. Increase strongly odoured fat and protein in the diet.

ENERGY REQUIREMENTS DURING LACTATION

When a cat is producing milk her energy needs are up to four times greater than those of an inactive cat. During this time, increase the kilocalorie energy level of your cat's food to minimize weight loss.

ADULT WEIGHT	2 KG	4 KG	6 KG	8 KG
Lactation weeks 1-2	220	440	660	880
Lactation weeks 3-4	300	600	900	1,200
Lactation weeks 5-6	420	840	1,260	1,680

NATURAL DEVELOPMENT

NATURAL TRAINING

NATURAL NUTRITION

NATURAL HEALTH CARE

HEALTH DISORDERS

THE IMPORTANCE OF MICRONUTRIENTS

WHILE PROTEIN, FAT, CARBOHYDRATE, and fibre make up the large "macronutrients" necessary for a healthy life, small quantities of other items are also vital. These are the "micronutrients", the vitamins and minerals that work at the cellular level, helping the cat's body to function with maximum efficiency. The importance of some of these trace nutrients is only now being discovered.

OBTAINING NUTRIENTS

Both dogs and people can survive on plant-derived protein because they can obtain from plant protein all the essential amino acids their bodies need. Through evolution, with meat always available, the cat lost the ability to manufacture the essential amino acid taurine and, to a lesser extent, arginine. Cats obtain these vital nutrients from meat, poultry, and fish tissue.

Insufficient taurine in a cat's diet leads to blindness, heart failure, and other serious diseases. The microbial flora of the gut varies according to what a cat eats. Somehow, wet foods promote bacteria that break down more taurine. Reputable manufacturers of quality cat foods ensure that their canned foods contain at least twice as much taurine (in excess of 2 g per kg) as their dry foods.

Cats are extremely sensitive to even a single meal low in arginine. Vomiting, muscle spasms, and sensitivity to touch rapidly ensue. Fortunately, arginine is present in all diets containing adequate levels of protein.

THE ROLE OF VITAMINS

Vitamins have many roles to play in cat nutrition. For convenience, vitamins are divided into fat-soluble and water-soluble

groups. Although vitamins from each group can have similar functions (for example, water-soluble vitamin C and fat-soluble vitamin E both act as antioxidants), their roles in the cat's body differs according to whether they are fat- or water-soluble.

FAT-SOLUBLE VITAMINS

Unlike humans, a cat cannot manufacture vitamin A. It needs to consume preformed vitamin A, found in fish-liver oils and animal livers, and use it to maintain good retinal health. Excess vitamin A causes bone deformities, especially in the bones of the neck, leading to pain and lameness.

Cats need vitamin D, together with a proper balance of calcium and phosphorus, in their diet for skeletal development and growth. Excess leads to skeletal deformities. Natural vitamin D is high in the viscera of marine fish, posing a health hazard if a cat is fed large quantities of marine fish.

Vitamin E, together with the mineral selenium, acts as an antioxidant, neutralizing chemicals called "free radicals" that damage cell membranes. A deficiency of vitamin E leads to pansteatitis, causing fever and loss of appetite. Cats consuming high levels of fish oil will need an increase of daily vitamin E.

Vitamin K is necessary for blood coagulation. Natural deficiencies rarely occur. Eating a rodent killed with the anti-blood-clotting rodenticide warfarin may create a sudden and unattainable demand for vitamin K. Cats on prolonged antibiotic therapy benefit from a vitamin K supplement.

WATER-SOLUBLE VITAMINS

There is little risk of overdosing with the water-soluble vitamins. If food is deficient in vitamin B complex, yeast-based tablets are a safe supplement. Thiamine deficiency may occur in cats fed large quantities of certain species of raw fish that contain an enzyme that destroys thiamine. Deficiencies in folic acid lead to an increase in circulating levels of the amino acid homocysteine, recently recognized to be an important factor in

TASTY BUT WRONG
Cats do not necessarily eat what is nutritionally best. Tuna contains an enzyme that destroys thiamine and may eventually lead to clinical thiamine deficiency. Do not let your cat dictate what it eats, and vary its diet to prevent micronutrient deficiencies or overdoses.

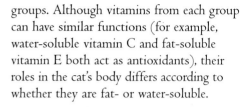

human heart disease. Excess folic acid may cause gastrointestinal problems in cats.

The cat manufactures its own vitamin C so take care if giving a vitamin C supplement to your cat. Excess vitamin C is excreted in the urine as a substance called oxalate. In the last decade, there has been an increase in the incidence of oxalate bladder stones in cats.

MINERALS

Like vitamins, minerals play vital roles at the cellular level. Calcium and phosphorus are necessary for growth and maintenance of the skeleton and for cell membrane and neuro-muscular function. Meat-only diets (low in calcium) lead to over-stimulation of the parathyroid gland and eventual swollen, painful joints. Lactation can result in low blood calcium leading to eclampsia, but too much calcium during pregnancy may increase the risk of eclampsia during lactation. Excess dietary calcium may induce zinc deficiency if fed over a prolonged period.

Magnesium has been implicated as a cause of lower urinary tract disease in cats, although recent evidence suggests that it is not singularly responsible for the disease (see pages 140-141). Magnesium deficiencies may be associated with certain heart conditions.

Selenium is an essential part of the enzyme systems that maintain healthy body tissue. It may also play a role in the immune system, and help neutralize carcinogens.

WHAT ARE NUTRACEUTICALS?

The increasing acceptance that certain nutrients such as fatty acids can be therapeutic resulted in the development of what are called "nutraceuticals". The North American Veterinary Nutraceutical Council has been formed to monitor whether products contain the ingredients listed on the label, are safely manufactured to high standards, and do what the labels claim they do. Until standards are set, nutraceutical products can be marketed as miracle cures. Be wary of all miracle cures for your cat.

Iron is vital for red blood cell production, while sodium is an essential nutrient, vital for transporting elements across cell membranes.

ESSENTIAL FATTY ACIDS

Important discoveries have been made in the last decade that explain the vital role of essential fatty acids (EFAs) in controlling allergy, arthritis, inflammation, heart disease, auto-immune disease, kidney and nervous system function, dermatitis, and even cancer. Many of the EFAs called omega 6 are associated with cell inflammation, and some may also suppress the immune system. Another group called omega 3 are associated with reduced cellular inflammation. Omega-3 EFAs do not suppress the immune system. In both people and cats, dietary omega-3

"Selenium is an essential part of the enzyme systems that maintain healthy body tissue. It may also play a role in the immune system."

fatty acids, working at the cellular level, may enhance the efficiency of the immune system.

While other animals manufacture EFAs from their food, cats cannot. They need to eat animal-sourced arachidonic acid and linoleic acid. Linoleic acid is necessary for body growth, wound healing, and liver function. Arachidonic acid is necessary for blood clotting, coat condition, and efficient reproduction. Some of the substances called eicosanoids, derived from arachidonic acid, stimulate inflammation. Feeding diets rich in omega-3 fatty acids results in changes in the compostion of cell walls. As a consequence the cell is less at risk of becoming inflamed.

SUPPLEMENTS
A balanced diet seldom needs vitamin, mineral, or EFA supplementation. Only consider supplements if your cat is elderly, pregnant, or unwell, or when there is a specific need for additional micronutrients. Never exceed the dose prescribed.

ANTIOXIDANTS

An antioxidant is a substance, such as vitamins C or E, that destroys free radicals. Free radicals are atoms in the body that destroy cell membranes. Cats have their own natural free-radical scavenging systems. Consuming additional antioxidants may boost these natural systems.

MINERAL SUPPLY
Iron is essential for red blood cell production. If you feed your cat fresh food, make sure you include an iron supply such as spinach.

PREPARING HOME RECIPES

HOME-MADE DIETS are easy to prepare. Start with high quality, uncontaminated ingredients. Prepare quantities of your cat's food at no more than three-day intervals, and keep meals refrigerated. Bring the food to room temperature before offering it to your cat. Increase or decrease the energy and micronutrient levels of the food according to seasonal changes and your cat's health.

RAW OR COOKED?

Kittens fed raw meat have slightly better growth rates than kittens fed cooked meat. This is not surprising considering that their digestion evolved to cope with raw rather than cooked meals, but there are disadvantages to uncooked meat. Because of modern abattoir methods we simply have to assume that any raw meat, even though it is "fit for human consumption", may be contaminated with harmful Salmonella bacteria. Consuming these bacteria may or may not cause illness in your cat, but it may become a carrier of bacteria harmful to us.

Uncooked freshwater fish can carry a tapeworm (*Diphyllobothrium latum*). Uncooked oily fish like herring has a high level of thiaminase, which breaks down the vitamin thiamine, leading to clinical disease. Almost any form of uncooked meat can harbour the protozoal parasite *Toxoplasma gondii*. Again, this may not cause harm to your cat but is

a potential health hazard to us. Finally, raw mince has a poor calcium-phosphorus ratio. Siamese kittens, in particular, may be prone to juvenile osteodystrophy, a painful developmental joint disease. Because of all these potential problems, there is little to recommend feeding raw food to your cat.

GOOD INGREDIENTS

When selecting what to feed your cat, always use ingredients fit for human consumption. Meat alone is not a balanced food unless fed in whole carcass form including the skeleton and viscera. Plain meat and fish are rich sources of protein and fat but they are low in calcium, vitamin A, and vitamin D.

Below is a recipe for an average-sized adult cat. Because of its universal availability and levels of unsaturated fatty acids I have chosen chicken as a good source of protein.

A STANDARD HOME-MADE DIET

- Chicken ....140 g
- Liver ....30 g
- Uncooked rice ....70 g
- Sterilized bone meal ....10 g
- Iodized salt ....5 ml
- Sunflower or corn oil ....2 g

Cook the rice, bone meal, salt, and corn oil in twice the volume of water. Simmer for 20 minutes. Add the chicken and liver, simmering for another 10 minutes. Blend thoroughly to prevent your cat separating the meat from the rice. This recipe produces about 800 kcal of energy, enough to feed a 3.8 kg (8 lb) cat for three days or a 5 kg (11 lb) cat for two days.

For weight control, replace medium-fat chicken with very lean poultry or flaky white fish. Reduce the vegetable oil by half. For extra fibre, add 40 g (⅔ cup) of wheat bran to this recipe and increase the water for cooking by 50 per cent. If you are feeding any cereal grains for added fibre, remember that these are poorly digested by cats. Cook a cup of grain in 2.5 cups of water for 75 minutes over low heat. If you see any grain

NOURISHING TREATS
If you love your cat, it is likely that you love giving it treats. It is simply human nature. There is nothing wrong with treats unless you give them in excess. Never let treats make up more than 10 per cent of the energy in your cat's diet and take account of these calories when preparing the rest of its daily food.

in your cat's stool, it has not been digested properly. Try soaking the grain in water overnight, cooking it longer, using more water, or using cracked grain instead of whole grain.

FOODS TO AVOID

Tofu can be difficult for cats to digest, causing them to produce loose, pasty stools. Tofu may also increase mucous congestion in a cat's lungs. It is unnecessary to give milk to adult cats. They lack an enzyme necessary to digest it. Siamese cats are especially prone to milk intolerance. If your cat develops diarrhoea on cow's or goat's milk, give it lactose-free milk, available for lactose-sensitive children, from supermarkets.

GOOD SUPPLEMENTS

Supplements are unnecessary if a diet is well balanced. If you are unsure whether the diet you have prepared is balanced, a single supplement can be prepared from liver, bone meal, iodized salt, and fish oil. This contains all the micronutrients a cat needs.

If feeding individual supplements, do not exceed the following amounts. Brewer's yeast is an excellent source of B-group vitamins and minerals: feed 2.5 g (½ tsp) daily per 5 kg (11 lb) body weight. Vitamin E in the form of "d-alpha tocopherol" is given at 25 IU (International Units) per 5 kg (11 lb) daily. Kelp (*Fucus vesiculosis*) is rich in minerals, especially iodine, which stimulates the thyroid gland: give no more than 1.25 g (¼ tsp) daily. Avoid giving kelp to cats that are prone to

GIVING BONES

Cats eat their entire natural prey including the bones. Bone itself has an ideal ratio of calcium and phosphorus for skeleton maintenance. If introduced early in life, the bones in well-cooked chicken necks are a good source of nourishment for most cats. Be cautious with cats that wolf down their food like dogs. These cats, often Siamese or their close relatives, have developed a competitive manner of eating and are likely to swallow dangerous splinters of bone.

GOOD MANNERS
Show your understanding by providing your cat with a suitable bowl, wide enough for its whiskers. If it does not like the food bowl, it will lift food from it, drop it on the floor, and eat it from there. Do not stand over your cat. Cats prefer to eat in privacy rather than be watched.

hyperthyroidism (*see pages 150-151*). Cod-liver oil and halibut-liver oil contain the antioxidants vitamin E and beta carotene. Feed no more than 100 mg per 5 kg (11 lb) daily.

HOW TO FEED

Offer food at somewhere between room temperature and "mouse temperature" – about 35° C (95° F). Put the meal in your cat's bowl, which should be placed out of the way of passing feet, then leave the cat alone to eat in privacy. Do not fall for your cat's histrionics when you offer a perfectly nutritious and palatable diet and it pretends it would rather die than eat such fare. Whether you use a ceramic, glass, stainless-steel, or plastic bowl, make sure it is wider than your cat's whiskers. Cats dislike narrow bowls and remove food from them to eat off the floor. Thoroughly wash your cat's food and water bowls daily but avoid bleaches or detergents with citrus or pine smells. They are likely to repel rather than attract your cat.

A VEGETARIAN DIET?

The answer is simply, "No!" It is unnatural, unbalanced, and potentially deadly to feed a cat a vegetarian diet. Don't do it.

HEALTHY TREATS

Too many "treats" can unbalance your cat's diet. Offer treats only occasionally and in small amounts. Use brewer's yeast tablets or small cubes of microwaved liver as training rewards. Make sure that treats make up less than 10 per cent of your cat's daily intake.

ALGAE-BASED SUPPLEMENTS

Blue-green algae such as spirulina are protein-rich compared to other plants. Algae also contain high levels of B-complex vitamins and iron, as well as traces of manganese, selenium, and zinc. Blue-green algae are safe at certain times of year but have seasonal "toxic blooms" causing gastrointestinal upset when eaten, and skin irritation upon contact.

NATURAL DEVELOPMENT

NATURAL TRAINING

NATURAL NUTRITION

NATURAL HEALTH CARE

HEALTH DISORDERS

COMMERCIALLY PRODUCED FOOD

IT IS AN UNFORTUNATE FACT that most cat owners simply do not have the time to develop an understanding of their cat's nutritional needs and then meet them with home-cooked foods on a daily basis. Some commercial pet food companies understand this dilemma and use the healthiest products, safest manufacturing processes, and, most important, carry out extensive feeding trials.

CHECKLIST

- Using a calculator, work out the nutrient content of cat foods on a dry-matter basis.
- Only use products tested by extensive feeding trials.
- Telephone the manufacturer to get ingredient information that is not on the label.
- Only buy products from manufacturers who have carried out long-term programmes of research.
- Pay attention to your cat's opinion about any food.

WHAT IS IN CAT FOOD?

Reputable pet food manufacturers only use surplus nutrients from the human food chain in their products. Less reputable manufacturers may use products that have been deemed unfit for human consumption. At the premium end of the commercial cat food market, manufacturers compete with human-food producers for ingredients.

Whether canned or dry, cat food recipes follow either variable or fixed formulas. Fixed formulas remain constant and form the premium end of the market. Manufacturers make no substitutions. A variable formula product is not necessarily inferior as long as the variety of ingredients remains of high quality and nutritional value. What is in cat food is listed on the label. Unfortunately, this often needs interpretation direct from the manufacturer.

HOW TO INTERPRET A LABEL

Labels give information on:
Typical or Guaranteed Analysis This usually lists the minimum amount of protein and fat and the maximum amount of fibre and moisture. This says little about the quality of a product. Manufacturers may list other ingredients such as taurine and ash. Ash refers to the food's total mineral content, including magnesium. Magnesium has been associated with urinary problems in some cats but its role is questionable. For example, magnesium oxide probably increases the risk of urinary problems, while magnesium chloride actually reduces it.
Ingredients This gives you more information on quality but usually fails to be specific.

"LOW CALORIE" AND "LITE"

Manufacturers seldom state the calorie content of their cat food, even when it is promoted as "low calorie" or "lite". In EU countries it is actually not permitted to state the energy content on the majority of cat foods! As a rule of thumb, assume that a "low calorie" food has about 15-25 per cent fewer calories than the average from that manufacturer. If a label gives only "minimum" information and you want to know the "maximum" level for fat or other ingredients, telephone the producer. If a label does not state the metabolizable energy per kilogram of product, manufacturers should provide you with this information.

Constituents are given in descending order of weight. Meat means muscle. Meat by-products or derivatives means viscera, bone, and marrow, natural components of a cat's diet. Meat meal means dry products rendered from animal tissues.
Feeding Guidelines These recommendations are suggestions based on an average cat in ideal condition. Your cat is an individual who may need more or less than is recommended.
Nutritional Adequacy Statement Look for the phrase "animal feeding tests" on North American manufactured foods. If it says "formulated to meet the nutritional profiles..." the manufacturer is relying upon laboratory analysis, not feeding trials, to determine the food's nutritional content.

SELECTING A COMMERICAL FOOD

Most of the world's commercial cat foods are manufactured either in Europe or North America or to standards that have been set on those continents. European foods are always labelled according to EU directives. They must state what preservatives have been added, although they are not required to state what preservatives are present in "preprocessed" ingredients. All European cat foods include a "best before" date that usually corresponds to the shelf life of the fat-soluble vitamins in the product. In the

United States, cat foods and their labels conform to regulations prepared by the Association of American Feed Control Officials (AAFCO). In Canada, a voluntary certification scheme is monitored by the Canadian Veterinary Medical Association. Manufacturers who comply with these standards provide more information on their food labels about ingredients and must substantiate any claims they make.

Manufacturing processes expose foods to a range of "stresses" such as pasteurization. While these procedures make food safer, there can be nutritional losses in food preparation. However, the greatest potential problem with commercially produced food will be spoilage in the package.

SHELF LIFE

Heat, humidity, light, even oxygen can spoil cat food. Of all the nutrients your cat eats, fat spoils fastest. Heat sterilization and vacuum sealing prevent spoilage of canned food but dry cat food needs preservatives. Antioxidants are excellent preservatives. Vitamin E (tocopherols) and vitamin C (ascorbic acid) are usually called "natural" although they are sometimes synthesized. Truly synthetic antioxidants, such as BHA, BHT, and ethoxyquin, are also used. BHA and BHT in excess may be associated with liver and kidney problems.

Food containing 180 parts per million (ppm) of ethoxyquin is associated with increased liver pigment in lactating female dogs. The United States Food and Drug Administration has recommended that the maximum allowable levels of ethoxyquin in pet food should be reduced from 150 ppm to 75 ppm.

Natural antioxidants do not last as long as synthetic ones. To avoid feeding your cat potentially rancid food, buy commercial foods from retailers with a high inventory turnover. Whenever possible, use dry food products within six months of their manufacture date. Store your cat's dry food in a sealed container in a cool, dry location.

FEEDING TRIALS
Laboratory analysis is not sufficient to reveal unexpected problems with any commercial diet. Only feed your cat commercial food that has undergone extensive feeding trials. It is in the interest of reputable manufacturers that they discover potential problems before you do.

NATURAL CAT FOODS

Some manufacturers use the word "natural" on their processed cat foods . Of course, a cat's "natural" diet is fresh, warm, small rodents and birds. Manufacturers of "natural" cat foods include natural rather than man-made antioxidants to their dry foods. In the United States, the world's largest source of cat food, the Food and Drug Administration has no official definition of what "natural" or "preservative free" means, although guidelines will be developed.

URINARY PROBLEMS

Dry cat foods were once believed to be the cause of feline lower urinary tract disease, but veterinary studies suggest that each cat responds individually. A food that is reliable for one cat may predispose another to urinary problems (see pages 140-141).

TYPES OF FOOD

CANNED FOOD
Canned food is palatable to most cats but gives little exercise to teeth and gums. It is best for cats to chew and crunch food. Wet food is prone to contamination if not eaten immediately.

DRY FOOD
These foods are cooked under pressure, then dried. Fat is applied to the surface of the particles for palatability. Nutrients can be lost after a package is opened, so buy it in small packs and use immediately.

NATURAL HEALTH CARE

Over millions of years the cat evolved natural ways to maintain its health. When conditions permit, organs, cells, even molecules repair themselves. We should harness these evolutionary defences, not depress them, when providing health care. Throughout our history we developed numerous ways of caring for ourselves, involving touch or movement, medication, and techniques for influencing our mind and emotions. Some of these methods may be beneficial for cats, too. The objective of any form of therapy is to enhance natural defences and promote repair. Use a therapy to treat a cat only if it clearly meets these objectives.

Exercise is as important as uninterrupted rest to your cat.

THE ORIGINS OF GOOD HEALTH

GOOD HEALTH DEPENDS ON THE BODY being able to repair itself whenever the need arises. All parts of a cat's body are capable of defence, self-diagnosis, and renewal. Organs, cells, even molecules recognize when damage occurs and proceed to remove, recondition, or replace the damage. A cat's body is on guard every second of every day. Only when its natural defences fail does illness ensue.

NATURAL HEALING

My role as a veterinarian is not to heal animals. Cats are outstandingly efficient at healing themselves. A vet's job is to create the circumstances in which an animal's body is best able to repair itself. This can be done by recommending a good diet, by prescribing medicines to help the body overcome attack or organ failure, by surgical interventions such as setting a broken bone, and (this is the complex part) by creating a positive environment that promotes natural healing.

Obvious healing occurs at the visible level. Let us say a cat suffers a skin puncture in a fight with another cat. Over the next two weeks the skin naturally repairs itself. You can watch and marvel as the damage disappears. All of us are familiar with the

"Cats are efficient at healing themselves. A vet's job is to create the circumstances in which an animal's body repairs itself."

inflammation that occurs around a puncture, the formation of a scab, and the growth of new skin under the scab to fill the defect. The real repair, however is less visible.

GUARDIANS OF GOOD HEALTH

At all times, white blood cells circulate in the bloodstream, waiting for accidents to happen. When an injury occurs, such as the skin puncture wound, the "infantry" arrive. Cells called neutrophils, the body's most populous white blood cells, converge at the spot where the defensive line of the skin has been breached. They kill germs that have got through. This creates debris, but almost immediately other white blood cells, called macrophages, quite literally "big eaters", arrive, engulf, and digest the debris. Pus consists of white cells that have committed suicide defending the body. Meanwhile, cell formation begins anew at the margin of the wound. New cells grow across the wound, under the protection of the carapace-like blood clot that has formed. New blood vessels sprout from the closest intact vessels and grow with the new cells.

HARMONIOUS ACTIVITY

All of these activities are controlled by recently discovered chemical regulators called cytokines, proteins so small and so scarce they are almost impossible to detect. Some cytokines stimulate cell growth, while others inhibit it. There is a natural, well-regulated balance between these opposing cytokines. If you consider that the entire lining of your cat's digestive system is virtually renewed several times each week, that gives you an idea of how coordinated these activities are. This natural balance of cytokine activity is influenced by hormones and by the nervous system, by the "state of mind". One state of mind encourages a homeostatic balance of cytokine activity. Another state of mind results in cytokine disharmony. This is how "stress" affects good health.

CELLULAR GOOD HEALTH

The wall of a cell is, like a cat's skin, its first and most important line of defence. It is not a permanent structure, but a membrane made up of proteins embedded in a fatty substance. Recent research into omega-3 (anti-inflammatory) and omega-6 (pro-inflammatory) fatty acids has shown how a cat's diet influences the levels of these fatty acids in cell membranes. Cells with more omega-3 fatty acids in their walls are less likely to become inflamed than those with a preponderance of omega-6 fatty acids. Cell walls are covered with special receptor sites that are designed to recognize and bind important nutrients, hormones, and other substances to the cell. To ensure that the receptor sites are always kept in pristine condition, bits of the cell wall with their receptor sites are continually withdrawn into the cell where they are examined, repaired if necessary, and then returned to the cell's surface. Inside the cells, scavengers called lysosomes recognize and eliminate defective sections of the cell wall. This is natural healing at the cellular level.

MOLECULAR GOOD HEALTH

Cats have trillions of cells in their bodies and millions are replaced every single day. Cells make new cells by passing on their genetic information, their DNA, from one generation to the next. Technically, DNA also transcribes information into another related molecule called RNA that can travel out of a cell nucleus. RNA translates the information it acquired from DNA and directs cells to manufacture specific proteins that will determine the form and function of all aspects of life. These processes of replication, transcription, and translation of information are the most basic processes of life and are profoundly "homeostatic".

THE ROLE OF ENZYMES

Overseeing DNA activity is a special group of proteins called enzymes. Enzymes cut up DNA molecules, dissect out bits, add other bits, and put it all back together with amazing precision and speed. But lots can go wrong. A DNA molecule might be injured by radiation, or ultra-violet light, or any of hundreds of chemicals to which the body is exposed. When this happens, it makes a mistake when it copies itself. The new cell is "wrong". If it is not detected, it multiplies "wrong" and could become a cancer. But molecular troops are waiting for mistakes to happen. When DNA copying goes wrong, special enzymes snip out the damaged bit of DNA, fill the gap with a correct version, then paste the system back together.

Molecular mistakes occur daily and each one is a potential cancer. Virtually all are caught in time. This is natural good health at the molecular level. Your cat's body has evolved to heal itself. Your responsibility in caring for your cat, and mine as its vet, is to ensure the best circumstances for the maintenance of good health, but also to work with natural defences when help is needed to overcome adversity.

WOUND REPAIR

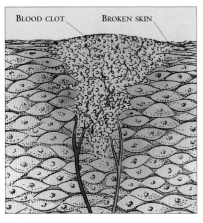

THE SKIN
When skin damage occurs, defensive white blood cells converge at the site of injury. Some kill germs that have invaded the injury, others digest debris.

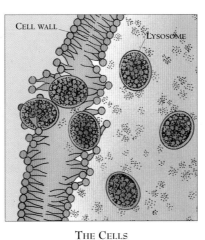

THE CELLS
The wall of each cell protects the interior. Inside each cell, scavengers called lysosomes monitor the health of the cell wall, eliminating defective sections.

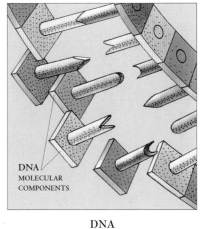

DNA
Within each cell's nucleus DNA copying is carried out. If it goes wrong, special enzymes snip out the damage and fill the gap with the correct version.

WORKING WITH NATURAL DEFENCES

CATS PROVERBIALLY HAVE NINE LIVES for good reasons. They are splendidly efficient at repairing themselves. Cats have superb natural defences against disease, but by keeping cats in unnatural environments, and in our rush to accept all the benefits of modern medicine, we sometimes forget that the essence of restoring good health is to work with those natural defences.

ADVANCES IN MODERN MEDICINE

In the 20th century, spectacular advances in drug therapy have created a vast armoury of weapons we can use to treat diseases. These treatments, though, have their downside. Drug therapy has misled us into thinking in a simple "cause and effect" way. If vomiting occurs, give an anti-emetic. If a cat coughs, give an anti-tussive. If histamine is released in an allergic reaction, give an antihistamine. If a painful inflammation occurs, give an anti-inflammatory. Treating the clinical signs of disease is simple, but when we do so, we may be suppressing the cat's natural defences. We forget that these defences evolved to fight injury and infection.

CONSERVING ENERGY
This kitten is off its food and running a high fever, both components of a cat's natural defences. Fasting and a high temperature make life more difficult for bacteria. If, through forced feeding and medication, we interfere too aggressively, we will weaken the sick kitten's natural defences.

THE CAUSE AND EFFECT OF ILLNESS

Some of the most common problems vets are asked to treat are vomiting, diarrhoea, coughing, and limping. None of these are diseases – they are a cat's natural defences, reacting when confronted with something that upsets its equilibrium. Cats naturally swallow hair when they groom themselves. Vomiting is the most efficient way to rid the stomach of hairballs, but also of other potentially harmful substances. Diarrhoea serves the same purpose. Toxins in the intestines are explosively removed as quickly as possible. Intestinal irritants may be covered in mucus when expelled, a good clue that the large intestine is reacting defensively.

Coughing actively expels from the air passages any material that has accumulated as part of the body's natural defence against infection. Coughing may also occur when a cat's heart is not functioning well and fluid has accumulated in the lungs. Limping is a natural way to rest an injured limb. Bearing weight on the other legs gives the injured leg a chance to heal. A common mistake we all make is to suppress these natural defences rather than work with them to fight the threat to equilibrium.

TREATING THE WHOLE CAT

A permanent struggle exists between your cat's natural defences and elements that, if left unchecked, could overcome them. Cancer cells multiply if natural defences don't recognize their presence. Germs enter the body and cause disease unless natural defences detect and destroy them. When we think about how to work with a cat's natural defences, regardless of the type of threat to a cat's health, we need to answer a few simple questions:

1. Is the medical condition genetic or inherited?
Cures are not possible when conditions are genetic. Our best way to enhance natural defences is to avoid selective breeding that leads to known inherited illnesses. If a cat carries the genetic potential for an inherited

disease, it will not necessarily develop that condition – environmental factors play a role. We can help the cat avoid the circumstances that allow the genetic potential for a problem to develop, although we seldom know exactly what those circumstances are.

LESS DEFENCE
Breeds with a small genetic base inherit predispositions to illness. This Himalayan cat may develop cataracts, a hereditary problem in this breed.

2. Have design changes increased susceptibility?
The risk of suffering from some medical problems increases when we deviate away from natural cat design. For example, cats with flat faces, such as Persians, are more prone to complications when they suffer from upper respiratory tract infections. We can enhance their natural defences through good nutrition and daily hygiene.

3. Does the cat's environment cause the problem?
In nature, cats only meet when they fight or mate. Close living in catteries is an unnatural lifestyle that their immune systems have not evolved to cope with. The risk of catching a transmissible infection is high. We can help safeguard a cat's defences by avoiding risk situations and by preventatively vaccinating against transmissible diseases (*see pages 120-121*).

4. How is the problem manifested?
Using pneumonia as an example, difficulty in breathing is a manifestation of the harm done to lung tissue by an infectious virus, bacteria, or fungus.

5. What part of the condition is the cat's defence?
Using the same example, coughing is the cat's natural defence to help expel mucus and debris, by-products of the cat's defensive systems, from its air passages. Rather than suppressing a cough, we should work with it.

6. What are the cat's natural defences?
A cat might have a fever and lose its appetite when it has an infection. These are natural defences, reducing the ability of the germs to multiply. We should not eliminate these defences but rather work with them and allow the cat to heal itself.

7. How does the illness outflank the cat's defences?
Diseases constantly evolve to cope with the threats directed at them. For example, bacteria are in effect being selectively bred for resistance to antibiotics. We need to be aware of the tactics of the enemy when planning to assist a cat's natural defences.

HELPING SELF-REPAIR
In this age of drug therapy we tend to think that drugs alone are responsible for recoveries from illness. When an abscess is treated with antibiotics and the abscess disappears, we credit the antibiotic therapy with the recovery. Antibiotics are powerfully important drugs but they only ever reduce the number of bacteria. They will give the immune system the time it needs to prepare its counterattack, to deploy natural killer cells, macrophages, and other components of the natural defence system. The real source of the cure is the immune system, aided and abetted by antibiotics.

HEALING FROM WITHIN
Drug therapies do not cure. They facilitate self-repair. Through medical or surgical interventions, modern veterinary medicine removes obstacles to healing. Treatments originate outside the body but healing comes from within. Before the development of modern technologies, medicine relied upon the drugs in plants and the power of the mind to overcome disease. The fact that something as intangible as emotion can modify the behaviour of your body cells – and modify the efficiency of your immune system – is accepted in human medicine. It raises the question whether complementary forms of veterinary medicine, too, are able to enhance your cat's natural defences.

CHECKLIST

Selective breeding can have the effect of reducing natural defences. This leads to hereditary health problems such as:

- Cataracts common in Himalayans
- Hip dysplasia in Maine Coons
- Progressive retinal atrophy common in Abyssinians
- Patellar luxation in Devon Rexes
- Deafness in blue-eyed white cats
- Bladder stone formation in various breeds.

NATURAL DEVELOPMENT

NATURAL TRAINING

NATURAL NUTRITION

NATURAL HEALTH CARE

HEALTH DISORDERS

WHAT IS COMPLEMENTARY MEDICINE?

CONVENTIONAL MEDICINE treats the body as an exquisitely evolved piece of machinery, while complementary medicine approaches health from a more spiritual viewpoint. The objectives of both forms of medicine are the same: to return the body to a state of balance. Implementing the spiritual aspects of complementary medicine, however, is more problematic when applied to cats than to humans.

WHY SO LITTLE RESEARCH?

Double-blind studies in which neither the vet nor the cat owner (nor, of course, the cat) know what substance is being used therapeutically, are difficult to set up for many forms of complementary medicine. Also, until recently, there has been little impetus for research from within the fields of complementary or conventional veterinary medicine.

DEFINING MEDICINE

How you define what medicine is or does influences your attitude to different forms of diagnosis and treatment. A dictionary might define medicine as the science of diagnosing and treating disease or damage to the body or mind. Carvel Tiekert, executive director of the American Holistic Veterinary Medical Association defines medicine as "anything that works". To clarify what I am writing about, here are the definitions I use.

Conventional veterinary medicine, also known as orthodox, scientific, modern, or Western medicine, uses scientific principles and techniques to diagnose and treat illness. It is the form of care that is most readily available to cat owners in the West.

DIFFERENT SYMBOLS, COMMON MEANING
Equilibrium is the aim of all forms of medicine. The Western emblem of medicine, the intertwined snakes of the caduceus (left), and the Chinese symbol of yin and yang (above, centre), both represent opposites held in harmonious balance.

Complementary, integrative, or alternative veterinary medicine covers a wide variety of systems of diagnosis and treatment that are separate from conventional veterinary medicine. Treatments are less interventionist than conventional treatments, and often have a spiritual component. Most complementary treatments are fully compatible with those of conventional medicine.

Traditional forms of veterinary medicine use historic methods that may pre-date the scientific era for the diagnosis and treatment of illness. Traditional veterinary medicine includes Far Eastern forms such as Chinese and Japanese, Indian (Ayurvedic), European folk medicine, and indigenous forms of medicine that are still practised in Africa, the Americas, and elsewhere. In poor regions of the world, traditional veterinary medicine still remains the most common form of care for agricultural animals. It is a major branch of complementary veterinary medicine.

HOLISTIC VETERINARY MEDICINE

Holistic medicine (the word is derived from the Greek *holos* meaning "whole") recognizes the interplay of mind, body, and spirit and considers that the whole is greater than the sum of its parts. There is a common belief that holistic medicine is the preserve of the complementary therapies, but in fact it is rapidly being integrated into conventional veterinary medicine. Practising vets know that nutrition, environment, and social relationships can affect health.

While conventional veterinarians talk of "homeostatic balance", vets who practise complementary therapies are interested in "harmony". Conventional vets want to know and understand, right down to the molecular level, what happens when things go wrong in the body, and the homeostatic balance is upset. Complementary vets, and people who choose complementary therapies for themselves or for their cats, feel uneasy with this approach because, by simply breaking down disease into its biochemical components, it denies the influence of the soul.

To describe medicine in this mechanical way is to deny the spirituality of life, the essence of many complementary forms of medicine.

The European medical philosophy that evolved into modern medicine has its origins in the 17th-century tension between the Church and the emerging notion of factual science. The philosopher René Descartes accommodated factual science and religious belief by creating the mind-body philosophy that still influences Western medicine today. Care of the mind, in the form of the soul, was given to the Church, while care of the body was given to medical science. Under this division, medicine evolved to regard illness as a mechanical breakdown of body parts. Spirituality – the mind and the soul – played no role, as these aspects of life and personality previously did, and still do in traditional forms of medicine.

Descartes' philosophy was cruel to animals because without a soul (only humans had souls) animals are automata, functioning by instinct, incapable of experiencing pleasure or pain. His philosophy survives today. When I carried out a survey of British vets' attitudes to pet death, one out of four practising small-animal vets answered that cats are not sentient beings – they are unaware of their own feelings and emotions. When the same survey was applied to veterinarians in Japan, not one of them believed that to be true.

SYMPTOMS AND SIGNS

With words we describe how we feel. I might say I have a headache, or cannot sleep, or feel depressed. These are my symptoms, my subjective feelings. My doctor might then take my pulse or look at the colour of my tongue. My heart rate or pallidness are my clinical signs. Like paediatricians, vets cannot ask their patients about their symptoms. If I see a cat that is holding its head low and squinting in bright light, I might guess that it has a headache, but it is only a guess. Cats cannot tell us about their symptoms. Vets rely completely on clinical signs when making diagnoses.

WHAT ABOUT THE EVIDENCE?

There is a proverb, sometimes attributed to the Chinese, at other times to the Jewish Talmud, that says, "To be uncertain is to be uncomfortable, to be certain is ridiculous". In veterinary medicine, the clinician's state is one of uncomfortableness. Whenever I make a diagnosis, I have to be a little uncertain.

In the early 1990s, a fresh concept, called evidence-based medicine, was developed at McMaster University's Medical School in Canada. The concept suggests that doctors (or vets) have to accept uncertainty. It explains that for many medical questions good research findings will never be available. In these circumstances, we need to rely upon our own, an expert's, or collective experience for the evidence that a treatment is useful.

CONSTANT REASSESSMENT

The McMaster clinicians say that doctors and vets need to constantly assess what they are doing and the outcomes of their actions. Let me give you an example: Cystitis or bladder inflammation causes a cat to urinate more frequently. If I give antibiotics, the frequency of urinating diminishes. Logically, I assume that the antibiotic killed the bacteria causing the medical condition. But it is now known that a bacterial cause for cystitis is, in fact, rare. Yet cats improve on antibiotics.

The answer may be that the antibiotic happens to do something else that, by sheer good fortune, is beneficial. Some antibiotics reduce urinary tract spasm and provide relief from discomfort. Evidence-based medicine says we should evaluate not only what we know, but what we do not know. If treating a cat for cystitis with a herbal remedy results in the cat straining less, evidence-based medicine says use it, rather than wait for the explanation to be found.

Throughout history, people who have practised medicine have used treatments long before understanding them. A considerable problem with our cats, however, is to know which of the complementary therapies we should use and in what circumstances.

SPECIFIC OR HOLISTIC?
Conventional veterinary medicine often aims to restore equilibrium or balance by targeting specific problems with specific drugs. Complementary therapies also aim to restore balance, or harmony, but often use combinations of substances as found in whole herbs.

NATURAL DEVELOPMENT

NATURAL TRAINING

NATURAL NUTRITION

NATURAL HEALTH CARE

HEALTH DISORDERS

COMPLEMENTARY THERAPIES

A VARIETY OF COMPLEMENTARY therapies are available to preserve our good health or to treat illness. However, not all of these therapies can or should be applied to cats. Remember, not all cats enjoy being handled a lot. For any therapy, ask "Is it safe?", "Does it work?", and also, "Is it fair to my cat to use this therapy?" Use therapies that complement the best that conventional medicine offers.

ONE OR THE OTHER?

In 1942, one of the most articulate fathers of modern medicine, Sir William Osler, wrote, "The philosophies of one age become the absurdities of the next and the foolishness of yesterday has become the wisdom of tomorrow". Do not be dogmatic about what is best for your cat. Conventional medicine can be mechanical and dispassionate, but it saves lives. It has been inherently suspicious of complementary therapies but is beginning to adopt Osler's open mind. In 1996, the American Veterinary Medical Association reclassified acupuncture as a conventional rather than a complementary therapy.

CHECKLIST

- Complementary therapies often work on the assumption that disease is a result of interaction between the cat and its environment.

- Complementary therapies are particularly useful for dealing with chronic conditions.

- Just because a form of therapy is "natural", it does not follow that it is safe. Some herbs are toxic to cats.

- If your cat is ill or in pain, always consult your vet before embarking on any form of home treatment.

THE RISE IN POPULARITY

The success of conventional veterinary medicine may be partly responsible for the rising popularity of complementary therapies. When I began practising veterinary medicine almost 30 years ago, every week I saw a cat with viral enteritis. Most died from the disease. Today, because the majority of cats where I practise are vaccinated against enteritis, cases are rare. Because the disease no longer appears to be a threat, some people turn to nosodes – homeopathic remedies – for protection and, because their cats do not develop viral enteritis, feel that the nosode offers protection (*see pages 92-93*).

RELYING ON FAITH

While most of us are reluctant to allow any conventional therapy to be used on ourselves or our cats until the procedure or drug has been subjected to vigorous studies, many of us will happily take complementary therapies on trust. We are attracted to the idea that swallowing something natural, or undergoing

COMMON CAUSES FOR A VISIT TO THE VET

When veterinarians at the University of Minnesota surveyed American veterinary clinics they learned that cats are taken to vets mostly for minor reasons. Here are the most common reasons for cats of different ages being taken to the vet.

0–7 YEARS OLD		7–10 YEARS OLD		OVER 10 YEARS OLD	
No medical problems	34%	Mouth problems	20%	Mouth problems	20%
Mouth problems	10%	No medical problems	19%	No medical problem	12%
Ear mites	5%	Cat bite abscess	3%	Kidney failure	2%
Fleas	3%	Skin problems	2%	Weight loss	2%
Cat bite abscess	3%	Overweight	2%	Heart murmur	2%
Respiratory infection	2%	Animal bite	2%	Overactive thyroid	2%
Tapeworm	2%	Ear mites	1%	Tumour	2%
Eye inflammation	2%	Respiratory infection	1%	Diabetes	1%
Roundworm	1%	Vomiting	1%	Cat bite abscess	1%
Skin problems	1%			Vomiting	1%

a form of medical therapy that is thousands of years old, will enhance good health. We know the pitfalls of conventional medicine – the drug reactions, dispassionate treatment of pets as "illnesses" rather than individuals, the aggressive desire to prolong life length without thought for quality – but we should be equally questioning of complementary medicine. Blind faith in any therapy is not in your cat's interest. Ask questions. How long will it take to see results? If there appears to be no improvement, at what point do you accept that the therapy may not be working?

CONVENTIONAL MEDICINE

Most conventional vets treat all medical problems in the same "fire-brigade" way: there is a fire burning, so douse it. This is by far the best way to treat some but not all conditions. Conventional veterinary medicine should always be your treatment of choice in the following circumstances:

- To manage physical injury and trauma
- To treat medical and surgical emergencies
- To treat acute bacterial and fungal infections and parasitic infestations
- To immunize and prevent infectious disease
- To diagnose and correct hormonal upsets

Conventional medicine is not as good for curing a variety of chronic conditions. These are the areas where, increasingly, cat owners turn to complementary therapies for help:

- Chronic pain and degenerative disease
- Viral diseases and chronic infections
- Chronic allergic disorders
- Heart disease
- Debility and fatigue
- Behavioural and psychosomatic disorders
- Cancer

Owners of cats with any of these problems are often willing to try to tackle the root of the problem by, for example, altering their cat's lifestyle. They want therapies that do not harm other parts of their cat's well-being.

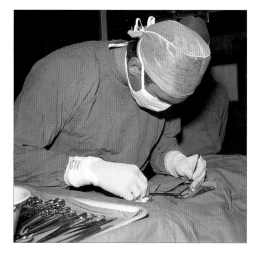

CONVENTIONAL
TREATMENT
*Conventional medicine is at
its finest when confronted
with acute emergencies.
Surgical interventions, or the
use of powerful drugs such
as antibiotics for infections,
are overwhelmingly better at
saving lives than any form
of complementary therapy.*

COMPLEMENTARY THERAPIES

When someone asks me about treating their cat with a complementary therapy, it indicates to me that the owner has a specific philosophy of life and wants to apply it to his or her cat. It also tells me the owner is prepared for a lengthy treatment and does not expect an instant cure. This is not practical with some forms of complementary medicine.

Complementary therapies can be divided into three categories; touch and movement (physical), medicinal, and mind and emotion. Touch and movement therapies are only beneficial with those cats that actively enjoy physical attention from their owners. When animals are manipulated against their will, the stress inhibits their natural killer cells from performing their defensive functions. Never *force* your cat to undergo any form of physical therapy. By doing so, you are weakening its immune system.

If you plan to use any medicinal therapies, remember that a cat's physiology is different to ours. A herb that is safe for us may be toxic to cats. Whenever possible, use supplements or nutrients in appropriate quantities for cats. These can be quite different from the quantities that are beneficial for us.

Mind and emotion therapies depend upon an ability to think in the abstract. The mind-body relationship is increasingly understood by conventional medicine, but what is good for our inner needs does not necessarily apply to cats. Never force a cat to undergo any type of mind-body therapy it does not enjoy.

WHERE TO GO
Cats have different
nutritional, medical,
and emotional needs
from our own. The
best way you can
help your cat is to
seek the advice of a
qualified veterinarian
who understands the
different needs of
pets. He or she will
refer you to a vet
who specializes in
the most appropriate
complementary
therapy.

NATURAL DEVELOPMENT

NATURAL TRAINING

NATURAL NUTRITION

NATURAL HEALTH CARE

HEALTH DISORDERS

THE MIND-BODY RELATIONSHIP

THE RELATIONSHIP BETWEEN mind and body, and between personality and good health, has long been recognized in Eastern medicine and is becoming accepted by conventional medicine. Positive, extrovert personalities cope better with poor health than negative, introverted personalities. Although it is difficult to study this phenomenon in cats, there is no reason why it should not apply to them too.

A CHANGING ATTITUDE

It is true that until recently, conventional veterinary medicine used to be interested primarily in physical cause and effect. Little attention was paid to the influence personality has on behaviour, health, or illness. This is now changing. There is a converging interest in the role that stress and personality play in a cat's health.

MIND AND BODY MEDICINE

The interrelationship between mind and body has been accepted for centuries in traditional forms of medicine throughout the world. In traditional Chinese medicine, the life force, *qi*, directs and co-ordinates the flows of energy and is central to a cat's health, personality, and individuality. Practitioners of traditional Indian medicine believe that three *doshas* "vital energies" — *vata*, *pitta*, and *kapha* — not only govern health but also shape the personality.

In modern veterinary medicine, the branch called psychoneuroimmunology (PNI) examines the interrelations between an animal's mind ("psycho"), its nervous and hormonal systems ("neuro"), and its immune system ("immuno"). PNI investigates 24-hour circadian rhythms, biofeedback, and neuroendocrines and cytokines (proteins that stimulate or inhibit cell growth).

The differences in the explanations of traditional medicine and modern Western medicine may seem overwhelming. *Qi* and *doshas* are mysterious, even spiritual, while

PNI is dry, arcane, and pedantic, but both Eastern and Western medical systems make a connection between the mind and body.

In all forms of traditional medicine, the way you think and feel is believed to have a direct effect on how your body responds to illness. In conventional medicine, it is known that the number of circulating natural killer cells, vital for good health, is affected by emotion. When university students are under the stress of exams, the fighting power of the killer cells in their immune systems is known to drop temporarily.

Abhorrent experiments carried out in the early 20th century showed that cats were able to learn helplessness, and that this adversely affected their health. Cats are naturally a highly resilient species, but when cats, like the university students, are put under emotional stress, the efficiency of their immune system is adversely affected.

THE PLACEBO RESPONSE

In highly sociable species such as humans, the mind-body relationship can be affected in many ways. One of the most intriguing ways is through the placebo response. In both human and veterinary medicine, any new therapy produces benefits when it is first introduced, even when that therapy ultimately is found to lack any special value.

In human medicine, surgically tying an artery in the chest in individuals with angina eliminated pain for many of them. But so too did just surgically opening and closing the skin without tying the artery. Ultrasound was found to reduce wisdom-tooth pain, but so did the ultrasound machine when it was set to produce no ultrasound. Dr Harold Koenig from Duke University in North Carolina discovered that churchgoers have better functioning immune systems than non-churchgoers.

These are examples of placebo responses, or benefits that arise for non-physical or non-material reasons. Whether you believe in God, in orthodox Western medicine, or in complementary therapies, belief itself seems

SWEET PLACEBO
When mice were given, with saccharin, a drug by mouth to suppress their immune system, their defensive capacity faltered. Later, just giving the saccharin without the drug caused immune failure. Animals are capable of experiencing a placebo response.

to play a role in the body's natural defences. All of us, regardless of our own individual personality, can benefit from the placebo response. There is one common factor, however, which is expectation. A doctor's or a veterinarian's expectation is infectious. If your doctor is convinced that a treatment will work, and convinces you, the treatment has a better chance of working. A difficult question to answer is whether cats can experience expectation, the basis of the placebo response.

PLACEBO RESPONSE IN ANIMALS

Expectation is a learned or conditioned response. Writing about the placebo effect in the *Textbook of Pain*, the neuroscientist Patrick Wall eloquently says, "'Mummy will kiss it better' is a wonderful, beautiful, and effective treatment." Even physiological body processes can be changed through expectation. Over 20 years ago, studies of mice showed that when they were given insulin, which lowered their blood sugar, they responded by producing more sugar. Later, salt water injections instead of insulin injections also stimulated them to produce more sugar. The salt water was a placebo that provoked a physiological response. The mice had been "conditioned" to experience a surge in blood sugar, even though salt water would not cause this effect.

UNDER YOUR INFLUENCE?

Studies of dog owners in the United States and Britain show that their personality can have a direct effect on their dog's behaviour. Among Cocker Spaniel owners, tense, shy, and anxious people are more likely to have aggressive dogs. What this interesting study showed was the possible relationship between how you treat an animal and its attitude towards life. I am sure that most people who work with cats understand that an owner's personality affects a cat's behaviour. Whether your relationship with your cat can affect its state of mind and its health is not known. I see no reason why it should not.

SIAMESE TWINS?
Selective breeding creates cat breeds whose members all have similar personality profiles. Siamese cats, for instance, are vocal. However, individual personalities do still vary within each breed.

YOUR VALUE AS A PLACEBO

People with a natural desire to please others are more likely to enjoy a placebo effect, while hostility reduces the placebo response. Does this mean that people-oriented cats are more responsive to the placebo effect than feral cats that have never been handled? The experiments with mice (*facing page*) suggest that the placebo effect is conditioned.

If this is the case, the placebo effect can perhaps be experienced by people-oriented cats, conditioned as they are to accept our interventions. Through selective breeding, we have perpetuated the kitten in cats, and through early learning we make them reliant on us for food and security. The more "kitten-like" your cat, and the more sociable it is, the more open it will be to being conditioned to benefit from the placebo response. In contrast, a feral cat may be stressed by well-meaning interventions.

YOUR CAT'S IMMUNE SYSTEM

In Britain, where for decades the common cold was studied, only 20 per cent of the volunteers exposed to the cold virus became infected. Of these, 25 per cent developed symptoms. Your chance of catching a cold depends in part on your personality. How optimistic you are, and even whether you are extroverted or introverted, affects how well your immune system works.

Similarly, a group of cats can be exposed to a calici flu virus but not all the cats will develop the disease. The efficiency of a cat's immune system plays a vital role in whether or not it picks up an infection. Just as they are for us, our cats' personalities and states of health are interrelated.

NATURAL DEVELOPMENT

NATURAL TRAINING

NATURAL NUTRITION

NATURAL HEALTH CARE

HEALTH DISORDERS

ASSESSING YOUR CAT'S PERSONALITY

NATURAL DEVELOPMENT

NATURAL TRAINING

NATURAL NUTRITION

NATURAL HEALTH CARE

HEALTH DISORDERS

THE DISTINCT AND UNIQUE personality of your cat is an important factor to consider before embarking upon any form of conventional or complementary therapy. Assessing your cat's personality will help you to decide which, if any, of the different therapies may provide benefit to it, and which should be avoided unless there are no suitable and effective alternatives.

CHECKLIST

- A cat's personality is partly inherited and partly formed by its environment.
- For thousands of years, cats' lives have been solitary and self-reliant.
- Generic personality differences exist between breeds and between the sexes, as well as the differences that exist between individual cats.
- Selective breeding can enhance or diminish a cat's natural ability to defend its good health.

THERAPY AND PERSONALITY

In his book, *How the Mind Works*, Professor Steven Pinker explains how evolutionary pressures shaped not just how an animal's body functions but also how it thinks. He explains how emotions are part of the interlocking systems that evolved to help individuals survive. This suggests that your cat's personality plays an integral role in its state of health, one that it is vital to take into account when your cat is not well.

Many traditional therapies will consider the personality type or constitution before deciding on the treatment. Personalities are described by statement, rather than critique, as "strong" or "weak". Types of herbs, or even the amount of pressure applied during manipulations, are altered according to an individual's personality. For instance, in the Ayurvedic system, cats are divided into three personality groups: so-called *kapha* cats are well-muscled, strong, stable, patient, and possessive; *pitta* cats are evenly proportioned, confident, and aggressively competitive; and *vata* cats are lithe, lanky, quick, and creative but energy-wasting. More generally, cats are described as having "excess" or "deficient"

"DEFICIENT" INDIVIDUAL
The introverted nature of the "deficient" cat may make it prone to illness. Active therapies may stress these individuals. They may benefit from benign therapies that enhance the immune system.

personalities. An "excess" cat is assertive, hard-muscled, confident, with a strong voice, quick, lithe, and demanding attention. A "deficient" cat is shy, timid, introverted with a quiet miaow, and suffers poor digestion and frequent illness. If overweight, it will have pudgy fat and weak muscles. If thin, it has a slight bone structure and small muscles.

"EXCESS" INDIVIDUAL
These confident, attention-demanding, well-muscled, assertive cats have strong personalities that make them more open to a variety of complementary therapies.

QUESTIONNAIRE

The questionnaire below is designed to help you assess the personality of your cat. Does your cat greet your guests, or does it disappear until visitors have left your home? Is your cat always hunting and playing, or is it content to sit in a warm spot for hours on end? The questionnaire also addresses your cat's nutrition and general health in order to assess the efficacy of its immune system.

Different factors are presented in the column on the left, while on the right you will find lists of related statements. Consider your cat and score each statement accordingly, using the scoring system given in the box on the right. When you have finished, add up the scores and check the total in the box at bottom right. Your cat's result will indicate how it is likely to respond to complementary therapies.

SCORE	
Almost always	5
Usually	4
Sometimes	3
Rarely	2
Almost never	1

FACTOR	ASSESSMENT
SOCIABILITY WITH PEOPLE Many therapies involve active participation by people. Therapies such as acupuncture and massage should only be used on cats that have high scores on sociability with people.	*My cat:* • Likes to be with its human family • Greets strangers who visit • Enjoys being stroked • Actively asks to play
LEVEL OF ACTIVITY Just as our own physical fitness is an important factor in overcoming ill health, active cats are best equipped to maintain good health, and to recover quickly from injury or illness.	*My cat:* • Enjoys physical activity • Plays games with its human family • Gets active daily exercise outdoors • Demands attention
RISK-TAKING A risk-taking cat increases its risk of physical injury, but a risk-taking individual's curiosity and enthusiasm may help it to recover most efficiently from states of poor health.	*My cat:* • Willingly investigates new surroundings • Approaches other animals without fear • Is relaxed when visiting the vet • Is not frightened by new experiences
HEALTH General good health is the best sign that a cat's immune system functions efficiently. A high score here means that your cat's defences have generally been working well.	*My cat:* • Is physically well • Recovers quickly from minor illnesses • Is uncomplaining about minor injuries • Seems only normally sensitive to pain
NUTRITION Good nutrition is the basis of good health. Mother's milk provides early protection from diseases she has been exposed to. High-quality nutrients provide the building blocks for life.	*My cat:* • Has been well-fed from an early age • Willingly eats a variety of foods • Has a healthy digestion • Is fed high-quality foods with no additives
SOCIABILITY WITH OTHER CATS Sociability with other cats indicates a positive attitude. Through selective breeding and early learning we try to perpetuate sociability in cats. This trait may act as a spur to recovery.	*My cat:* • Enjoys the company of other family cats • Accepts the presence of visiting cats • Has its own outdoor "cat friends" • Shares its resting places with other cats

INTERPRETATION

24 – 55 Your cat's personality and its lifestyle suggest it will not enjoy many conventional or complementary therapies.

56 – 89 Taking into account where your cat has scored highest, it can benefit selectively from some complementary therapies.

90 – 120 Your cat has a confident and outgoing nature. It will be able to accept a wide range of forms of complementary therapy.

NATURAL DEVELOPMENT

NATURAL TRAINING

NATURAL NUTRITION

NATURAL HEALTH CARE

HEALTH DISORDERS

NATURAL HEALTH CARE

70

NATURAL DEVELOPMENT

NATURAL TRAINING

NATURAL NUTRITION

NATURAL HEALTH CARE

HEALTH DISORDERS

TOUCH AND MOVEMENT THERAPIES

TOUCH IS A CAT'S MOST PRIMITIVE SENSE. A newborn kitten first finds its mother through touch, maintaining contact with her and the rest of the litter for warmth and security. Harry Harlow's inhumane experiments with macaques at the University of Wisconsin in the 1950s showed how vital touch is to good health. Using a glass partition, Harlow separated newborn macaques from their mothers at birth. The baby macaques were well nourished but had no physical contact with their mothers or any other animals. When they matured, they developed physical, behavioural, and medical problems.

Throughout kittenhood, mothers lick their young and both are physically and psychologically rewarded by their actions. In feral circumstances, touching comes to an end when the litter is dispersed. Touch only continues between relatives, usually females who live together near a good food source. These individuals continue to touch each other through mutual licking or by simply lying in close physical contact. Our intervention in the life of the house cat potentiates the value of touch. Petting from people early in life moulds personalities that thrive on contact comfort later in life.

TTOUCH THERAPY
TTouch was initially developed by Linda Tellington-Jones as a training method for horses. Later she adapted her methods for all animals. The gentle, rhythmic stroking relaxes and focuses them.

Most of us understand intuitively that touch is beneficial. In the 1970s, Dr Aaron Katcher, a psychiatrist at the University of Pennsylvania, found that pet owners experience a drop in

ACUPUNCTURE
Frequently used for arthritis, back pain, and tendon injuries, acupuncture is known to stimulate the body's endorphins, bringing natural pain relief.

blood pressure when they stroke their pets. Later, Dr Constance Perin at the Massachusetts Institute of Technology suggested that when we touch our pets we are subconsciously reminded of our own infancy, and feel the same rewards that we experienced when we were in physical contact with our mothers.

Touch and movement therapies are especially appealing to cat owners who turn to complementary therapies as a refuge from the unwanted side effects and technological obsessions of conventional veterinary medicine. Acupuncture and acupressure are the most widely available of all these therapies. Veterinary chiropractic is more widespread than osteopathy. Trigger point therapy is mainly found in Australia and China. Hydrotherapy is used for dogs to treat a wide range of conditions in Japan, and as a physiotherapy wherever a swimming pool is available, but its suitability for cats is limited.

Many cats resent physical therapies simply because, while natural for dogs and us, they are unnatural for cats. The most common touch therapy, massage, is probably the least stressful therapy for cats because it can be carried out at home. Massage is perhaps the simplest and the most effective of all the contact treatments.

THERAPEUTIC MASSAGE
As well as reducing stiffness and pain, massage can diminish anxiety and stress, which in turn helps the immune system to function efficiently.

NATURAL DEVELOPMENT

NATURAL TRAINING

NATURAL NUTRITION

NATURAL HEALTH CARE

HEALTH DISORDERS

NATURAL DEVELOPMENT

NATURAL TRAINING

NATURAL NUTRITION

NATURAL HEALTH CARE

HEALTH DISORDERS

ACUPUNCTURE

ACCORDING TO TRADITIONAL Chinese Medicine (TCM), all forms of life are shaped by the dynamic interaction of *yin* and *yang*, the opposite aspects of life. The basis of good health is the appropriate balance of *yin* and *yang*. An imbalance results in illness. Acupuncture, the insertion of needles in the body, developed out of this philosophy. Some cats resent this form of complementary therapy.

CHECKLIST

Consider the following questions before taking your cat for acupuncture treatment.

- Is my cat going to resent treatment?

- How long does a session last?

- How will I know if my cat's health is improving?

- How many sessions are likely to be needed?

- Are there going to be after-effects?

- What will it cost?

HISTORY

Veterinary acupuncture is probably as old as acupuncture itself. A treatise on the use of acupuncture on elephants, thought to be 3,000 years old, was found in Sri Lanka in 1979. In China, a rock carving that is over 2,000 years old depicts soldiers performing acupuncture with swords on their horses. Outside China, modern interest in veterinary acupuncture developed during the 1970s, and the International Veterinary Acupuncture Society (IVAS) was formed in 1975. This organization provides extensive courses for veterinarians, and a vet who has completed IVAS training has a good understanding of the theory and practice of acupuncture.

HOW IT WORKS

There are two radically different theories, Chinese and Western, about how acupuncture works. In Traditional Chinese Medicine, acupuncture is one element in a range of recognized therapies that also include herbs, acupressure, exercise, and diet. Fundamental to the philosophy of TCM is the concept of a vital force called *qi*, an invisible "life energy" that flows along meridians, or channels, through the body. *Qi* is maintained by *yin* and *yang*, opposite but complementary forces whose perfect balance keeps the body in harmony. Along the meridians are points where *qi* is concentrated. Humans have 670 acupoints; in cats there are 112 traditional acupoints. Inserting a fine needle at any of these points stimulates or suppresses the flow of energy. The role of the traditional acupuncturist is to determine the imbalance of *qi* and to use appropriate acupuncture points to stimulate or suppress it.

In Western veterinary acupuncture, vets may find the philosophy of TCM appealing, but they will also make a diagnosis by using the scientific means at their disposal: a

TREATING AN INJURED FORELEG

1 The practitioner first examines the patient, and a full history of the current problem, plus details of previous illnesses and injuries, is taken from the pet owner. The cat is examined for signs of pain or discomfort, or imbalance in any part of its body.

2 On the basis of the examination and history, the practitioner selects the smallest possible number of points for treatment. Selection can also be based on experience, intuition and, especially in the case of cats, the animal's tolerance of being handled and restricted.

WHERE IT IS AVAILABLE

Acupuncture for cats is a medical procedure and can only be performed by a qualified veterinary acupuncturist. Do not have the procedure carried out by someone who performs acupuncture solely on people. Your veterinarian should be able to recommend a colleague who carries out this procedure. If not, write to the International Veterinary Acupuncture Society for practitioners in your locality. Do not use acupuncture as an alternative to drugs or surgery for the treatment of severe or acute pain, and do not take a cat in pain on long car trips for acupuncture therapy. The journeys might increase your cat's discomfort.

physical examination, laboratory tests, x-rays, and other techniques, such as ultrasound. Once the diagnosis is made, acupuncture is performed at points individually selected for treating the disease or pathological condition. The typically Western approach is to insert the needles in the region where the animal feels chronic pain, rather than in one of the classic acupoints elsewhere on the body.

VETERINARY OPINION

Painkilling drugs work by mimicking the brain's painkilling chemicals, the endorphins. Acupuncture stimulates the release of the brain's endorphins, bringing natural pain relief. In 1996, the American Veterinary Medical Association said: "Veterinary acupuncture and acutherapy are now considered an integral part of veterinary medicine." Its most frequent application is for problems such as arthritis, back pain, tendon injuries, and physical problems of the nervous system. Although most commonly used as a non-chemical method for reducing pain, some veterinary practitioners use acupuncture to promote healing of damaged tissue.

Some cats accept the insertion of needles surprisingly well, becoming relaxed and tranquil, even falling asleep while the needles remain in place. Cats that are particularly sensitive are more likely to be upset by the procedure, especially when it takes place in strange surroundings. Independent cats may resent treatment. Acupuncture should not be used on a cat that resents or is upset by the procedure. It causes more harm than good.

NEEDLES
The thin, flexible acupuncture needles used on cats range in length from 1-4 cm (0.5-1.5 in).

HOW OFTEN?

Therapy usually begins with weekly sessions for a month, and continues with further sessions at longer intervals in cases where more therapy is beneficial. If no improvement is seen after the first three sessions, it is unlikely that further acupuncture will be beneficial.

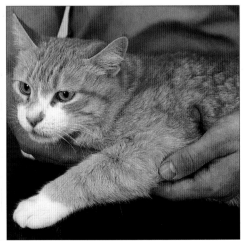

3 Needles are placed at various depths according to location and size of patient. The patient is left as quiet as possible during the treatment, which may last up to half and hour. Most pets relax deeply, some even sleeping soundly during the session.

4 After the treatment, the needles are removed. Some cats need a little time to "wake up" and a gentle massage helps to complete their treatment. Most cats finish each treatment in a relaxed state and often happily accept their next treatment.

NATURAL DEVELOPMENT

NATURAL TRAINING

NATURAL NUTRITION

NATURAL HEALTH CARE

HEALTH DISORDERS

ACUPRESSURE

ACUPRESSURE IS BELIEVED to predate its sister therapy, acupuncture (*see page 72*), but is less well known in the West. It works on the same principle, that *qi*, "life energy", flows along meridians around the body. Pressure is applied with the fingers to points on the meridians. It is perhaps more suitable for cats than acupuncture, and has the advantage that, with training, cat owners can apply it at home.

CHECKLIST

- Done incorrectly, a manipulation can increase pain and make the patient worse. Ask the practitioner to show you how to apply finger pressure.

- Do not try to use a manipulation therapy to control overt pain.

- To control your cat's discomfort, use pain-killing medications that you know to be effective.

- Never persist with the use of a manipulation therapy that your cat resents.

HISTORY

Many Chinese doctors practise acupressure, and it is a popular form of self-help, but it is infrequently used in veterinary medicine. Historically, several styles of acupressure developed, the most common of which is *tuina*, which involves finger pressure but also rubbing, kneading, and rolling. The Japanese form of acupressure, *anma*, developed into what is now called shiatsu (*see page 75*).

HOW IT WORKS

Your cat's muscles are rather like slings, ropes, and pulleys that move various parts of its body. Muscles lie in layers that run in certain directions. You can liken them to the pile of a carpet that, if rubbed one way, becomes smooth, and if rubbed the opposite way, becomes rough. Acupressure, using straight fingers, presses muscles in the "right"

PRESSURE APPLIED
Acupressure is easily performed at home and is a useful way for owners to continue and become involved in their cat's treatment. The use of finger pressure on the more superficially located points can be a relaxing treatment.

direction. Touch begins on the acupoints in natural "valleys" in the musculature, using the middle finger and and forefinger, or the thumb and forefinger. Pressure intensifies until the cat's muscles start to resist. At this point the pressure is relieved slightly, and then held on the point for five seconds.

Other variations of the sister therapies, acupuncture and acupressure, are used on people but are rarely applied to cats. Moxibustion is as old as acupressure. The herb mugwort, *Artemisia vulgaris*, called moxa in Chinese, is dried, cured, and mortar-ground. Applied as a cone-shaped plug to the top of an inserted needle, the moxa is set alight, heating the needle and causing local skin inflammation.

A modern variation of this heat therapy is electro-acupuncture. Electrodes are attached to inserted needles and a low-voltage electric current passes into the cat's body. Laser light is also sometimes used as an alternative to the physical insertion of needles or to finger pressure (*see page 83*). The laser equipment is expensive and its usefulness depends upon a cat remaining still long enough for the laser to be positioned and used. Laser therapy is used more on horses than on other animals. No conclusive evidence has been published showing the benefits of these therapies.

VETERINARY OPINION

Acupressure is sometimes used on cats that resent the insertion of acupuncture needles. Veterinarians consider acupressure to be a form of massage, and will often use it to relax a cat before it undergoes acupuncture. No evidence has been published that proves acupressure does anything more than relieve pain by relaxing muscles.

WHERE IT IS AVAILABLE

Veterinary acupuncturists sometimes use acupressure as part of their therapy. They will often show cat owners how to apply finger-tip or even finger-nail pressure to acupoints. This is believed to maintain the value of therapy between veterinary visits.

SHIATSU

SHIATSU, A FORM OF finger-pressure therapy, has its basis in Traditional Chinese Medicine and follows the same philosophical principles of "life energy" and meridians as acupuncture and acupressure. Therapists use fingers and thumbs, applying pressure at the key points to stimulate muscle relaxation and blood circulation. Shiatsu for cats is mainly practised in Japan, Australia, and the United States.

LISTEN TO YOUR CAT

Let your cat tell you whether or not to continue with acupressure or shiatsu. Both these forms of manipulation will be comforting to some cats but aggravating to others. Always reward relaxed behaviour with kind words and, whenever possible, a food snack.

HISTORY

Shiatsu, Japanese for "finger pressure", has its origins in Traditional Chinese Medicine, which was introduced into Japan 1,500 years ago. Early in the 20th century in Japan, a massage practitioner named Tamai Tempaku combined the millennia-old practice of acupressure with a modern understanding of medical anatomy and physiology, creating shiatsu. Shiatsu has been successful in Japan and is now widespread there. It has become a popular therapy in Australia, and on the west coast of North America, but is less commonly practised in Europe.

TAKING THE PULSE
Shiatsu practitioners readily use modern techniques, such as monitoring the pulse, both to diagnose a problem and to assess the effects of their therapy.

HOW IT WORKS

There is a considerable gulf between the theory and practicality of shiatsu for cats. Some Japanese practitioners consider that it works in just the same way as acupuncture, by stimulating the same "life force", *ki* (*ki* in Japanese, *qi* in Chinese) along the meridians. Australian and other Western practitioners, on the other hand, tend to use physiological terms to describe the effect of their therapy, claiming that shiatsu massage enhances the body's self-healing capabilities by aiding relaxation and by regulating the components of the circulation system.

Shiatsu massage covers the whole body. The practitioner stretches and massages the cat's trunk, limbs, and head. Manipulation begins gently but becomes firmer if the cat allows. The end of a session, which usually lasts 20 minutes, is followed by a rest period to allow the cat to absorb the benefits of its treatment. Needless to say, the cat decides whether or not to accept shiatsu.

VETERINARY OPINION

Shiatsu is believed to release muscle tension, promote deep relaxation, and aid healing by improving circulation. There have been no published studies of its value. It is not well known in Europe. Practitioners in Australia claim that it is superior to acupressure because it is based upon modern knowledge of feline anatomy. Practitioners ask the owner about the cat's medical history, its diet, and personality, and watch the cat's movement as it walks around, before taking its pulse and beginning the shiatsu massage.

WHERE IT IS AVAILABLE

Shiatsu is available from therapists with a knowledge of feline health, anatomy, and behaviour. There are forms of shiatsu, for example, *Do-in* finger pressure, that rely on self-assessment by the patient, for example of indigestion or a headache. Because it is difficult to diagnose these states in cats accurately, such forms of shiatsu are hard to apply in veterinary care.

NATURAL DEVELOPMENT

NATURAL TRAINING

NATURAL NUTRITION

NATURAL HEALTH CARE

HEALTH DISORDERS

TRIGGER POINT THERAPY

ALTHOUGH MUSCLE ACCOUNTS for 40 per cent or more of your cat's weight, muscle problems receive scant attention in conventional veterinary textbooks. Muscle is subject to daily wear and tear, but veterinarians usually concentrate on the body's "superstructure" – the bones, joints, and ligaments – when treating pain. Trigger point (TP) therapy is a physical treatment of the sites of pain in muscle.

OTHER TRIGGER POINTS

While the most common TPs are in muscles, other TPs can develop on the surface of bone (the periosteum), in the ligaments, scar tissue or, particularly, the skin. A positive skin rolling test over your cat's back, and no skin problems, might indicate active TPs in the muscles below.

HISTORY

Trigger point therapy comes from China and is now beginning to be accepted in Western conventional medical teaching. Until recent decades, if physicians found no laboratory or radiological evidence for the source of a patient's muscle, or "myofascial", pain, they would consider it to be in the person's mind rather than the muscles. The discovery that pain is often felt, not at the site of injury but at a different or "referred" site, led to TP therapy being re-evaluated.

While classic acupuncture points are always located at specific sites, TPs are not. However, over 70 per cent of common TP points are near classic acupuncture points. It seems possible that the Chinese physicians who originally determined the acupuncture points for pain also found and included a number of the more common myofascial TP locations. If this is so, acupressure often works because it affects TPs.

HOW IT WORKS

Scientific research suggests that trigger points in muscles are sites of increased metabolism and nerve sensitivity, but of reduced blood circulation. Muscle consists of two types of fibres, called "slow" and "fast". Throbbing pain comes from "fast" fibres. TP therapy stimulates these fibres, adds to pain for an instant, then relieves it. Left untreated, the muscle cells could become damaged and a source of chronic pain.

A cat naturally shifts its weight to avoid using a painful limb. It may also tense its muscles as a way of coping with discomfort in the joints. Either way, it overuses certain muscles, which then develop painful trigger points. If a cat permits, firm finger pressure is applied on these TP points.

The response to local therapy is usually immediate for recent tenderness. Chronic pain takes longer to control. Hot packs are sometimes applied to the muscle for a few minutes after therapy, to reduce muscle soreness and enhance circulation. Relief is more likely to be long-lasting if all the treated muscles are used in their full range after a therapy session.

VETERINARY OPINION

Working at Murdoch University's veterinary school in Perth, Australia, Dr Liz Frank uses TP therapy on dogs, to relieve discomfort associated with pathological damage and for pain relief in young dogs that have exercised too vigorously. TP therapy is used when a taut, and probably tender, band can be felt in a specific muscle. Dr Luc Janssens in Belgium concentrates his treatments on seven specific trigger points and describes them as feeling "like marbles in mud". Therapy in cats is difficult because few cats permit the finger pressure necessary for therapy.

WHERE IT IS AVAILABLE

Muscle injury is a significant but neglected cause of pain, and TP therapy has limited availability. Experienced therapists work in Australia, Belgium, and the United States.

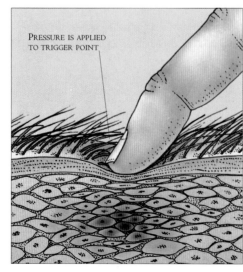

PRESSURE IS APPLIED TO TRIGGER POINT

POINT OF PAIN
Trigger points are found in the neck, shoulders, and hips. Pain is not necessarily felt at a trigger point, but projected to a "referred" site. TP pain is dull, deep, and aching in people. The pain is temporarily heightened when finger pressure is applied, before being relieved.

TTOUCH THERAPY

TTOUCH IS AS MUCH a training method as it is a therapy. It was developed, initially for horses, by Linda Tellington-Jones. This form of simple, circular touch evolved from the light movements that had been used in the Feldenkrais Method to increase people's body awareness. Circular finger movements are used over a cat's body to relax it, either as an aid to healing or to reduce fearful behaviour.

TTOUCH TECHNIQUES

To make learning easy, TTouch uses animal names to describe different methods. For example, Raccoon TTouch is quick, gentle, and light while Bear TTouch is deep and slow. The basic circular touch used most often on cats is called Clouded Leopard, signifying softness with strength.

HISTORY

In 1972 the Israeli engineer and writer Moshe Feldenkrais published a book called *Awareness through Movement*, in which he promoted his concept that the brain learns to direct the body to move in certain ways, and that these ways are not necessarily the best ones. Linda Tellington-Jones, a Canadian horse-trainer, successfully adapted the Feldenkrais Method to horse training. In 1978, she created the so-called TTEAM (Tellington-Jones Equine Awareness Method). When her training techniques were applied to dogs and cats, the words behind the acronym were changed to Tellington-Jones Every Animal Method. In 1984, she introduced TTouch, a method of gentle, rhythmic stroking that relaxes and focuses the awareness of animals by stimulating the nervous system.

HOW IT WORKS

TTouch therapy manipulates only the skin, not deeper tissues. With relaxed fingers the cat's skin is gently and slowly pushed around in a small, tight circle, beginning at the six o'clock position and completing a circle and a quarter, finishing at eight o'clock. These circling actions are done in connected lines over the cat's body. Pressure is adjusted for different cats and different parts of the body, depending upon what is comfortable and non-threatening to the cat.

VETERINARY OPINION

While there is no formal evidence that TTouch has therapeutic value, trainers who use it say that animals become relaxed and more focused on their training sessions.

Zoos in San Diego, California in the United States, and in Zurich, Switzerland, include Tellington-Jones methods in their programmes for large cats and other animals. Domestic cats that enjoy contact comfort will find this form of touch therapy relaxing. Frightened or nervous cats that need to be handled may be calmed with TTouch because the movements tend to be slow, repetitive, and non-threatening.

WHERE IT IS AVAILABLE

TTouch practitioners are widely available in Canada and the United States, and they can also be found in the UK. However, a professional therapist is not always needed for this treatment. TTouch is not difficult to learn. The gentle strokes and manipulations can be applied by cat owners to their own pets or by veterinary nurses to hospitalized individuals. Books and videos are available that explain the techniques.

GENTLE MOVEMENT
To relax and calm a cat that is nervous, stroke its ears gently with your thumbs, and make tiny circles at the corner of its mouth with your fingers.

Chiropractic

Chiropractic had dubious beginnings but has matured into an effective form of physical therapy and may have applications for cats. It considers the backbone or spinal column as the defender of the spinal cord and structural focus of the body. When the spine and other parts of the skeletal system function smoothly, the entire system of bones, joints, and muscles works in harmony.

DO-IT-YOURSELF?

Trained veterinary chiropractors and osteopaths know and understand feline anatomy. They know where muscles are attached to bones, and where nerves, ligaments, and tendons are located. Never attempt to use thrusting or rapid manipulations on your cat. A careless manipulation can cause pain. In some circumstances, it can cause paralysis.

HISTORY

Chiropractic was developed in Canada in 1895 by Daniel Palmer and perpetuated by his son, B.J. Palmer. Early chiropractors invented a curious terminology and theory of action for their work that led to it being condemned, in the 1960s, as an "unscientific cult". Condemnation forced chiropractors to carry out properly controlled studies on their clients. The results, worldwide, were so encouraging that chiropractic manipulation is today accepted as a safe technique for alleviating conditions such as lower-back pain. In the 1950s, John McTimoney, a British chiropractor, developed a gentle form of manipulation and applied it to animals. His is the most popular form of veterinary chiropractic in Britain.

HOW IT WORKS

Modern chiropractors examine the spinal column and pelvis and also look at other relevant joints for misalignments or muscle

DANIEL PALMER
Canadian-born Daniel Palmer (1845–1913) founded the Palmer School of Chiropractic in Iowa in 1898. He was jailed in 1906 for practising medicine without a licence, but his son, B.J., continued his work.

spasm. Using hands only, the problem areas are treated with palpitation and manipulation. Aftercare usually involves rest or very limited exercise for several days. Depending upon the injury, one or more treatments may be needed, with half-yearly or yearly re-examinations.

VETERINARY OPINION

In 1996, the American Veterinary Medical Association reported, "Sufficient clinical and anecdotal evidence exists to indicate that veterinary chiropractic can be beneficial." Chiropractic can be used for canine athletes. Greyhounds racing on tight tracks, in one direction only, put abnormal strain on their spinal columns. Agility dogs encountering difficult obstacles on tight courses may also suffer from spinal-column tension.

Chiropractic can be therapeutic for cats during the recovery stage after road traffic accidents and other physical mishaps.

WHERE IT IS AVAILABLE

Few veterinarians are trained in chiropractic manipulation. The American Veterinary Chiropractic Association holds courses both for veterinarians and chiropractors in the United States and Canada. In Britain, the McTimoney Chiropractic Association trains and certifies animal chiropractors. Its practitioners only work on animals that have been referred to them by a qualified vet.

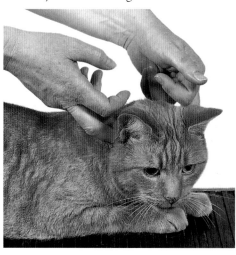

ASSESSMENT
The chiropractor begins the manipulation at the "atlas", behind the cat's ears. The area is palpated to assess what adjustment is necessary, before moving onto the spine.

OSTEOPATHY

OSTEOPATHY AND CHIROPRACTIC are the most widely practised forms of human complementary medicine in the West. Controlled studies show that manipulations based upon a firm understanding of anatomy are effective for limiting human back pain. Because of its superb natural anatomy, the cat suffers from a smaller incidence of spinal-column discomfort than do short-legged dogs, or people.

HISTORY

Osteopathy, like chiropractic, evolved out of bone setting. While chiropractic initially concentrated wholly on the spinal column, osteopathy used touch and manipulation to treat all parts of the musculo-skeletal system. This therapy was developed by Dr Andrew Taylor Still. He was an Army doctor in the American Civil War who later in life, in 1892, founded the American School of Osteopathy. A British School of Osteopathy was founded in 1917. Osteopaths have not been as organized as chiropractors in their approach towards treating cats and other animals. In Britain, some osteopaths are members of the recently formed Association of Chartered Physiotherapists in Animal Therapy (ACPAT). Individuals belonging to this group will only take animal referrals from practising veterinarians.

HOW IT WORKS

Osteopaths are interested in why there is a fault in the musculo-skeletal system, as well as the best way to overcome or cope with it. The techniques that they use are manual, and are sometimes similar to those used by chiropractors to improve the mobility of muscles and joints. But while chiropractic concentrates mainly on the manipulation of misaligned joints, osteopathy places more emphasis on soft-tissue treatment. The aim of this treatment is to bring back mobility by making the muscles relax. Equine osteopaths occasionally use ropes as well as their hands to manipulate joints, but practitioners manipulating felines use methods similar to those used on people.

VETERINARY OPINION

Virtually no research has been carried out on the value of osteopathy for cats, but there is anecdotal evidence: veterinarians who refer individuals with back pain to osteopaths often say they are pleased with the results. Osteopathic procedures may be helpful in the recovery phase after trauma incurred in road traffic accidents, especially injuries involving fractures. Because cats suffer from fewer degenerative joint diseases than people or dogs, osteopathic treatment for these conditions is less vital. The natural role of osteopathy in conventional veterinary medicine has not yet been seriously examined.

WHERE IT IS AVAILABLE

Now established alongside conventional medicine in North America, and practised in Europe and Australasia, osteopathy is widely available for us but still limited in availability for cats. Manipulations are similar to those used by chiropractors, so your veterinarian may refer you to either, depending upon which is available.

PRECAUTIONS

Never force a cat to undergo any kind of physical manipulation. If it does not enjoy the experience, you will do more harm than good. Be aware of the danger that you may force discomfort on your cat in your efforts to give it therapy. For example, a car journey in a carrier to the chiropractor may make your cat's condition worse. If you know that rest is important to recovery, let it take precedence over any manipulation. Manipulations are only appropriate after the rest stage of recovery.

SUPPORT SYSTEM
Practitioners emphasize that the musculo-skeletal system supports the body's vital organs. If bones and joints are correctly aligned, the rest of the body will be healthy.

NATURAL DEVELOPMENT

NATURAL TRAINING

NATURAL NUTRITION

NATURAL HEALTH CARE

HEALTH DISORDERS

THERAPEUTIC MASSAGE

WATCH A MOTHER CAT vigorously lick her kittens and you see the origins of therapeutic massage. Her tongue not only cleans her young, it stimulates the kitten's muscles, blood, and lymph circulation. Later in life, massage can help to disperse pain and restore mobility and flexibility. Massaging your cat also helps you to be more aware of changes in your cat's behaviour and physical condition.

HISTORY

Massage may be the oldest and most natural form of medical care. It is an important element of all forms of medicine, including Traditional Chinese, Ayurvedic, Persian, Arab, Greek, and ancient Roman. In modern Western medicine, the practice of massage was restored to favour by the Swedish gymnast Per Henrik Ling at the end of the 19th century. His Swedish massage methods became the basis for physiotherapy. Massage is used more frequently on dogs than on cats, not only because it is more readily accepted by dogs but also because a dog's form and lifestyle predispose it to greater need. Massage oils are not used on cats.

HOW IT WORKS

Touch is perceived through the skin, the cat's largest sensory organ. Gentle massage triggers the release of cytokines, chemicals that exist in such small quantities that they were not known to exist until 20 years ago. These chemicals affect the cat's hormonal system, bringing down the levels of stress hormones that weaken the immune system.

Massage also stimulates blood circulation, which increases the amount of oxygen that reaches tissue and flushes out toxins and waste. Massage probably induces cells at the site being massaged to release cytokines. The cytokines then instruct the brain to release painkilling endorphins.

Different forms of massage can be used, depending on a cat's need. The most common is "effleurage" (stroking in one direction); this is used at the beginning of a therapeutic session as it calms the cat. "Petrissage" involves specific skin and muscle tissues being stretched, rolled, gently pinched, kneaded, even ever-so-slightly wrung. Hand movements may be circular or transverse. Percussive forms of therapeutic massage such as tapping may

TOUCH HEALING

Almost every nation in the world has a tradition of healing by "laying on of hands". Most touch healers are ordinary people who say they discover accidentally that they have special gifts which work not only on humans but on other animals too.

MASSAGING A CAT

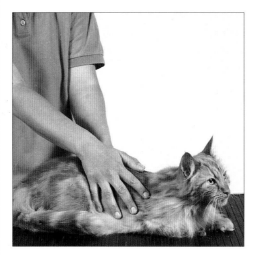

1 The first stage of massage is effleurage, which entails stroking the cat gently in one direction. Slow stroking aids relaxation, while fast stroking will stimulate the cat. Steadily slow the pace until your cat is completely relaxed.

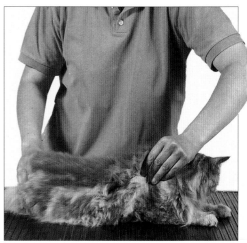

2 Once your cat is relaxed, move on to petrissage, an aid to circulation. "Kneading" involves applying circular pressure with the palm, all over the cat's body. Follow this with "picking up" the soft tissues between your fingers and thumb and then releasing.

be used occasionally, but the more physically robust actions of clapping and hacking, which are commonly used for people, and sometimes for dogs, are considered too harsh for the feline frame.

VETERINARY OPINION

Early and frequent touch leads to reduced glucocorticoid production later in life. Translated out of medical jargon, cats that are frequently touched when they are young experience less stress when they are older. In theory, this means that cats that are routinely massaged should have fewer immune-system problems than other cats.

Massage is therapeutic at a variety of different levels. On its own, it can reduce pain and discomfort, and increase blood circulation. On a secondary level, regularly massaging your cat helps you uncover early signs of problems such as muscle tenderness, swelling, or shrinkage. On a third level, if you massage your own cat, it strengthens the bond between you and your pet, and is actually good for you too, dropping your heart rate and lowering your blood pressure.

PRECAUTIONS

Never massage inflamed, infected, swollen, torn, or bruised areas. Similarly, never massage a cat with a fever, in clinical shock, or suffering from heatstroke. Do not massage near tumours, bone fractures, dislocations, or ligament tears. Never massage an injured neck or back. Unwittingly, you may make the condition far worse.

From the point of view of the therapist, cats that accept regular massage tend to make better patients. They are easier to examine and treat because they are relaxed about being handled and manipulated.

WHERE IT IS AVAILABLE

Massage can be carried out at home if your cat is willing and in general good health. If your cat is recovering from an injury and needs remedial massage, it should only be administered by a registered therapist who is familiar with feline anatomy. Your vet should be able to refer you to a therapist in your area.

3 If your cat still appears happy with the massage, move onto "wringing", gently pushing and pulling the skin in both hands, followed by "rolling", the final stage of petrissage, where the skin is pushed away and then pulled towards you.

4 After the petrissage is complete, your cat should be totally relaxed. If your cat allows, you can gently stretch its limbs. Cats do not like to be held by their paws, so hold the limbs just below the knee. The front and back legs are stretched forwards and then backwards, each stretch being held for no more than six to 10 seconds. Stretching will wake up your cat, so finish with effleurage to relax it again

NATURAL DEVELOPMENT

NATURAL TRAINING

NATURAL NUTRITION

NATURAL HEALTH CARE

HEALTH DISORDERS

HYDROTHERAPY

MODERN HYDROTHERAPY, in which swimming pools with whirlpools and waterjets are used as a medium for physiotherapy, should only be used on the small number of cats that have a natural affinity for water. Traditional hydrotherapy, in which water in all its forms – hot or cold, steam or ice – is used to revitalize and restore parts of the body, is beneficial for treating local conditions.

PRECAUTIONS

Ensure the water is not too hot. A cat's coat retains heat and exaggerates the effect of overheated water. Avoid whole body hydrotherapy for cats that find getting wet distasteful. Avoid any form of heat therapy for cats with high blood pressure.

HISTORY

Many mammals enjoy the feeling of floating in water and will, of their own free will, enter ponds, lakes, rivers, or the sea for the sensual satisfaction of wading, splashing, or swimming. Cats generally do not. The Turkish Van cat is alleged to like water but this appears to be a learned behaviour of Turkish Vans in Turkey. It is not perpetuated in all individuals that are kept as pets.

Historically, warm-water bathing has been used therapeutically throughout the world wherever there are natural hot springs.

HOW IT WORKS

Water is an ideal vehicle for heat and cold. Cold water stimulates surface blood vessels to constrict, inhibiting blood flow and the cascade of chemical events that causes inflammation. External cold water redirects blood towards the internal organs, helping them to function more efficiently. Warm water dilates blood vessels, increasing blood flow to the skin and muscles and easing stiffness. Improved circulation brings more oxygen and nutrients, and elements of the immune system, to the body's cells. It helps remove waste products. Increased blood flow to the skin also reduces blood pressure. Cats are unlikely to accept immersion in water, but water locally applied, either in a warm poultice or cold compress, can bring relief to inflammation and swellings.

VETERINARY OPINION

Conventional veterinarians understand the value of buoyancy and water resistance for exercising injured dogs but have ethical reservations about its use for cats. Japanese veterinarians use natural sulphur springs for treating skin conditions such as oily seborrhea.

WHERE IT IS AVAILABLE

Topical hydrotherapy, using heat or cold to stimulate an injured part of the body, can be readily applied at home.

NATURAL SWIMMERS
By nature, most cats avoid water and swim only if it is absolutely necessary. The exception is the Turkish Van, which willingly goes for a paddle. This appears to be a learned behaviour. Pet Vans lose this habit if they do not learn it from their parents.

OTHER PHYSICAL THERAPIES

A PHYSICAL THERAPIST thinks of an injury as a process, rather than an event. The process often begins acutely and continues for a variable length of time. The therapist modifies his or her treatment during the course of the process, rather than maintaining a standardized therapy throughout. A variety of new technologies are used as complementary forms of physical therapy for cats.

PRECAUTIONS
All of these physical therapies have limitations and carry the potential for doing harm. Increasing tissue temperature is supposed to increase the pain threshold, but, in excess, these therapies destroy tissue. Do not apply them to your cat yourself.

HISTORY
In 1973, in his book *Horse Injuries*, Charles Strong first advocated the use of electrical stimulation to treat pain in animals. Since then, other physical therapies, including laser, electrical stimulation, magnetic therapy, and therapeutic ultrasound have been advocated as therapies for cats. The American Veterinary Medical Association now includes these technologies, as well as hydrotherapy, stretching, and massage in its definition of physical therapies.

HOW THEY WORK
A wide variety of technical appliances are available to veterinarians but all have the same purpose – to relieve pain. Therapeutic lasers first appeared on the market about 30 years ago. In human medicine, since 1990, over 2,500 articles have been published on the use of low-level laser therapy (LLLT). LLLT is the internationally accepted term for lasers that do not burn. These devices do not raise cell temperature but are thought to cause chemical reactions within cells. They are more frequently used in horses than cats.

Various high- and low-voltage electrical stimulators are marketed for pain relief. The most popular are low-voltage, transcutaneous, electrical nerve-stimulator units or TENS units. These provide sensory stimulation in much the same way that electro-acupuncture does (*see page 74*).

Small ultrasound units make use of ultra-high-frequency sound waves to "heat" tissue such as ligaments, tendons, or scar tissue. The intensity of ultrasound varies according to what the practitioner wants to achieve.

Lower intensities are used to reduce pain, to relieve spasms, and to disperse excessive inflammation. Higher intensities are used to heat tissues before stretching and massage. Ultrasound is usually applied to damaged tissue through a gel.

VETERINARY OPINION
Laser light is capable of penetrating tissue, but there is some doubt as to whether LLLT radiation can penetrate to a sufficient depth to be therapeutic. Electrical stimulation does appear to stimulate blood flow. It has been reported to have increased the contractile force of muscle fibres, giving new strength to muscles after an injury.

While advocates say that LLLT reduces pain, clinical trials have not substantiated this suggestion. TENS units are probably used more commonly than other physical therapies and they may well stimulate a cat's endorphins, much as electro-acupuncture does. A report published in 1995 found that ultrasound reduced the formation of excess fibrous tissue in dogs with femur fractures. However, in clinical trials "sham ultrasound" (with the machine switched on but not set to give out ultrasound) was just as beneficial as therapeutic ultrasound.

WHERE THEY ARE AVAILABLE
If you are interested in these therapies for use in controlling your cat's pain, find a vet who is experienced with the equipment used in the therapy in question. If experience is not available, use another therapy that is known to be effective and does not carry the potential risks of these treatments.

CHECKLIST
- Lack of exercise causes muscles to shrink and joints to tighten.
- Physical therapies are useful methods of manipulating muscles and reversing atrophy.
- Pain does serve a useful purpose. It conditions a cat to rest the injured part of its body.
- Excess pain may be controlled by various forms of physical therapy.

NATURAL DEVELOPMENT

NATURAL TRAINING

NATURAL NUTRITION

NATURAL HEALTH CARE

HEALTH DISORDERS

MEDICINAL THERAPIES

THE BASIS OF GOOD HEALTH is well-balanced body biochemistry. Illness is associated with abnormal body biochemistry. In many circumstances, abnormalities are corrected by providing the body with specific substances. Throughout history, people have used a variety of natural products as medicinal therapies; Western culture takes this tradition in a scientific direction, purifying specific substances. The objective of all forms of medicine, complementary and traditional, is to return the body to a state of equilibrium. However, there are philosophical differences in how this is best achieved.

Western medicine investigates how the body works, down to its most elemental level. Scientists want to know what is happening, not just to organs or cells but to molecules. They believe that if they understand how the body's balance is upset at the most basic level of life, they can formulate specific therapies at that level. Complementary veterinarians say this is fine as long as the diagnosis is correct, but the very nature of illness means that diagnostics remains "educated guesswork". They argue that more general manipulative, herbal, or mind therapies are safer and more realistic than target-specific therapies.

NATURE'S MEDICINE CHEST
Evolution taught cats that eating certain substances is beneficial. In the wild, cats consume part of the intestines of their kills, which contain essential nutrients not found in muscle-meat alone.

GIVING MEDICINE
Historically, we have shared our medicines with our cats. This is not always in their interest as they have less resistance to toxins than we have.

Herbal medicine has evolved wherever people lived. Today, over 75 per cent of the world's population still rely upon herbal medicines for basic body care. In many countries, for financial reasons, agricultural veterinary medicine is still almost wholly herbal. In the United States, the Department of Agriculture has information on the folk uses of over 80,000 plants in its data base on botanical plants.

The pharmaceutical basis of Western medicine evolved from herbal traditions. It might be interesting to speculate what would have happened if the concept of purified plant pharmaceuticals had developed in China rather than Europe and North America. A 1975 report of the American National Academy of Sciences suggests that Chinese herbal medicine has a 50 per cent "success" rate, higher than any other form of indigenous herbal medicine that has been studied. For example, Amerindian herbal medicine has a 25 per cent success rate. However, we need to be careful when translating to cat care the herbs that benefit us. Cats are not as good as we are at detoxifying herbs. What is beneficial for us may be dangerous to a cat.

ITCH RELIEF
A conventional vet may prescribe antihistamines and corticosteroids to relieve itching caused by parasites. Complementary vets prefer to avoid drugs, believing that they depress the immune system.

NATURAL DEVELOPMENT

NATURAL TRAINING

NATURAL NUTRITION

NATURAL HEALTH CARE

HEALTH DISORDERS

NUTRITIONAL THERAPIES

UNTIL COMPARATIVELY RECENTLY, cats captured and ate their own naturally balanced meals, but since they have relied on people to feed them, diet-induced problems such as taurine deficiency have appeared, while nutrient sensitivities and other feeding-related disorders have grown in magnitude. With a better understanding of feline health, nutritional therapy is now practical and necessary.

HISTORY

The concept of nutritional therapy evolved out of naturopathy, which is the science of treating disease and promoting good health through nourishing, non-allergenic foods, clean water, fresh air, and an uncontaminated environment, achieving equilibrium and good health in the body's internal environment. The basic concept of naturopathy has been adopted by conventional veterinary medicine and is the basis of preventative medicine today. Nutritional therapies concentrate on overcoming health problems through fasting and clinical nutrition.

HOW THEY WORK

Not eating, a central component of "nature cures", appears to be an excellent adaptive strategy that all animals developed over the centuries to help overcome illness. Medical studies show how fasting is beneficial during the initial stages of an infection. When a cat is challenged by infection, cytokines in its brain temporarily turn off the brain's hunger centre. Consequent fasting benefits the ill cat in two ways. By not eating, bacteria that invaded the body are starved of the minerals

FOOD SENSITIVE
Itchiness and diarrhoea are common manifestations of food sensitivity. A diet that is good for most cats but induces a disorder in one individual reveals that this cat is suffering from a nutrient sensitivity.

they need. More important, a fasting cat will not use up precious energy looking for food. The cat rests, conserves energy, reduces heat loss, and fights infection.

Controlled fasting is beneficial for most mammals. Mice that are fasted for two days before an infection are more likely to survive the infection than mice that are not fasted. Controlled fasting can also be used as a method of clearing the system, so that the vet can investigate whether a health problem is diet-induced, an allergy, or feeding-related.

DIET-INDUCED PROBLEMS

A cat's diet may be the actual cause of a medical or behavioural problem. A diet may be deficient in macro- or micronutrients. It may be toxic to a cat, contaminated with hazardous materials, contain anti-nutrients, or be imbalanced. Diet-induced problems can be caused when we, or the manufacturers of cat foods, formulate diets incorrectly. Processing problems and post-processing mistakes also lead to diet-induced problems, usually deficiencies. Severe diet-induced problems are uncommon in cats, while the incidence of minor dietary problems simply is not known. Some veterinarians feel that cats are especially susceptible to diet-induced problems because they are less efficient at detoxification than are omnivores like dogs.

NUTRIENT SENSITIVITIES

Each cat is a unique individual with its own idiosyncratic responses to the foods it eats. Some individuals tolerate almost any foods, while other cats develop a variety of food intolerances. Nutrient-sensitive diseases occur, not when there is a defect in the diet, but rather when there is a defect in the cat.

Nutrient-sensitive diseases include food allergies, heart, liver, and kidney diseases, and some forms of bladder and urinary tract disease. Food sensitivities occur more frequently in some breeds. For example, Himalayans and Persians are more inclined to diet-induced calcium oxalate urolithiasis than are other breeds (*see page 140*).

Even relatively common problems such as gum disease can be induced by food sensitivity. Treating a nutrient-sensitive disease can be risky because the needed diet change is usually a permanent one. Without careful planning, a nutrient-sensitivity problem can be turned into a nutrient-deficiency condition.

FEEDING-RELATED DISORDERS

Overfeeding is the most common feeding-related disorder in cats. A feeding-related problem is a responsibility of the owner, rather than of the cat. And, frustratingly, the only treatment for this nutritional problem is to educate the owner, a far more difficult task than changing a cat's diet. Feeding-related problems include obesity, lameness, growth disorders, and reproductive failure.

VETERINARY OPINION

Historically, veterinarians have understood the link between nutrition and health, but it is only in the last 20 years that nutritional therapy has become a component of clinical veterinary care. Food grown in poor soil may lack nutrients, crops sprayed with pesticides may contain toxic chemicals, or meat that has been passed as unfit for human consumption can end up in cat food. Poor food may alter the balance of bacteria in the gut, and this is thought to be one cause of the increased incidence of allergic conditions in cats.

MEGAVITAMIN THERAPY

Pioneered by the Nobel prize-winning scientist Linus Pauling, megavitamin or orthomolecular therapy involves giving large doses of vitamins as a medication rather than as nutritional therapy. In his book *Vitamin C and the Common Cold*, Pauling argued that large doses of the antioxidant vitamin C mopped up free-radical molecules that cause cellular damage. While we obtain our vitamin C only from what we eat, cats manufacture their own. A megadose may do no harm, but it may upset the balance of acid and alkali in a cat's body.

WHAT DIETS ARE AVAILABLE?

In reaction to information concerning the way livestock are treated, what drugs they are given to promote their growth, and what risks of disease meat poses to us, increasing numbers of people are giving up meat and eating vegetarian diets. However, we must remember that any form of vegetarian diet is harmful as well as unnatural for cats. A cat needs meat to live.

Macrobiotic diets, developed in the 1950s to contain calming *yin* foods such as green vegetables and strengthening *yang* foods such as fish and root vegetables, have had little impact on feline nutritional therapy. Some cat owners feel that raw food diets are most natural. This is true, although cats have difficulty digesting raw grains and vegetables. Raw meat contains all its nutrients unaltered by cooking but also contains potentially harmful bacteria such as Salmonella and parasites such as *Toxoplasma*, which are killed by heating.

Beginning in the 1980s, and accelerating rapidly in the 1990s, pet food manufacturers produced a range of therapeutic diets for cats. While the earlier diets were only mildly different from other commercial cat foods, therapeutic diets today are radically different. Responding to a more refined demand, cat food manufacturers use ingredients from the "human food" chain in their therapeutic cat foods, and avoid additives such as synthetic preservatives and colorants. The best of the therapeutic diets are thoughtfully prepared and palatable, and they utilize the therapeutic nutritionist's knowledge of practices such as modifying gut flora to secure health benefits. Some cat food manufacturers have responded to owner concerns about nutrition faster than human convenience-food makers.

Regardless of what nutritional therapy your cat needs, any strict diet fed over a long period may lead to malnutrition. Always talk to your vet and obtain a feline nutritionist's advice before embarking on any form of nutritional therapy for your cat, especially if it is growing, pregnant, or elderly.

BENEFICIAL BACTERIA
Certain types of bacteria in the intestines, such as Lactobacillus brevis (above), aid digestion, and some of them actively enhance the immune system. An incorrect diet alters intestinal bacteria and reduces natural defences.

CHECKLIST

- Use nutritional therapy as a means of supporting the immune system.

- Never force a cat to eat when it does not want to.

- Always obtain the advice of a good veterinarian before changing a cat's diet.

Understand what you are feeding your cat. Differentiate between:

- Diet-induced problems caused by the diet itself.

- Particular nutrient sensitivities that are personal to an individual cat.

- Feeding-related disorders which are caused by how we feed cats.

HERBALISM

HERBS ARE A MAJOR SOURCE of modern pharmaceuticals, but herbal remedies differ from conventional drugs in using parts of the whole plant rather than isolating single ingredients. In traditional Chinese and Indian herbalism, the choice of herb depends upon the cat's personality as well as its illness. In modern herbalism, there is greater emphasis on the chemical constituents of the herb itself.

DANGERS IN NATURE

All medicines, whether they are natural herbs or synthesized by pharmaceutical companies, are potentially toxic in excess. The difference between therapeutic and dangerous doses for cats can be very small. "Herbal" does not mean safe. Use all medications for cats with caution.

HISTORY

From the earliest stages of their evolution, animals learned that eating certain types of vegetation made them feel better. Cats know to eat grass in order to induce vomiting and rid themselves of hairballs.

Classical herbalism developed in all early human cultures but was best recorded in the ancient Hindu texts, the *Vedas*, starting about 4,500 years ago. Ayurveda, the traditional holistic healing system of the whole Indian subcontinent, shares herbs with Traditional Chinese Medicine (TCM), where legend tells how animals guided humans to discover the medicinal values of plants. Herbalism also flourished in Europe and was augmented by Persian and Islamic physicians.

When Europeans arrived in the Americas, Africa, and Australasia, their herbal armories were expanded by herbs in use among native peoples. The first 'flu epidemics in the new American colonies were treated with sage

HERBALISM AND FOODS

Traditional associations with herbs influenced regional cuisine. Indian cookery reflects Ayurvedic alchemy. The water-generating nature of coriander is used to balance the heating qualities of chilli, while cardomon reduces the mucus-forming qualities of other foods.

CHILLI

CARDOMON CORIANDER

(*Salvia officinalis*) and boneset (*Eupatorium perfoliatum*). Even today, in most parts of the world, the use of herbs remains a vital ingredient of veterinary care, but it is only recently that it has been applied to cats.

HOW THEY WORK

In traditional forms of medicine, herbal treatments are tailored to an individual's personality. Ayurvedic medicine stipulates the need for balance between the "energies" within and without the body. Ayurveda's five elements – ether, air, fire, water, and earth – are contained in three *doshas*, or energies, that every person, animal, food, and environment is made up of in varying degrees. Because each animal is a unique composite of *doshas*, its illness is treated with herbal prescriptions not only according to the disease, but also according to its combination of *doshas*, its age, and even the time of day.

The herbal therapy in Traditional Chinese Medicine follows similar patterns. All illness is regarded as a "pattern of disharmony". Particular herbs are given to induce healing actions such as sweating, vomiting, draining downward, warming, clearing, reducing, harmonizing, and tonifying. The herbs are used in varying amounts, according to the blend of *yin* and *yang* both of the patient and of the herbs, in order to restore harmony. For example, ginseng is believed to tonify the *yang* tendencies of the body, which are male and assertive.

SYMBOLISM IN MEDICATION

Like conventional drugs, the dispensing of herbs is imbued with symbolism, much of which is understated but nevertheless understood both by the herbalist and the cat owner. A herb can be:

- A token of the herbalist's power to heal
- A symbol of the mystical power of the herbalist
- A sign that the cat is "really ill"
- A fulfilment of the contract between you, as the owner of the cat, and the herbalist

- A sign that you can control the cat's health
- An indication of the herbalist's degree of understanding of and concern for the cat
- An additional way in which the herbalist can communicate with you
- A way of satisfying your goal to use traditional medicine such as herbs
- A source of satisfaction for the herbalist

There is far more to the dispensing of a herb or a drug than just the substance itself.

VETERINARY OPINION

Modern herbalism, under its scientific name of phytotherapy, is the basis of conventional drug therapy. While many modern drugs have been isolated from herbal extracts, for example, aspirin from willow tree bark, modern herbalists contend that therapeutic herbal plants are complex mixtures of chemicals, all of which contribute to the beneficial effects of their use. Herbalists argue that chemicals which have been isolated and refined from herbs are much more likely to be toxic than their botanical sources; they produce effects that have a rapid onset and a greater intensity, which can lead to unwanted side effects.

Conventional veterinarians understand and accept the medicinal values of herbal therapies but find it difficult to accept the ancient concepts that underlie traditional herbalism. They find the herbalist's emphasis on promoting "homeostasis" by means of preventative health care, diet, and lifestyle fully compatible with modern trends in conventional veterinary medicine.

However, cats are a lot more sensitive to a wide range of substances than are dogs or people. Because toxic doses for cats have not been calculated for most herbs, vets are concerned about possible side-effects of certain remedies.

In most parts of the world, traditional herbalism remains the treatment of choice for livestock animals, although this form of traditionalism has been abandoned for pet animals, which are now generally treated with modern pharmaceutical therapies. When I had the opportunity to visit East Java recently, veterinarians there told me that with the advent of Western veterinary medicine, centuries of trial-and-error understanding of the value of local herbs for treating animals would probably die out within one generation.

WHERE THEY ARE AVAILABLE

Herbs are available worldwide and often are promoted for benefits that have never been evaluated or proven. In most countries, there is little control over how herbs are sold. In Germany, on the other hand, the Federal Health Authority's "Commission E" publishes information on the composition, use, interaction with other drugs, side effects, and dosages of marketed herbs. This allows herbs to be marketed as "over-the-counter" drugs in Germany, and enables doctors and veterinarians to use common sense and to prescribe what they feel is best for their patient. In Germany, 50 per cent of the total sales of herbal products are prescribed by doctors, and more St. John's wort (*Hypericum perforatum*) is purchased as an anti-depressant than Prozac. Where such information is not available, be cautious when considering herbal treatments for your cat. Few have been evaluated. Some are dangerous, even life-threatening.

STILL ACTIVE?
Herbs have a short shelf life. Use products labelled with a harvest or expiration date. The label should explain the parts of the herb used and list any other ingredients, such as fillers or containers.

CHECKLIST

- Herbal therapies provide chemical building blocks for body cells.
- They interfere with dangerous micro-organisms.
- They maintain effective defences.
- As knowledge increases, herbal therapies evolve.
- Herbalism evolved into modern pharmaceuticals.
- The nutrient side of herbalism is now evolving into "nutraceuticals" (*see page 51*).
- Proven therapies are the best kind, irrespective of whether they are old ones or new.

WILLOW LEAVES

WHOLE HERBS
Many herbalists use whole herbs, for instance, the bark of the willow tree (right). Others feel that toxins in herbs decrease the activity of the desired ingredients and prefer to use synthesized ingredients. Willow bark is a source of salicin, from which aspirin is derived.

WILLOW BARK

ASPIRIN

HERBAL THERAPIES

HERBAL THERAPIES ARE OFTEN used to correct body functions and are given as short courses. Most cats are not disposed to eat fresh or dried herbs, so herbal tablets tend to be used. Herbs may be excellent as skin treatments for people but are potentially dangerous for cats, as they may lick them off and poison themselves. Only use herbs under close veterinary supervision.

HAWTHORN

PEPPERMINT

MOTHERWORT

CHECKLIST
- Be extremely cautious with herbs.
- Only apply herbs to your cat's coat that you know are safe if ingested.
- Cats do not have good natural systems to detoxify a range of natural substances.

HERBAL PREPARATIONS

Medicinal parts of plants can be prepared in a variety of ways. Infused oils, ointments, and creams are made for topical use (applied to the surface of the body).

Decoctions, tinctures, and infusions are more appropriate than topical preparations for cats because they are made from herbs that are safe for the cat to take internally. Decoctions are prepared by boiling in pure water the tough parts of plants such as bark, roots, and berries. The liquid is strained and consumed either hot or cold. Tinctures are made by soaking a herb in alcohol and water, usually for a few weeks, and then straining it. Tinctures are usually stored in dark bottles and can be kept for up to two years. Infusions are made like tea, from the leaves and flowers of the herb.

THE USES OF HERBS

In order to survive, plants produce chemicals for their own protection. Some of these chemicals are beneficial for other forms of life, including cats. For example, garlic, the world's most popular herb, contains at least 200 different compounds, many of which are said to be useful for cats. Garlic lowers blood pressure, accelerates the breakdown of waste matter from cells, and may even act as a mild flea repellent. Ginkgo (*Ginkgo biloba*) leaves contain substances called flavonoids that are said to be effective at scavenging free radicals. Siberian ginseng (*Eleutherococcus senticosus*) may help regulate blood sugar and affect the adrenal glands. *Ashwaghanda* (*Withania somnifera*), popular in Ayurvedic herbalism, is reported to increase haemoglobin and red blood cell counts, countering

HERBAL HOME-CARE KIT

Some herbal remedies are especially effective for minor accidents and illnesses. These herbs have been used with safety on cats and constitute a basic home-care kit. They can be found at most pharmacies and herbal shops. Only use herbs recognized as safe for cats, preferably those specially prepared for veterinary use.

COMFREY

Comfrey (Symphytum) *is soothing and healing. Used to help heal wounds, burns, bruises, and strains.*

LAVENDER

Lavender (Lavendula) *is claimed to be antiseptic and calming. Used on the site of insect bites and for burns.*

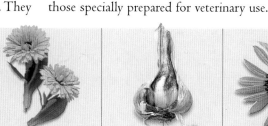

MARIGOLD

Marigold (Calendula) *is used to soothe inflamed skin. Infusions are given for digestive disorders.*

GARLIC

Garlic (Allium sativum) *is given for mild infections, upper respiratory conditions, and digestive disorders.*

ECHINACEA

Echinacea (Echinacea purpurea) *may act as an antibiotic and stimulate the immune system.*

FIELD HORSETAIL

BARBERRY BARK

CINNAMON BARK

anaemia. Oil of cedar (*Cedrus*) is reported to have antibacterial, antifungal, and acaridical (mite-killing) properties. Seed oil from neem (*Azadirachta indica*) is antibacterial and, according to published reports, inhibits ringworm. Scientific studies suggest that aloe vera has anti-inflammatory, analgesic, and anti-microbial effects, while studies in horses suggest it stimulates the immune system.

Many cancer treatments have been developed from herbal products. For example, the Madagascar periwinkle (*Catharanthus roseus*) contains vincristine, a chemical used to treat feline lymphomas. When vincristine was available only as a plant extract it was very expensive. Since it has been synthesized, thousands of cats have benefited from successful treatment with this product.

PREPARING A HERBAL INFUSION

For immediate soothing and antiseptic use for wounds or skin infections, or for the relief of mild gastroenteric problems, an infusion of peppermint leaf or Roman chamomile flower can be made at home:

- Heat a clean (well washed and rinsed) cup with boiling water.

- Pour away the water and add 1 tsp of dried or 2 tsp of fresh herb to the heated cup.

- Fill to three-quarters level with boiling water.

- Cover and leave to steep for 10 minutes.

- Remove the cover, pouring condensation inside the cover back into the cup.

- Strain and use or store covered in a cool place.

COMMON HERBAL THERAPIES

If not used correctly, herbal substances can be just as dangerous as wrongly prescribed modern drugs. Do not make your own diagnoses or use any of these herbs without professional guidance.

CONDITIONS	HERBAL THERAPIES
CANCER *(prevention)*	• Lemon balm *Melissa officinalis* • Mistletoe leaf *Viscum album* • Barberry bark *Berberis vulgaris* • Roman chamomile flower *Chamaemelum nobile* • Comfrey leaf *Symphytum officinale* • Echinacea root *Echinacea purpurea* • Fenugreek seed *Trigonella foenum-graecum*
ITCHY SKIN	• German chamomile flower *Chamomilla recutita* • Burdock root *Arctium lappa* • Curled dock root *Rumex crispus* • Liquorice root *Glycyrrhiza glabra* • Southernwood *Artemesia abrotanum*
SKIN ABRASIONS	• Turmeric root *Curcuma longa* • Yarrow *Achillea millefolium* • Peppermint *Mentha x piperita* • Comfrey leaf *Symphytum officinale*
COLITIS	• Marsh mallow root *Althaea officinalis* • Nutmeg seed *Myristica fragrans* • Turmeric root *Curcuma longa*
HEART DISEASE	• Hawthorn *Crataegus laevigata* • Motherwort *Leonurus cardiaca* • Dandelion leaf *Taraxacum officinale*
URINARY TRACT DISORDERS	• Stone root *Collinsonia canadensis* • Field horsetail *Equisetum arvense* • Couch grass *Elymus repens* • Bearberry leaf *Arctostaphylos uva-ursi* • Juniper berry *Juniperus communis* • Marsh mallow root *Althaea officinalis*
KIDNEY IMPAIRMENT	• Cinnamon bark *Cinnamomum zeylanicum* • Rehmannia root *Rehmannia glutinosa* • Comfrey leaf *Symphytum officinale* • Celery seed *Apium graveolens*

WARNING

Be wary of imported Chinese herbs. The desired herb may be contaminated with other herbs that are potentially toxic to cats. Only use herbs from reliable, established suppliers who carry out batch assessments for consistency and quality control.

HOMEOPATHY

HOMEOPATHY IS ENJOYING A REVIVAL in both North America and Europe. The American Veterinary Medical Association says: "Clinical and anecdotal evidence exists to indicate that veterinary homeopathy may be beneficial." About 60 per cent of the 2,500 homeopathic remedies come from plants. Current understanding of biology cannot yet explain how homeopathy works.

WARNING

Do not prepare your own homeopathic medicines. Some are deadly if not prepared properly. Don't experiment. Only use products recommended by an experienced homeopath, and produced in safe conditions. The greater the dilution, the safer the solution.

HISTORY

The idea that "like cures like" is found in many forms of traditional medicine and was revived in the late 18th century by the German doctor Samuel Hahnemann. Critical of the invasive treatments, such as leeches and violent purges, used by his contemporaries, he developed "homeopathy", from the Greek *homoios* (same) and *pathos* (suffering). Homeopathic treatment of animals was later introduced by Baron von Boenninghausen in the early 19th century.

HOW IT WORKS

The body is in a constant state of self-repair, with all organs and cells constantly renewing themselves. Homeopaths believe that a "vital force" regulates the body, and maintains health. Clinical signs of disease

DO NOSODES PROTECT?

Some owners choose not to use biological vaccines to protect their pets from deadly diseases such as leukaemia and rabies and rely upon homeopathic nosodes to render protection. At a recent meeting of the American Holistic Veterinary Medical Association, Dr Susan Wynn gave the results of a study in which dogs were given nosodes to protect them against canine parvovirus. When exposed to parvovirus, all the dogs developed this serious disease. Feline enteritis is a feline parvovirus. Homeopathic nosodes do not stimulate a dog's or a cat's immune system to form protective antibodies.

are seen as indications that the body is fighting illness or injury. The homeopath determines how the body is trying to defend itself, before prescribing, according to the principle of "like cures like", a remedy that stimulates self-healing rather than suppresses the signs of disease. The result may be that symptoms work their way along the body from head to tail; or they move from inside to outside the body; or they move from the more important organs to the least important. Historically, "like cures like" has been called the "law of similars". This was and remains

POTENTIZATION

Hahnemann believed that the more a substance was diluted, the more potent it became. Remedies are made from plant, animal, and mineral extracts. The extract is chopped or ground and then soaked in a mix of 90 per cent alcohol and 10 per cent distilled water. This mixture is shaken from time to time to dissolve the material.

1 Once the mixture has stood for two to four weeks, the mixture has become infused. It is strained into a dark glass bottle, and becomes known as the "mother tincture".

2 One drop of the tincture is then diluted in 99 drops of alcohol, then shaken rapidly – a process called succussion. Dilution and succussion are repeated.

3 After dilution and succussion have resulted in the required potency, a few drops are added to a jar of lactose tablets, which absorb the potentized remedy.

the central principle of homeopathy. The remedies consist of substances that, if taken undiluted by a healthy person, would cause symptoms similar to those of the disease being treated. For example, poison ivy, *Rhus toxicodendron*, naturally causes local irritation of the skin, so diluted *Rhus tox.* is used to treat a skin irritation, caused, for example, by flea bites. All substances used in homeopathic remedies are diluted many times.

When used preventatively, homeopathic remedies are called nosodes. Nosodes are available to prevent infectious diseases such as respiratory infection and viral enteritis (*see box, left*). Diluting doses repeatedly limits possible harmful side effects and is believed to increase the potency of the solution. This is called the "law of potentization".

MODERN EXPLANATIONS

Chaos theory, which proposes that minute changes lead to huge differences, has been used to explain how homeopathy works. So too has resonance theory, which says that all matter consists of and radiates energy. Some homeopaths believe that water, the substance in which homeopathic medicines are made, is capable of storing energy. Others argue that diluting and shaking homeopathic remedies creates an electromagnetic state, and magnetite, an electromagnetic substance found in cats' and other mammals' brains, is hypersensitive to the resulting mixture.

VETERINARY OPINION

An extensive review, published in the *British Medical Journal* in 1991, analyzed 107 controlled studies involving homeopathic medicines. It concluded that, although the studies were not well designed, 81 showed homeopathic medicines to be effective, 24 showed they were ineffective, and 2 were inconclusive. In 1994, a double-blind study published in the medical journal *The Lancet* reported that homeopathy was more useful than a placebo in treating hay fever. No high-calibre studies of homeopathic medicines have been carried out on cats.

The number of veterinarians who include homeopathic remedies such as *Arnica 6c*, *Aconite 6c*, and *Hypericum 6c* in their medical arsenals is increasing in Europe, North America, and Australasia. Although they find it difficult to accept homeopathic theories, many vets are willing to accept evidence from owners that homeopathic remedies work. Most vets feel that, because homeopathic treatments are administered in such minute amounts, they can do no harm and will not upset any therapies directed at returning the body to homeostatic levels, for example, through intravenous fluid therapy. They do not consider remedies to be therapeutic.

WHERE IT IS AVAILABLE

Most homeopathic remedies are available in liquid and in pill form. Cats sometimes resent the alcohol in liquids. Pills are more suitable for cats because, unlike those used in conventional medicine, homeopathic pills are intended to be dissolved in the mouth rather than swallowed. My nurses give *Arnica 6c* to all surgical cases while animals are anaesthetized, placing the tiny pills under the tongue. Unfortunately, because a cat's mouth often becomes dry during anaesthesia, these pills may take a long time to dissolve.

SAMUEL HAHNEMANN
In a lecture delivered in the early 1800s to the Leipzig Economic Society, Samuel Hahnemann, the founder of homeopathy, referred to the similarity of his methods as applied to animals and humans. Homeopathic treatment of animals was formally begun around this time by Baron von Boenninghausen.

HOMEOPATHIC HOME-CARE KIT

Because homeopathic remedies are so diluted, there is little possibility of them causing side-effects. These homeopathic remedies can be kept at home to form a basic home-remedy kit.

CONDITIONS	HOMEOPATHIC THERAPIES
Panic attacks and emotional stress	*Aconite 6c*
Flea bites and wasp stings	*Apis 6c*
Bruises and swelling	*Arnica 6c*
Flatulence and digestive disorders	*Carbo veg. 6c*
Skin grazes and superficial wounds	*Hypericum 6c*

NATURAL DEVELOPMENT

NATURAL TRAINING

NATURAL NUTRITION

NATURAL HEALTH CARE

HEALTH DISORDERS

BIOCHEMIC TISSUE SALTS

BIOCHEMIC TISSUE SALTS, sometimes called Schüssler salts, are homeopathic remedies prepared from mineral rather than animal or vegetable sources. While they are prepared in the same way as homeopathic remedies, rather than using them according to the homeopathic philosophy of "like curing like", biochemic tissue salts are given to correct perceived mineral deficiencies.

HOW THEY WORK

Therapists believe that an imbalance or lack of specific salts causes a range of medical conditions from emotional upsets to allergies. They believe that a small "homeopathic" dose, where the minerals are diluted so that they are no longer measurable, is easily absorbed by the body, restores balances, and helps the body to heal itself.

NATURAL DEVELOPMENT

NATURAL TRAINING

WARNING

Biochemic tissue salts are often made up as lactose-based tablets. If your cat has loose stools when it drinks milk, it may be "lactose-intolerant", sensitive to the natural sugar, lactose, in milk. In these circumstances do not give lactose-based tissue-salt tablets.

HISTORY

The concept of using tissue salts to correct the body's mineral imbalances was developed in the 1870s by a German homeopathic physician, Dr. Wilhelm Schüssler, who also created the terms "biochemics" and "tissue salts". He named 12 essential salts, and described the medical conditions that his remedies should be used to treat, either singly or in combination. Biochemic tissue salts were incorporated into the existing range of organically-derived homeopathic remedies.

VETERINARY OPINION

Conventional medical research has shown that mineral salts are vital for good health, and conventional vets routinely measure mineral levels in the blood, especially those of sodium and potassium, to monitor a variety of illnesses. However, they feel there is no evidence that biochemic remedies, if diluted to homeopathic levels, will have any effect. Homeopathic vets will often prescribe biochemic tissue salts, along with nutritional advice, as treatment for minor illnesses.

NATURAL NUTRITION

BIOCHEMIC TISSUE-SALT TREATMENTS

Tissue salts are used singly or in combination to treat conditions that a homeopathic vet believes are associated with specific mineral deficiencies. Tablets are given more frequently for new clinical signs and less frequently but for longer durations for chronic conditions.

NATURAL HEALTH CARE

CONDITION	NAME	SOURCE
Poor dental health	*Calc. fluor.*	Calcium fluoride
Bone problems	*Calc. phos.*	Calcium phosphate
Catarrh	*Calc. sulph.*	Calcium sulphate
Early stage of inflammation	*Ferrum phos.*	Iron phosphate
Later stages of inflammation	*Kali mur.*	Potassium chloride
Emotional strains	*Kali phos.*	Potassium phosphate
Breathing problems	*Kali sulph.*	Potassium sulphate
Lower bowel conditions	*Mag. phos.*	Magnesium phosphate
Mouth problems	*Nat. mur.*	Sodium chloride
Upper bowel conditions	*Nat. phos.*	Sodium phosphate
Allergies	*Nat. sulph.*	Sodium sulphate
Neurological disorders	*Silica*	Silicon dioxide

HEALTH DISORDERS

BACH FLOWER REMEDIES

FLOWER ESSENCES ARE increasingly popular with cat owners and are used to treat feline emotional states, thought by the developers of flower essences to be the main cause of disease states. Although similar to homeopathics in that they are physically dilute, flower essences are closer in form to herbal decoctions in that they are produced in relatively concentrated 1:10 or 1:100 dilutions.

ARE FLOWERS CALMING?

The relationship between emotion and disease is studied in psychoneuroimmunology (PNI). Some vets believe that Rescue Remedy reduces panic in some cats. Others assume that giving a remedy causes the PNI effect: cat owners become less tense, which has a positive effect on their pets.

HISTORY

In the 1930s, an English bacteriologist and homeopath, Edward Bach, concluded that harmful emotions lead to physical disease. "Treat the mood of the patient," said Dr Bach, "and the disease will disappear." He believed that essences from flowers could affect an individual's state of mind. Dr Bach developed the first range of flower essences. He identified appropriate non-toxic flowers by cupping his hands over blooms of many varieties and intuitively divining which had healing properties. In 1936, the Bach Flower Remedies were commercially marketed in Britain, fulfilling Bach's belief that patients should heal themselves. In the 1970s, a range of Californian Flower Remedies were marketed in the United States, and a decade later Australian Bush Flower Remedies were successfully launched in Australia.

HOW THEY WORK

Dr Bach developed 38 flower essences, each of which is meant to deal with a specific emotional state or behavioural problem. For shock, panic, and hysteria he produced a multiple flower essence called Rescue Remedy, overwhelmingly the most popular flower essence given to cats. Remedies are prepared by infusing flower heads and other flower parts in spring water for three hours in direct sunlight. The solution is preserved in brandy and sold in 10 and 20 ml phials.

VETERINARY OPINION

Clinical trials of Bach Flower Remedies began at the University of California's veterinary school in the early 1990s but the results were so discouraging that the project was dropped. No other clinical trials have been carried out. When Flower Remedies are analyzed, only spring water and alcohol are detected. Proponents attribute the beneficial effects of Flower Remedies to "molecular imprinting", one of the theories that is also applied to homeopathy.

WHERE THEY ARE AVAILABLE

Bach Flower Remedies are now available in health food shops and pharmacies around the world. Californian and Australian Bush flower remedies are primarily available in their countries of origin.

AWAY FROM LIGHT
Bach Flower Remedies come in airtight bottles made of dark glass with a pipette to measure the prescribed dose. They should be stored in a cool, dark place.

BACH FLOWER REMEDIES

It is easier to interpret your own emotional state than your cat's. A sudden change in your cat's behaviour may have a physical cause. Consult your vet before prescribing any complementary therapy.

STATE OF MIND	FLOWER REMEDY
Shyness	Mimulus
Apathy	Wild rose
Fear on behalf of the family	Red chestnut
Lack of self confidence	Larch
Lack of concentration	Clematis
Melancholy	Mustard
Aloofness	Water violet
Excessive desire for companionship	Heather
Over-protectiveness	Chicory
Dominance	Vervain

MIND AND EMOTION THERAPIES

HISTORICALLY, VETERINARY MEDICINE has ignored the cat's emotions as a cause of illness. In 1995, evidence was published that suggested that there is a relationship between the cat's mind and clinical disease. Certain cats with cystitis, a bladder inflammation, were relieved of their clinical signs when treated with an anti-anxiety drug. Since then, mind and emotion therapies have been applied to various medical and behavioural problems, so far with intermittent success. By understanding how the mind and emotions affect disease, and by using therapies that address the mind and emotions, it may be possible to treat certain conditions without resorting to drugs.

The cat's emotions are really ancient mechanisms for marshalling the body's forces. Emotions, and the physiological changes that are associated with them, developed to cope with the vagaries of life, including threat. A perceived threat stimulates a cascade of chemical reactions in a cat's body that help it to cope with that threat. Even short-lived depression may be a beneficial coping mechanism to deal with stress successfully. In the 1940s, Professor Hans Selye at McGill University in Montreal, Canada, showed how chronic threat caused heart problems, gastric disorders, and a breakdown of the immune system in animals.

EXERCISE
Both physical and mental stimulation are vital to a cat's health. Outdoor cats occupy themselves patrolling territory and hunting. Indoor cats must be offered activities that utilize their natural energy.

PHEROMONES
Animals communicate by sniffing each other's facial gland secretions. If these secretions are harnessed, they can be used to control some forms of unwanted behaviour.

In experiments that would be ethically unacceptable today, he demonstrated that if the stress response is activated for too long, the response itself will eventually damage the cat's health. But stress is not always a bad thing. Cats thrive on positive, intermittent stress. Just think of the urgent anticipation your cat radiates when a moth flies by. The buzz of excitement, the stimulation of challenge, these are positive emotions for cats. A safe, boring life can be a chronic negative stress for some cats. Cats evolved to cope with intermittent stress, not chronic stress. Chronic stress reduces natural resistance.

Relaxation techniques, controlled breathing, and uninterrupted sleep are known to be good for our health. Recently, these therapies have been applied to cats. Biofeedback therapy is also used. Scent has a powerful effect on our emotions and has been used for thousands of years. In this century, scent research led to the development of the field of aromatherapy. More applicable to cats is the new study and remarkable success of the influence on the cat's mind of pheromones – natural body odours secreted by all animals. Other therapies aimed at influencing the cat's mind are also used to enhance well-being in non-invasive ways.

ESSENTIAL REST
Cats sleep for up to 18 hours a day. Just as exercise is vital for mental and physical health, so is uninterrupted sleep.

NATURAL DEVELOPMENT

NATURAL TRAINING

NATURAL NUTRITION

NATURAL HEALTH CARE

HEALTH DISORDERS

RELAXATION THERAPY

IF THERE IS AN ANIMAL that can show us how to relax, it must be the cat. Physiologists discovered 30 years ago that when we look at resting cats our state of arousal diminishes. However, because of the unnatural lifestyles we expect from our cats – living indoors and with a traditional enemy – some will experience stress. With a little effort, it is possible to train your cat to relax.

RELAXATION IS REWARDED
When a cat is tense, the owner avoids eye contact and makes no physical response until the cat relaxes. Relaxation is rewarded by kind words and physical contact from the owner, which further reduces the cat's state of arousal.

CHECKLIST

- Provide active daily exercise for all indoor cats.
- Play games that require mental as well as physical co-ordination.
- Practise relaxation techniques, and always reward your cat for relaxed breathing and calm demeanour.
- Allow your cat to sleep deeply and take care not to interrupt its dreams.
- Modify your indoor cat's exercise according to its age and abilities.
- Provide mind-stimulating games for elderly or convalescing cats.

HISTORY

Relaxation therapy has an important role in Eastern health systems, such as Traditional Chinese and Ayurvedic medicine. It did not begin to be taken seriously in conventional Western medicine until after the Mind/Body Medical Institute of the Harvard Medical School in Cambridge, Massachusetts, had carried out a study of the therapeutic effects of Transcendental Meditation. Now it is accepted that relaxation can affect the body's physiology and reverse the effects of stress.

At the beginning of the 1990s, Professor Karen Overall, head of animal behaviour at the University of Pennsylvania's veterinary school, adapted human relaxation techniques for dogs, showing how dogs respond better to training when they are relaxed. Because "conditioning" training is the same for all animals, her therapeutic relaxation methods can also be applied to cats.

HOW IT WORKS

When a cat is stressed, it will take short, shallow, rapid breaths and too much carbon dioxide is removed from the blood. Many owners will have seen their cats behave like this when they were taken in a car for the first time, or were taken to an unfamiliar environment. This tense behaviour can lead to physiological and behavioural changes, including a lack of concentration.

Cat owners are taught to use normal training techniques to condition their cats to relax. Techniques include watching a cat's ear position, eyes, and breathing rate and recognizing when it is stressed. A cat is rewarded when the ears relax, when the

expression in the eyes becomes less intense, and the breathing slows. The physiological responses to relaxation are substantial. Circulating levels of adrenalin, a stress hormone, drop, as do blood pressure and blood-sugar levels. As the cat's muscles relax, the level of lactic acid in them diminishes. Digestion improves, the immune system becomes more active, and alertness increases.

VETERINARY OPINION

Teaching *dogs* relaxation to increase their alertness and enhance obedience training has a marvellous logic. There appears to be excellent potential to incorporate this form of natural conditioning into conventional therapeutic regimes for a wide variety of medical problems. Vets understand that cat training is likely to be more difficult and acknowledge that relaxation therapy is less accessible for most cat owners.

WHERE IT IS AVAILABLE

Relaxation training is available primarily from the University of Pennsylvania's veterinary school, where it is used on dogs and cats referred to the university for behavioural conditions. Veterinarians elsewhere instruct cat owners in relaxation therapy particularly for cats recovering from surgery, where there are obvious health benefits from relaxing.

EXERCISE AND REST

WE DO NOT NEED TO WORRY about the amount of exercise and rest cats get if they have the opportunity to go outdoors. Each individual lives life at its own pace. But for many cats the outdoors is alien, as are the natural feline activities of patrolling territories and hunting prey. These deprived cats benefit from routine and planned daily activities that exercise the mind as well as the body.

EXCESSIVE EXERCISE

Take care when introducing increased physical exercise if your cat is overweight. Sudden exercise can be an overwhelming burden on the heart. Ask your veterinarian to devise a nutrition and exercise plan that is appropriate for your cat's age, weight, and state of health.

THE IMPORTANCE OF EXERCISE

The benefits of routine exercise have been thoroughly researched and evidence in its favour is overwhelming. Exercise increases circulation, improves heart and lung function, strengthens muscles, keeps joints mobile, cuts down the risk of diabetes, maintains natural weight, improves immune function, and encourages sound sleep.

You only need to look at the differences between sedentary indoor and active outdoor cats. Sedentary cats look, as well as act, less energetic than well-exercised felines. Routine outdoor exercise increases the body's ability to produce energy effectively.

WHAT HAPPENS DURING EXERCISE

Physical activity boosts a cat's brain-power. Keeping fit maintains oxygen supply to the brain and promotes mental alertness. If the brain does not receive sufficient amounts of oxygen and glucose, brain cells die. Some researchers believe that exercises requiring co-ordination and mental agility, such as having to overcome obstacles to find food, help to form additional connections between brain cells. Exercise is nature's antidepressant. During exercise, body temperature increases, giving a sense of warmth. Endorphins, the body's natural opiates, are released. Sustained exercise burns the waste products accumulated during stressful, inactive periods.

THE IMPORTANCE OF SLEEP

Relaxed sleep is just as important as routine exercise. Adult cats need about 16 hours of sleep each day. Sleep consists of two basic states, Rapid Eye Movement (REM) sleep, when dreams occur, and Non-REM (NREM) or deep sleep. Cats naturally take frequent "cat naps". If a cat is deprived of either sort of sleep it becomes confused and irritable.

WHAT HAPPENS DURING SLEEP

During dreamless (NREM) sleep, your cat's body repairs and regenerates itself. Kittens build their muscles and bones. The immune system strengthens and revitalizes. Kittens need more NREM sleep than adults and with advancing years the amount of NREM sleep diminishes. During a cat's dream (REM) sleep its eyes move behind closed lids, limbs twitch, and whiskers move. Up to 60 per cent of a cat's sleep is REM sleep, three times more than in our sleep. No one knows the exact purpose of sleep and dreams but both appear vital for cats, and both activities should be allowed to proceed without needless interruption.

NATURAL SLEEP
Cats dream more than people or dogs do, although why and what they dream remains a mystery. During light sleep, which consumes just under half of sleep time, the cat's body repairs itself and the immune system is revitalized.

AROMA AND PHEROMONE THERAPY

THROUGHOUT HISTORY, PEOPLE have used forms of aroma therapy to treat medical conditions or enhance a feeling of well-being. Recently, essential oils of plants have been used to treat illnesses in dogs and cats. The concept of influencing the mind-body relationship by using natural scent messengers has also gained popularity. By mimicking natural scents, pheromone therapy may modify behaviour.

ESSENTIAL OILS
Essential oils are extracted from the roots and flowers of plants. They can be heated, or diluted in steaming water, in order that they may be inhaled. If used for massage, they must first be diluted in a vegetable-based carrier oil.

TOXIC OILS

Remember that some essential oils used for massage aromatherapy on people are can, if swallowed, be toxic to cats . Never use aromatherapy oils on a cat without advice from an expert on whether they are toxic. Never carry out a complementary procedure on a cat that increases its level of stress or agitation.

HISTORY

Herbal oils have been used for centuries in many cultures to treat illness and promote well-being, but it was not until 1910 that the French chemist Réné-Maurice Gattefossé coined the term "aromatherapy". Since that time, doctors in France have sometimes used essential oils (made up of fatty acids) to treat medical and behavioural conditions.

In the 1980s, Dr Patrick Pageat, a French veterinarian who had studied pheromones in pigs, began to look at cats. He analyzed the secretions that cats produce in their facial glands, and found 40 different components. Most of these consisted of simple fatty acids. After several years of trial-and-error investigations he found that one subgroup of fatty acids, when concentrated and applied where cats were spraying urine, inhibited that unwanted behaviour. With the help of one of France's largest perfume makers, he had this subgroup of fatty acids synthetically reproduced. This product has been marketed as a natural pheromone analogue, used to dissuade cats from urine marking at home.

HOW IT WORKS

Pheromones are the odour signals that animals use to communicate with each other. In addition to a nasal membrane, cats have an additional "scenting" structure, called the vomeronasal organ, located above the roof of the mouth. Dr Pageat's work suggests that, when "urine-marking" pheromones are covered with "identification" pheromones, and natural facial secretions are spread in the environment, a cat's confidence is increased and its need to urine-mark reduced.

VETERINARY OPINION

Scents released by oils act on the part of the brain (the hypothalamus) that influences the hormone system. In theory, a scent might be able to affect mood or metabolism. Natural scents, such as pheromones, ought to be more effective than plant-derived scents for controlling a cat's mind. Studies on the use of pheromones to control unwanted behaviours such as urine-marking are promising.

Although aromatherapy is often requested by cat owners, there are drawbacks to its use. Inhalation can be difficult, as cats find many odours unpleasant, and massage can also be a problem. Massage without oil is best for cats as they resent odours in their fur and will roll vigorously to cover them. Pheromone therapy, on the other hand, has been well received in countries where it is available.

PHEROMONES TRANSFER INFORMATION
This cat is gathering scent information left by another cat in the household. In the animal world a just few molecules of scent (usually fatty acids) are all it takes for one member of a species to transmit potentially important information to another. We do not fully understand this process.

OTHER THERAPIES

A REMARKABLE ARRAY of mind-body therapies are used to help people stay healthy or enhance their body's response when they are unwell. Many of these therapies, for instance, colour therapy, have no practical application for cats. However, some complementary mind-body therapies, although impossible to study on creatures other than humans, may affect animals other than us.

WHERE'S THE EVIDENCE?
Many vets tend to view with suspicion information that does not fit existing theories, and demand higher levels of evidence to support new ideas. Remember that all through history we have found new treatments and used them before we have understood them. We do not know everything now.

MUSIC THERAPY
The eminent paediatrician Dr T. Berry Brazelton has shown that music influences human babies even while still in the womb, while German studies conducted in the 1990s suggest that certain rhythms may reduce stress in people by lowering heart rate, blood pressure, and respiration.

Dr Martin Seabrook at Nottingham University, England carried out research that demonstrated that dairy cows produce more milk when they listen to gentle music such as Beethoven symphonies than when no music is played in the milking shed. The effect of music on feline health and behaviour has not yet been studied.

LIGHT THERAPY
Natural light has been an important element in naturopathy (a therapy that emphasizes fresh air, sunlight, and exercise) for over a century, but it is only recently that medical science has discovered how light plays a role in regulating the cat's biological clock. The cat's daily or "circadian" rhythms, which are influenced by light, control sleep, hormone output, and other functions. Yearly rhythms too, such as those driving seasonal moulting or reproductive heat cycles, are influenced by increasing or decreasing daylight. There have been no studies of light therapy for cats.

MAGNETIC THERAPY
Some migrating birds successfully travel thousands of miles each year by following the position of the magnetic poles of the earth. Molecules of magnetite in the brain are thought to play a role in this "sixth

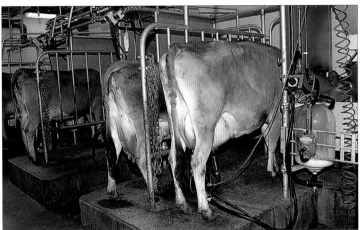

sense". Cats also have magnetite in brain cells but its function is unknown. Magnet therapy, utilizing electromagnetic fields, is used therapeutically in Europe, North America, and Australia to help heal bone fractures. Conventional veterinarians use magnetic resonance imaging (MRI) scans in diagnosis. They are safe and superior to x-rays, but more costly.

SPIRITUAL HEALING
Increased medical evidence shows that firm belief in your own religion, or in the powers of a spiritual healer, enhances your body's ability to defend itself. Faith healing is used on cats worldwide. Most reputable healers belong to national associations, for example, in the United Kingdom, healers follow a specific code of conduct, prepared by the Federation of Spiritual Healers, for the treatment of animals. How the positive value of spiritual belief affects animals in our care is unknown.

COWS RESPOND TO BEETHOVEN
If you ever hear the slow movement of Beethoven's Fifth Symphony as you enter a dairy farm milking shed, it means that the dairyman is familiar with studies indicating that cows release more milk when listening to soothing music.

THERAPEUTIC CARE

WHATEVER FORM OF THERAPY you choose for your cat, remember the most important rule of care, "Do no harm". The key to recovery from illness is lack of stress, good nutrition, and responsive immune and repair systems. Do not inadvertently stress your cat by using a therapy that seems appropriate for you but distresses your cat. Do not be afraid of using successful conventional therapies.

CHECKLIST

To reduce the risks entailed by any form of therapy, either conventional or complementary, ask your veterinarian these questions:

- What is the exact reason for using this therapy?
- How does the therapy work?
- Is the therapy absolutely necessary?
- What are the chances of success?
- Are there known potential side effects?
- Is a choice of different therapies available to you?
- Have you checked whether there are any recognized alternatives to this form of therapy?

CHANGES IN VETERINARY CARE

Many individuals can be exposed to an infection, yet only some will develop clinical signs of illness. If we take viral infections of the upper respiratory tract as an example, conventional veterinary medicine is excellent at diagnosing which infection a cat has, but it is not so good at explaining why a specific cat developed that specific disease in the first place. It is also not so good at creating an environment for recovery.

However, veterinary care is changing, and conventional and complementary forms of care are nowadays becoming integrated. The two approaches are no longer distinct and opposing philosophical entities.

ADVERSE DRUG REACTIONS

In the UK, the Suspected Adverse Reactions Surveillance Scheme recorded the following cases over the course of 1994.

DRUG	CASES
External anti-parasite drugs	104
Live vaccines	49
Inactivated vaccines	17
Anaesthetics	17
Antibiotic and antifungal drugs	14
Worming medicines	9
Non-steroid anti-inflammatories	5
Corticosteroid drugs	1
All other drugs	23

MARKET-DRIVEN CHANGES

Driven by public demand, conventional vets are now studying complementary therapies to deal with stress-related and degenerative problems. These are increasingly common in cats. As a result of effective vaccinations against killer diseases, and the move to an indoor lifestyle, cats are living longer and are more prone to degenerative disorders.

In my experience, most cat owners are sensible about what is best for their pets. They understand that cats are not people and that different ethical precepts exist for deciding how far you should go in treating a cat's medical condition. Compassionate cat owners understand that there are technological ways to prolong a cat's life but also ask, "What is best for the cat?"

CONVENTIONAL DRUGS

Owners are concerned about the incidence of adverse reactions to modern drugs. In many countries drug reactions are not centrally reported and compiled, but in the UK, the Suspected Adverse Reactions Surveillance Scheme recorded, in a typical year, that conventional drugs caused 239 suspected adverse reactions. The box (*see left*) gives the drug categories. Outwardly, these are remarkably low figures, considering that there are over seven million cats in the UK. However, the figures refer only to acute and severe adverse reactions. There are no statistics that collate long-term or chronic reactions to conventional drug therapies.

COMPLEMENTARY THERAPIES

A cat's needs are different to yours or mine. Only use someone recommended by your vet for any form of complementary therapy. Conventionally trained vets throughout the world practise all forms of complementary therapy, often openly alongside conventional treatments. Many national and international associations for veterinary acupuncture, homeopathy, and holistic veterinary medicine exist. Journals are published and yearly academic meetings are held.

A HEALING ENVIRONMENT

When your cat is recuperating from illness or injury, create a supportive environment conducive to recovery. Your cat will seek out a special area where it feels comfortable. Ensure that this location is comfortable, warm, and draught-free. Do not scold your cat for soiling outside its litter tray. Provide comfortable bedding, and make sure water and food are within reach. Unless advised otherwise, lean chicken is an ideal recovery diet. Do not expect your cat to play when it is ill, and do not allow children or other cats to pester it.

Statistics have not been compiled for acute or chronic adverse reactions to complementary therapies such as herbal medicines.

NATURAL AGEING

Age comes to all cats. A 10-year-old is like a 56-year-old human, and from then on each cat year is equivalent to four human years. Age brings deteriorating eyesight, reduced strength and agility, harder hearing, stiffness, and increasing medical problems. Anticipate the changes of ageing. Keep to daily routines. Groom your cat more because its skin glands produce less oil, and brush its teeth daily. Weigh your cat and report significant weight changes to your vet. Arrange for a yearly "older cat" health check-up. Use effective therapies to reduce the discomforts of old age.

CARING FOR AN ILL CAT

You know how *you* feel when you are ill. Respect your cat's desire to be left alone or to seek your company. Cats do not usually complain, so always assume that a condition that is painful for us is painful for them too. Cystitis, constipation, limping, difficulty in standing or walking are all painful. Take over cleaning responsibilities if your cat cannot groom itself while it is unwell.

When a comfortable life is no longer possible, think first of your cat's quality of life. When your cat's life is irrevocably low, do not wait for a "natural" death. We have it in our power to make pet death physically painless. Most vets will do whatever they can to make the sad event as easy as possible for you, your family, and your cat.

HOSPITALIZING YOUR CAT

Hospitalizing your cat is unavoidable whenever intensive care is necessary – when help is needed emptying the bladder or bowels, when pain control is critical, or when diagnostics or therapeutics require constant monitoring. Otherwise, cats recuperate best at home. Keep hospitalization to a minimum.

NATURAL DEVELOPMENT

NATURAL TRAINING

NATURAL NUTRITION

NATURAL HEALTH CARE

HEALTH DISORDERS

ADMINISTERING MEDICATION

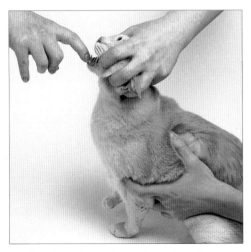

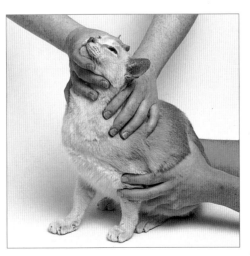

1 Cats dislike being given pills. It is best if someone can hold the cat still for you while you administer the pill. Hold the cat's head in one hand, and with the other pull the lower jaw down gently. Push your finger on the skin between the jaws.

2 As soon as you have dropped the pill in the cat's mouth, close the cat's jaws using one hand, and keep the jaw closed. Stroke the cat's throat and neck until you feel it swallow. If your cat licks its lips, you know that it has swallowed the pill.

HEALTH DISORDERS

There is a place for both conventional and complementary health care for your cat. Conventional medicine is at its best when acute conditions require treatment. Modern drugs and surgical techniques are the methods of choice to treat acutely painful or life-threatening conditions. Complementary procedures can play a supporting role and may be useful for chronic or long-term disorders for which conventional veterinary care appears to have no remedy. When opting for any treatment always consider the stress it places on your cat. What seems appropriate to you may not be right for your cat.

Cats tend to hide themselves away when they feel unwell, so owners must be alert.

CONFRONTING HEALTH DISORDERS

ONE OF THE MOST DIFFICULT problems, when a cat has a health disorder, is to recognize that there is a disorder in the first place. Cats tend to hide away from us if they are unwell, but this behaviour should warn us that something is wrong. In order to confront and overcome any health disorder we need to understand its "strategy": how it will try to combat or bypass the cat's natural defences.

CHECKLIST

Approach health problems in the following ways:

- As accurately as possible, define the problem.
- Minimize both physical and psychological stress.
- Try to create an environment conducive to recovery.
- Integrate the positive values of conventional and complementary therapies.
- Locate complementary practitioners through holistic veterinarians.

DIFFERENT FORMS OF DIAGNOSIS

In veterinary medicine it is often necessary to confront health problems without a clear understanding of what "the enemy" is, or what its tactics might be. This is where the diagnoses and treatments of conventional and complementary veterinary medicine differ.

Veterinary care is like paediatrics. Your cat's well-being depends upon you noticing that something is wrong, and describing to your vet what you have seen, or felt, or smelled, or heard. For example, you might notice that your cat has a swollen paw. A conventional veterinarian looks for clinical signs: a raised temperature might mean an infection; a soft swelling may suggest an abscess forming; a crackling feeling when it is manipulated can mean bone damage. Blood tests and x-rays might be arranged.

Your vet is looking for information that fits recognized patterns that enable him or her to name your cat's problem. When a specific disease is identified, there may be a specific treatment. However, sometimes it can be difficult to identify a disease. Your cat is certainly ill, but the disease cannot be identified. When this happens it is called an "undifferentiated illness".

AN ALTERNATIVE APPROACH

For complementary vets, the presence of recognizable clinical signs is important but the absence of an accurate diagnosis is less of an obstacle to treatment. For each type of complementary therapy, undifferentiated illnesses, usually pain or lethargy, and also stress-related conditions, are given unique diagnostic labels, such as "weakened vital force", "excess pitta", or "stuck liver qi". Complementary vets have both general and specific therapies for these conditions.

THE RISKS OF TREATMENT

The very first rule of medicine is just as important today as it was when Hippocrates formulated it and it is worth mentioning again: *Primum non nocere* – First, do no harm. This must be the basis for all therapies, both conventional and complementary. Your cat's body wants to be healthy and to maintain homeostasis. The body's self-diagnosis, repair, and regeneration is the success story of evolution. Your cat has magnificent ways of repairing itself but you can help it to confront health disorders by reducing risk and augmenting its natural defences. Prevention is better than cure. The best way to prevent disease is to reduce genetic and environmental risks (*see pages 108-109*).

CLINICAL SIGNS OF DISEASE

Do not treat your cat's clinical signs as the problem. Use them as a guide to the origin of the problem. Work with them rather than against them. A cough, for example, is a defence. It leads you to the throat, windpipe, lungs, and heart. Suppressing a cough could be life-threatening if, for example, there is unwanted material in the air passages. In the case of fluid in the chest cavity, the cough

"DO-IT-YOURSELF" IS DANGEROUS

Your cat's well-being depends entirely upon you. Complementary practitioners who are not qualified veterinarians are not trained to detect signs of disease in cats. Seemingly minor conditions can become life-threatening problems if not treated properly. When seeking complementary treatments for your cat, use the services of a veterinarian trained in complementary therapies or an individual recommended by a qualified veterinarian. When seeking advice, always tell your vet what complementary treatments you have given to your cat.

leads your vet to the true problem, and, once more, suppressing the cough is not in your cat's interest. Your cat's cough will reduce when its heart condition is treated effectively.

MIND AND BODY INTEGRATION

Psychoneuroimmunology (PNI), one of the most exciting fields of medicine today, investigates the connection between the mind and body. Each white blood cell circulating in a cat's bloodstream has receptor sites on its surface for all the chemical messengers from its brain. Behaviour, emotion, and psychology are all factors that should be considered and integrated into diagnosis and treatment. A medical problem may well be a physical condition but the root of the problem can be emotional or psychological.

USE SAFE TREATMENTS

Whenever possible, use the safest effective treatment. Some complementary therapies, for instance, homeopathy, are minimally interventionist, as are some conventional veterinary therapies such as bed or cage rest. Other therapies are more "invasive". Conventional drugs have potential side effects. An antibiotic either destroys bacteria or prevents their further multiplication. Some cats, when they swallow certain antibiotics, have a natural inclination to get rid of the "foreign" substance and vomit it back. This form of rejection applies to certain herbs, too. We might find them natural but cats don't. Do not define one form of medicine as safe and the other as dangerous. Assess the risks before deciding what is best for your cat.

TREAT CHRONIC CONDITIONS

Chronic problems are the backbone of complementary veterinary medicine. Long-lasting conditions of muscles, joints, the immune system, the gastrointestinal and urinary systems, and psychosomatic disorders are the fields where complementary therapies are most widely used. Other conditions, such as acute trauma and severe infections,

are best treated conventionally, while such procedures as surgery, dentistry, anaesthestics, and vaccinations are the rightful province of the conventional vet.

MAINTAINING GOOD HEALTH

Confronting health disorders should not be done on a "fire brigade" basis. Prevention is the most important way to maintain health. Feed a diet that contains not only all the nutrients that are necessary for life but also the ingredients that are known to bolster your cat's natural defences (*see pages 50-51*). There is no reason why the evidence that exercise is good for our health should not apply to cats too. Provide your cat with opportunities to exercise according to its wants and abilities. Mental and physical exercise nourish the mind and body. When each is nourished, the other benefits.

MAINSTREAM ALTERNATIVE

Many dietary treatments that are today an integral part of conventional medicine have their origins in alternative therapies. We have them to thank for the beneficial effects of fish oil on the immune system, of vegetable beta-carotenes in cardio-vascular problems, and *Lactobacillus* bacteria to avoid antibiotic side effects.

DEPENDENT ON YOU
Your cat will often need your help to confront and overcome health disorders. Get professional advice from a veterinarian you trust. Use a blend of conventional and complementary therapies that are appropriate for your cat's clinical condition.

NATURAL DEVELOPMENT

NATURAL TRAINING

NATURAL NUTRITION

NATURAL HEALTH CARE

HEALTH DISORDERS

THE CHANGING NATURE OF DISEASE

THE CAT SEEMS MORE SUSCEPTIBLE than other species to a wide range of influences. The range of cat illnesses that I treat today, including overactive thyroid glands, heart disease, and "new" infections such as feline infectious peritonitis, essentially did not exist in cats 50 years ago. Today, genetic, metabolic, geriatric, and new environmental disorders play dominant roles in cat health and disease.

INEXPLICABLE
It is popular to try to explain everything that occurs in the body as a result of natural evolutionary adaptation: for everything there is a reason. But perhaps this is not so. The natural historian Stephen Jay Gould argues that sometimes aspects of life may well be simply "accidental".

PARASITES AND MICROBES
The cat evolved as a lone hunter. Except for its early life with its litter, it spent little time with its immediate family and none with strangers other than during mating. The parasites, viruses, and bacteria that potentially could cause infection had to adapt to these circumstances.

As a result, curious life cycles developed. *Taenia taeniformis*, the common cat tapeworm, travels to its natural home, a cat's intestines, via the gut of the flea. This method of travel evolved because cats eat fleas when they groom themselves. Upper respiratory tract viruses use the sneeze, a natural defence that discharges mucus from the nose, as a method of transmission.

Because cat colonies were naturally small, consisting mainly of related females and a dominant male, these viruses could only affect limited numbers of individuals.

RAPID ADAPTATIONS
More recently, biological vaccines changed the nature of feline viral diseases. Viral enteritis, a parvovirus infection, was once a common cause of death in cats. This disease, sometimes called feline distemper, was the most commonly diagnosed serious infection in cats. Effective vaccination changed the nature of this disease but then, seemingly from nowhere, in the 1950s, feline infectious peritonitis (FIP) emerged. Its development coincided with the establishment of large groups of cats in breeding colonies and rescue centres. Initially, most cases involved a fatal inflammation to the lining of the abdominal cavity, but now cats in some countries have somehow adapted to the presence of this virus and have different clinical signs of disease. The nature of disease appears to change and adapt with remarkable rapidity in cats.

ANTIBIOTIC RESISTANCE
Antibiotics are used either to kill bacteria and fungi, or to prevent them from multiplying. Through unlimited and at times thoughtless use of antibiotics in circumstances that are arguably inappropriate, for instance, as growth promoters in farm livestock, we have created conditions that we cannot control.

Antibiotics have caused an acceleration of bacterial evolution. Microbe evolution is taking place right now at a faster pace than at any time in the history of life on earth. Microbes are evolving faster than we can isolate and create new antibiotics with which to control "antibiotic-resistant" forms.

The nature of bacterial illness continues to evolve, with the likelihood that bacteria that is resistant to all known antibiotics — a phenomenon that already exists in a human hospital strain of bacteria — will also occur in bacteria that affect cats.

DESIGN FLAWS
By breeding selectively to satisfy our own ideas of beauty, we alter the risk of disease for cats. Because of its unnaturally flattened face, this Persian has a far greater risk of upper respiratory tract disease, sinus conditions, and facial skin infections than cats with the natural face shape of their ancestors.

ENVIRONMENTAL PRESSURES

As we altered our own environment we have altered the nature of feline diseases. The cat evolved to live and hunt outdoors, obtaining nourishment by eating other animals. The cat's medical problems dramatically changed when we moved cats into our homes. Mixing cats from different backgrounds increased the risk of transmissible diseases. Cities have increased the dangers of road-traffic accidents. In some parts of some countries, air-rifle and gunshot wounds are a common cause of traumatic cat injuries. Simply living in our warm homes changed the nature of feline disease. In temperate zones, fleas are now a more significant cause of feline disease than they were previously, simply because fleas find our homes ideal for year-round occupation and breeding. This results in more fleas. At the same time, feline asthma is becoming a common problem.

GENETIC PRESSURE

In natural evolution, genetic mutations are always occurring. Survival of the fittest means that beneficial genetic mutations are retained while deleterious ones die out quickly. When we intervened in cat breeding, we influenced genetic pressures. Unwittingly, pedigree-cat clubs, through beauty contests and breeding to written breed standards, accelerated evolutionary genetic changes in cats in the same way. Many breeds today come from small genetic bases. Deleterious genetic changes in the nature of disease can occur because of the show success of a single individual in a breed. Its unknown genetic medical defects will be spread to a larger-than-normal population because of its popularity for breeding. Many breeds now have specific genetic problems. Himalayans may have hereditary cataracts. Abbyssinians potentially carry genetic predisposition to progressive retinal atrophy blindness, amyloidosis resulting in fatal kidney failure, and hemolytic anaemia. The Burmese is prone to hereditary deafness. Maine Coons can suffer from hip dysplasia. The number of known genetic diseases is increasing almost weekly. Ironically, only selective breeding will now be effective in eliminating these conditions.

GERIATRICS

At one time, a house cat's life expectancy was the same as a wild cat's, typically about 10 years. Individuals lived longer and the potential life expectancy was greater still, but the vagaries of life meant that few individuals passed this average age. Today, with our care and attention, many cats reach their potential of 15 to 19 years of age. Some individuals live even longer. But with advancing years come changes in the nature of disease — wear and tear, metabolic disorders, cancers, heart disease — a wider range of age-related disorders than ever before are now being diagnosed in cats. Even senile dementia, akin to Alzheimer's disease in people, now occurs in cats. Geriatric medicine is a new field in veterinary medicine, at least in part because of our successes in disease control, owner responsibility, and good nourishment.

CHANGING TREATMENT

Just as the nature of diseases constantly changes, so too does our approach to disease treatment. The veterinary medical establishment, aware that pet owners are concerned about drug side effects and expensive, unpleasant, or ineffective treatments, is showing increasing interest in complementary therapies. These factors were recognized by the American Veterinary Medical Association when it published new guidelines for alternative and complementary medicine in 1996. There is increasing integration of conventional and complementary systems in veterinary medicine.

OLD-AGE PROBLEMS
Geriatric illnesses, once uncommon in cats and often chronic in their nature, are now an important part of veterinary care. Many forms of complementary medicine are designed for geriatrics.

CHECKLIST
- The nature of disease varies for many reasons.
- The level of preventative medicine is determined by economics.
- Economics also determines how early in a disease process a cat receives treatment.
- Age, sex, breed, and individual temperament affect disease.
- Geography affects incidence and natural resistance.
- We dominate the nature of disease through our influence in genetics and the environment.

NATURAL DEVELOPMENT

NATURAL TRAINING

NATURAL NUTRITION

NATURAL HEALTH CARE

HEALTH DISORDERS

THE CAT'S NATURAL DEFENCES

YOUR CAT HAS SUPERB NATURAL DEFENCES, better than the dog's because, until recently, we did not compromise its defences through deleterious selective breeding. Good veterinary care will encourage these defences to fight off attack from illness. Do not mistake your cat's sneezes, vomiting, diarrhoea, or elevated temperature for its actual illness. These responses are its natural defences at work.

NATURAL DEVELOPMENT

NATURAL TRAINING

NATURAL NUTRITION

NATURAL HEALTH CARE

HEALTH DISORDERS

CHECKLIST
Good natural defences include:

- Cleanliness.
- Healthy natural barriers.
- Avoidance of known pathogens.
- If pathogens get through, an ability to attack, poison, starve, and ward off the dangers.

ALWAYS ON GUARD
The concept of recruiting the body's self-healing capacities, amplifying natural recuperative processes, and creating an environment conducive to well-being, has always been the premise of complementary veterinary medicine, but is now also a part of conventional veterinary medicine. The emphasis on restoring good health rather than removing sickness is increasingly embraced by conventional vets.

Most animals are uniformly exposed to the causes of medical conditions. For example, all cats in a household may be exposed to household fleas, but each cat responds in its own unique way. While one cat will not be bothered by flea bites, another may be driven to occasional scratching, while a third may be intensely irritated and develop secondary bacterial infection or even a systemic disease. The competence and reactivity of a cat's immune system ultimately determines what illnesses that cat will get and how it will cope with them, but there are other defences, too.

NATURAL BARRIERS
A pathogen is an organism or substance that causes disease. Any part of your cat that is easily accessible to pathogens, which means anything connected to the outside world, has a superb ability to repair and regenerate itself. Your cat's first line of defence is its skin. Skin acts as a barrier to pathogens and is a major organ in your cat's immune system. The hair that grows from the skin acts as an insulator and also offers physical protection.

The lining of the gut, and of the liver which is in open communication with the gut, has evolved equal powers of regeneration. The gut lining is the second largest organ in the immune system. Natural defensive actions take place throughout the gastrointestinal system. Pathogens are killed either by saliva or stomach acid. Toxic substances are denatured in the stomach or intestines or detoxified by the liver. The system is sophisticated and highly effective. Organs that are less accessible to pathogens, such as the brain and heart, have few natural regenerative powers.

NATURAL MECHANICAL REACTIONS
Coughing, sneezing, vomiting, diarrhoea, frequent urination, even scratching the skin, are all natural defensive manoeuvres to rid the body of dangers. These are evolutionary methods used to expel pathogens from body surfaces. Coughing, for example, is a highly complicated procedure involving co-ordination of the diaphragm, chest muscles, and voice box, but when it is successful, any foreign material that has entered the windpipe is either ejected or swallowed and destroyed by natural stomach acids. Grooming, including simple licking, rids the body of parasites and potential pathogens. When a cat limps it rests an injured leg, which creates the best circumstances for natural repair.

Many cat owners see symptoms such as coughing and sneezing as the problem itself and take their cat to the vet in order that these symptoms – in fact the cat's defences – can be suppressed. In fact, eliminating the defence is likely to create a greater problem.

CLEANSING THE SKIN
Your cat's skin is its first and most important line of defence. Grooming keeps this barrier clean. Antiseptic in saliva kills germs on the skin, while licking removes some parasites. Parasites such as the tapeworm take advantage of natural grooming by depositing their eggs in fleas, which are then likely to be swallowed.

THE DEFENCES IN ACTION

When a pathogen tries to invade your cat's body, your pet may respond in other ways that are also sometimes misinterpreted by owners. For example, your cat's brain may set its thermostat at a higher level to induce a defensive fever. A higher temperature is capable of killing certain pathogens, but it has its costs. A moderate fever increases metabolic rate by about 20 per cent and may also cause temporary male sterility. A higher fever can lead to seizures. Not eating is another natural defence: bacteria need iron in order to survive and multiply. Temporary fasting reduces iron available from the gut. During an infection, your cat releases a chemical called leucocyte endogenous mediator (LEM) that further inhibits iron absorption from the gut.

If a pathogen travels beyond the natural barriers of the skin, the lining of the gut, and the respiratory or urinary systems, and is not expelled mechanically, it is confronted by the second line of defence: white blood cells. The defensive capabilities of white blood cells are still being unravelled and the names of certain cells are aptly descriptive. Your cat's natural defences depend upon not only macrophages ("large eaters"), which circulate the body searching for bacteria, dirt, even cancer cells to engulf, but also upon "natural killer cells" and "armed helper T-cells" (*see pages 114-115*). The natural defence system is quite awe-inspiring. Only when this superb defensive system fails or is overwhelmed do invaders get through.

STRESS MANAGEMENT

Neuropeptides, the brain chemicals that can relieve pain, have powerful effects on a cat's health, level of energy, general constitution, and natural resistance to disease. These chemicals act like an invisible chemical nervous system that bridges the mind and body. When looking at feline disease, take account of a cat's psychological defences as well as the cat's physical state, environment, and social relationships. Early learning about how to cope with stress enhances a cat's natural defences.

DEFENSIVE REACTIONS
Cats use the same mechanisms that we do to rid themselves of potential infections and dangers. Coughing, sneezing, vomiting, diarrhoea, frequent urination, even limping are not diseases. These are natural defences that are used either to eliminate danger or to enhance repair.

OLD AND NEW ENEMIES

Your cat's natural defences evolved over the millennia to cope with the threats of its natural enemies. But in the last 100 years, modern science has created enemies against which cats have no defences. Nitrate food preservatives, heavy metals in water, dioxins, DDT, all of these are harmful because cats do not have natural ways to rid their bodies of these substances. Toxic materials such as PCBs are tasteless and odourless. They bind to fat, a body tissue in abundance in many cats, and accumulate, sometimes to toxic levels, affecting hormone balances. These toxic substances accumulate and are never expelled from the body because there are no natural enzymes to attack and destroy them.

Your cat's natural defences are at their most efficient during its prime of life. With time, they begin to falter. This is why auto-immune conditions (where the body attacks itself), cancers, overwhelming infections, and metabolic failures increase in frequency with advancing years.

PATHOGENS FIGHT BACK

Pathogens have natural methods of defence and preservation, too. Those that cause feline infectious peritonitis (FIP) actively multiply in your cat's white blood cells. Others, like intestinal worms, consume your cat's natural nutrients. Some pathogens use other agents, such as fleas, to get into your cat. Some manipulate your cat's natural defences and use defences such as sneezing or diarrhoea to spread themselves further. This war is sometimes called the "co-evolutionary arms race".

NATURAL DEVELOPMENT

NATURAL TRAINING

NATURAL NUTRITION

NATURAL HEALTH CARE

HEALTH DISORDERS

PAIN

NATURAL DEVELOPMENT

NATURAL TRAINING

NATURAL NUTRITION

NATURAL HEALTH CARE

HEALTH DISORDERS

CATS HAVE SUPERB painkilling systems, far more efficient than ours. They are reluctant to reveal to others that they feel pain because in the eyes of their enemies pain is a sign of weakness. Of course, cats do feel pain: it is part of their body's natural defences. Although pain is not an illness itself, it plays a major role in many feline health disorders and therefore should be looked at separately.

YOUR CAT'S PAIN

Cats are inclined to hide away if they are in pain. If your cat wants to be alone, don't stress it even more by forcing upon it a therapy that it resents. Never give a cat a painkilling drug or herb if it has not been licensed for use in cats, even if it is effective in other species.

HOW PAIN AFFECTS CATS

Pain is protective. Feeling pain causes a cat to avoid continuing dangers. Continued pain reduces use of damaged tissues, giving time for repair. Inactivity as a result of pain may assist the immune system's response to body damage. Pain has two separate dimensions — intensity and unpleasantness. The sensation of pain is not affected by a placebo but the unpleasantness of pain can be reduced by conditioning, and so is open to the placebo response. Your enthusiasm in treating your cat's pain may possibly help to control the unpleasantness of the experience.

ACUTE PAIN

Short-term pain ranges from benignly mild to so excruciatingly unpleasant that it causes a cat to go into clinical shock. Experience of pain is the natural way in which a cat learns that something should be avoided, or that something has gone wrong. Pain can have an obvious source. Nerve endings capable of receiving pain messages are everywhere but are concentrated on the skin. Curiously, the amount of pain a cat feels is not related to the amount of damage sustained. Your cat's brain monitors the inflow of all information and sets a biological priority to a fraction of that information. If your cat suffers painful, penetrating bite wounds from another cat, its response may be to suppress the pain and to bite back. Conscious, acute pain occurs only after other priorities have been met. The cat with deep puncture wounds from a cat fight may appear pain-free until its brain registers different priorities and pain sensation develops.

CHRONIC PAIN

Chronic pain is usually associated with bone and joint conditions, degenerative disease, and cancer. It is relentlessly uncomfortable, but most cats suffering from chronic pain behave stoically. Owners often notice only changes in behaviour, such as less agility or more resting. The degree of pain that a cat feels varies enormously. Some forms of chronic pain respond well to painkilling drugs but others cannot be alleviated by conventional treatments.

HOW PAIN IS TRANSMITTED

Nerve receptors throughout the body, in muscles, joints, and especially in the skin, are stimulated by temperature, pressure, or natural chemicals called prostaglandins, which are released by damaged cells. Once the receptors are stimulated, messages are relayed through nerves to the brain, where they are interpreted as pain. Each cat will interpret these signals in its own way, which is partly learned and partly inherited.

Individuals differ in how they feel pain. According to the "gate control" theory, information from nerve receptors travelling to the brain has to pass through "gates". A number of factors determine how wide open these gates become. Emotion certainly affects the size of the gate opening, probably by altering endorphins, the cat's natural painkillers. This is why, during the emotional intensity of a cat fight, cats are resistant to pain and will keep fighting despite serious injuries. An injection by the vet, on the other hand, may be registered as severe pain.

CONVENTIONAL TREATMENTS

Vets treat pain according to its cause. As well as a physical examination, vets use diagnostic tests such as blood and urine samples, x-rays, and ultrasound to pinpoint the source of pain. By monitoring a cat's resistance to or resentment of manipulation, the location and level of pain is assessed. Cats hiss or spit only with severe pain. Alleviating short-term pain in cats can be difficult. Paracetamol, which blocks pain impulses in the brain itself, is toxic to cats and should not be given. Aspirin works by inhibiting the production of inflammatory prostaglandins, but it takes a cat's liver about four days to remove a single small dose of aspirin from its body. At higher doses aspirin can be lethal.

Narcotic painkillers such as pethidine and morphine mimic natural endorphins, blocking pain impulses at specific body sites. In cats, morphine causes intense neurological excitement and can be a very dangerous drug. Newer and safer non-steroid anti-inflammatories are used to control mild to moderate pain. Corticosteroids are sometimes used when pain is associated with intense inflammation.

PERCEPTION OF PAIN
There are no specific "pain receptors" in your cat's body. Rather, information received by the brain from nerve receptors throughout the body is interpreted as pain. The brain constantly gives information different levels of priority, which is why, during a fight, cats don't feel pain.

COMPLEMENTARY TREATMENTS

ACUPUNCTURE The American Veterinary Medical Association and the World Health Organization both recognize acupuncture as a treatment for joint-related pain. Studies in humans show that acupuncture relieves joint pain, but studies in cats have never been carried out. Veterinary acupuncturists say that the more chronic the pain the more treatments may be necessary before pain relief is observed. *See pages 72-73.*

TRIGGER POINT THERAPY Pressure on specific trigger points in muscles is claimed to relieve severe pain associated with nerve inflammation as well as muscle and joint pain. Veterinary clinicians at Murdoch University in Perth, Australia, say that animals may initially resent pressure being applied but after therapy they have more mobility and fewer signs of discomfort. *See page 76.*

CHIROPRACTIC Correct manipulation of spinal joints and muscle tissues by chiropractors knowledgeable of feline musculature can ease acute pain. This is particularly useful in breeds such as the long-backed Maine Coon. Chiropractic tends to be less effective at easing chronic back and joint pain. *See page 78.*

THERAPEUTIC MASSAGE Gentle physical massage can alleviate muscle pain and also tissue-injury pain. This is only possible in dependent cats and only for short periods. Active attention from a cat's owner may have a beneficial psychological effect on a dependent cat, possibly stimulating natural endorphin release and further reducing pain sensation. *See pages 80-81.*

HYDROTHERAPY Ice packs can reduce pain caused by inflammation while cold compresses probably dull pain-sensing nerve receptors in the skin and underlying tissue. *See page 82.*

OTHER PHYSICAL THERAPIES Transcutaneous electric nerve stimulation (TENS) and other physical therapies such as pulsating electromagnetic field (PEMF) therapy may be effective for reducing the intensity of chronic joint or soft-tissue pain. British studies on dogs suggest that electro-stimulation is as effective as some pharmaceutical painkillers. *See page 83.*

NUTRITIONAL THERAPIES High levels of omega-3 fatty acids, such as those found in mackerel oil, appear to have a natural anti-inflammatory effect. Supplements of fish-oil concentrate are thought to reduce

discomfort from chronic skin and joint inflammation. It is possible that fish-oil supplement may reduce pain associated with an irritable bowel. *See pages 86-87.*

BACH FLOWER REMEDIES Rescue Remedy is said to diminish pain but there are no scientific or even extended anecdotal studies to confirm this. *See page 95.*

RELAXATION THERAPY Conditioning your cat to relax may be an effective way to reduce post-surgical pain in cats. Relaxation techniques are relatively simple to use. *See page 98.*

PHEROMONE AND AROMA THERAPY Natural pheromones, especially sex pheromones, work by distracting a cat from its pain, concentrating its mind on more intriguing matters. Eucalyptus and tea tree oil are said to stimulate the endorphin system when massaged on the body but studies on people found the effect no greater than that of massage alone. *See page 100.*

MACKEREL

THE IMMUNE SYSTEM

WITH ITS MILLIONS OF WHITE BLOOD CELLS, the immune system defends the cat's body against diseases. It can be activated by either physical or psychological causes, and should turn on and off as necessary. If the system doesn't turn on properly, a cat has a poor immune response and is "immuno-suppressed". If the system is over-sensitive, or doesn't turn off, allergy or auto-immune disease ensues.

antibody production when a job is completed. Appropriately named "natural killer cells" attack and destroy tumour cells and virus particles. Other lymphocytes, called memory T-cells, patrol the body, recognizing organisms they have met in the past, and mobilizing attack teams. Macrophages, the "big eaters", devour microbes and debris.

INCREASING AUTO-IMMUNE DISORDERS?

Auto-immune disease can be triggered by bacteria and viruses, drugs, tumours, and in rare circumstances, vaccines. Diseases such as auto-immune haemolytic anaemia and hypothyroidism are being diagnosed more frequently. Many vets feel that this is a result both of increased incidence and better diagnostic abilities.

HOW THE SYSTEM WORKS

White blood cells are the "attack soldiers" of the immune system. Their function is to guard and protect the body, to maintain homeostasis. An efficient immune system recognizes and destroys internal dangers such as cancer cells and external pathogens such as viruses, mycoplasma, bacteria, and yeast. Bone marrow, the thymus gland, lymph nodes, and the spleen are the visible internal elements of the immune system.

Immune system cells called helper T-cells prompt other white blood cells, called B-lymphocytes, to produce antibodies to neutralize harmful microbes. Suppressor T-cells instruct the B-lymphocytes to turn off

IMMUNITY AND IMMUNE DEFICIENCY

Under certain conditions, for example, feline immune deficiency virus (FIV) infection, suppressor cells become dominant and the immune system is weakened. A cat is then susceptible to secondary infections and to cancers. The opposite is equally harmful. If helper T-cells dominate, the immune system becomes overactive and loses its ability to differentiate between normal cells in the body (called "self") and real invaders. The immune system starts attacking its own body tissues. This produces an auto-immune disease. Renal amyloidosis (a type of kidney failure) is an auto-immune disease. Their excess helper T-cells have attacked and damaged their own kidneys.

ELEMENTS OF THE SYSTEM

All cats that live into old age will experience a decline in elements of the immune system, which include the immune cells in the skin and also the gastrointestinal tract. Old age is linked to this natural decline in immune competence, an increased incidence of cancer, infectious diseases, and auto-immune disorders.

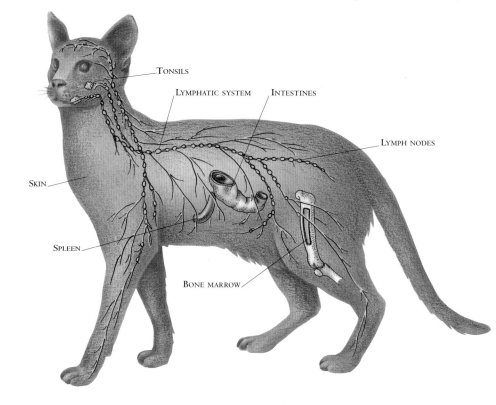

TONSILS

LYMPHATIC SYSTEM   INTESTINES

LYMPH NODES

SKIN

SPLEEN

BONE MARROW

Finally, the immune system may become over-sensitive, reacting to harmless substances such as flea saliva, dust-mite droppings, plant pollens, or foods. This is how allergic disorders, such as itchy skin conditions and feline asthma, develop (*see pages 116-117*).

CONVENTIONAL TREATMENTS

Conventional veterinary medicine manipulates the immune system in two ways. Inoculation introduces dead or modified germs into the cat's body, which stimulates the immune system to produce antibodies, "immunizing" against the dangerous form of that specific germ. Conventional vets also suppress the immune system when it becomes overactive, as it does in allergic reactions, asthma, and auto-immune conditions. They dispense corticosteroids and sometimes other, more powerful, immuno-suppressant drugs.

EXERCISE FOR IMMUNITY
In people, active exercise is known to increase total white blood cell numbers, natural killer cell numbers and activity, and levels of protective interferons. It is likely that there are similar benefits for cats. Mental and physical exercise can only be beneficial for cats.

NATURAL DEVELOPMENT

NATURAL TRAINING

NATURAL NUTRITION

NATURAL HEALTH CARE

HEALTH DISORDERS

COMPLEMENTARY TREATMENTS

Complementary practitioners claim that positive mental activity, a nutritious diet, and exercise support the immune system. Herbal remedies and nutritional supplements may enhance the immune system's ability to respond. Feelings and emotions influence immune processes, so mind and emotion therapies may also help.

THERAPEUTIC MASSAGE Gentle touch and massage can reduce stress and induce relaxation. They may also strengthen the immune system. *See pages 80-81.*

NUTRITIONAL THERAPIES Studies in people show that substances that act as antioxidants improve the immune response. Antioxidants neutralize excess free radicals, which are chemicals that can damage cell membranes. Antioxidants include the minerals selenium (toxic in excess) and zinc, vitamins A (as beta-carotene), C, and E, and bioflavonoids. Beta-carotene improves skin and mucous membrane defences and enhances antibody response. Vitamin C, which we must consume in our food but cats have the ability to manufacture themselves, increases antibody

levels, while vitamin E protects body cells, tissues, and organs. Some nutritionists believe that vitamin D, the B-complex of vitamins, iron, calcium, magnesium, and manganese all have roles to play in an efficient immune system. When auto-immune conditions occur, a cat's diet should contain sufficient glutamine and fibre (to allow production of short-chain fatty acids), both of which fuel and nourish cells lining the small and large intestines. EFA supplements (fish oil, oil of evening primrose) are also said to enhance immune function.
See pages 86-87.

HERBALISM Astragalus root, *Astragalus membranaceus*, a popular plant in Chinese medicine, is considered an immuno-stimulant herb. It is said to stimulate the development of cells in the immune system. The purple coneflower, *Echinacea purpurea*, one of the most popular of all herbs, is said to stimulate macrophages, especially in their action against yeast cells. According to research, both *Berberis* and *Aloe vera* stimulate an immune response.
See pages 88-91.

RELAXATION THERAPY Stress is known to have deleterious effects on the immune system. The stress of being restrained can inhibit the immune response in animals with infections. Any therapy that reduces negative emotions may boost the immune system's ability to cope with threat. *See page 98.*

PHEROMONE THERAPY Practitioners claim that a feeling of euphoria enhances the immune system by stimulating the occupation of cell receptor sites with natural body chemicals and preventing viruses from using those receptor sites to gain access to the cell. *See page 100.*

ALOE VERA

NATURAL DEVELOPMENT

NATURAL TRAINING

NATURAL NUTRITION

NATURAL HEALTH CARE

HEALTH DISORDERS

ALLERGIES

ALLERGY IS AN EXAGGERATED and unnecessary response of the immune system to non-infectious stimuli. Allergic reactions occur on a cat's skin, causing itchiness; on the lining of the air passages, causing difficult breathing; or on the lining of the gastrointestinal system, causing diarrhoea or vomiting. Allergic reactions, especially to certain foods and chemicals, are a 20th-century phenomenon.

CHECKLIST

To determine whether your cat is allergic, ask yourself these questions:

- Does the condition occur only at a particular time or season?

- Does the problem occur in a specific location?

- Do other members of the family have the same problem?

- Does the cat cause damage to its own skin?

- Does the cat have any lip ulcers?

- What does the cat eat?

- Is there any possible exposure to fleas?

WHAT IS ALLERGY
The word "allergy" was only coined in 1906, by Viennese paediatrician Baron Clemens von Pirquet. Allergies occur when the immune system reacts to a harmless substance as if it were harmful. Chemicals in insect bites (as in flea saliva), certain foods, drugs, plants, dust mites, plant pollens, fungal spores, even the skin that we shed (human dander) can set off an allergic reaction in your cat. A variety of feline disorders including dermatitis, eczema, colitis, hay fever, coughing, asthma, diarrhoea, and vomiting can all have allergic origins.

ALLERGY IS INCREASING
Hay fever, the most common form of allergy, is a relatively new condition. It was not even mentioned in medical literature until the early 1800s (by John Bostock at a lecture to the Royal Society in London). In 1950 it was still an uncommon condition. For example, less than one per cent of Japanese had hay fever then. Now over 10 per cent of the population suffer from it. In Australia, over 30 per cent of the human population have allergies. There has been a similar increase in allergies, especially asthma, in cats.

THE ALLERGIC RESPONSE
Pathogens, like viruses, normally stimulate the immune system to produce protective antibodies. Allergens such as flea saliva, dust-mite droppings, or human dander when inhaled, swallowed, or in contact with the body, mistakenly provokes the immune system to produce an antibody called immunoglobin E (IgE). In an allergic cat, IgE binds to receptor sites on specialized immune cells called mast cells that reside in the skin and the lining of the stomach, lungs, and upper airways. These cells are like primed mines, filled with chemicals waiting to explode. IgE causes the mast cells to release their chemicals, literally to explode, distributing inflammatory substances such as histamine and prostaglandins. The reaction takes eight minutes.

CONVENTIONAL TREATMENTS
Conventional vets recommend avoidance as the best treatment for allergies. Through history taking, allergy testing using skin tests or blood samples, reducing dietary protein, elimination diets, and sometimes temporary

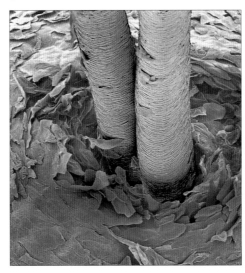

HUMAN ALLERGIES
Cats produce the protein Fel D-1, mostly in saliva but also in dry and flaky skin (see right). Fel D-1 makes some people sneeze and suffer watery eyes. A damp sponge will reduce the amount of this protein.

ASTHMA CAN BE LETHAL
Asthma is an allergic reaction in the bronchi, the air passages of the lungs. While asthma is uncommon in cats, it is increasing in frequency, especially in cats that live permanently indoors. Cats experience asthma that is almost identical to the type we suffer from, induced by wasp or bee stings, pollens, mould spores, house dust, even cigarette smoke. Food additives are also known to induce asthma in some people. The onset is acute and without immediate intervention with adrenalin or corticosteroids an episode can be fatal.

removal of a cat from its environment, they try to determine specific causes. For relief from allergy, veterinarians try to "turn off" the allergic reaction at its source.

Although many different chemicals are released when mast cells explode, only one of them, histamine, can be effectively controlled with an "anti-histamine". More recently an "anti" for another chemical, a leukotriene, has been licensed for use in people suffering from allergies and asthma.

Shampoos are recommended for skin allergies. Cats are relatively resistant to the side effects of corticosteroids when used short term, so they are often used. Vets increasingly recommend high-dose essential fatty acid (EFA) supplements. The EFAs are known to act at the cellular level, diminishing the intensity of mast-cell explosions.

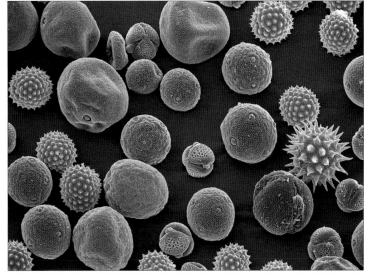

FALSE HAZARD
Microscopic pollen spores provoke an allergic cat's immune system to mistakenly produce an antibody that binds to its immune cells. The cells release inflammatory substances such as histamine. This allergic reaction takes about eight minutes.

COMPLEMENTARY TREATMENTS

Many holistic vets believe that problems in the gastrointestinal system are at the root of the increasing incidence of feline allergy. They argue that modern diets can lead to "leaky guts." Healthy food and undisturbed gut flora are at the root of many complementary therapies.

ACUPUNCTURE Some reports suggest that acupuncture temporarily relieves asthma in people. There have been no studies with cats. *See pages 72-73.*

HYDROTHERAPY Cold compresses or cooling baths may reduce skin itchiness and inflammation. *See page 82.*

NUTRITIONAL THERAPIES Holistic vets say that cats probably consume over 100 synthetic chemicals in their food and water each day and any of these may compromise a healthy immune system. They recommend filtering tap water, feeding antioxidant supplements, and avoiding commercial diets, even so-called hypoallergenic ones. Fresh diets, free from additives (take away even catnip toys), wheat, dairy products, and low in fish, beef, or chicken protein are often advised. Vitamin C and bioflavonoids are used. Vitamin E is said to reduce histamine reactions. (People exposed to ozone and sulphur dioxide from car exhaust were less sensitive to these pollutants after being on a five-week course of vitamins E and C.) Oily fish and fish-oil supplements rich in omega-3 fatty acids are thought to have an anti-inflammatory effect. Asthmatic cats may be deficient in vitamin B6 and niacin. *See pages 86-87.*

HERBALISM If the absorptive lining of the small intestines has been damaged, and is "leaking", gentle herbs such as fennel seed, *Foeniculum vulgare*, and cumin root, *Cuminum cyminum*, are given. Turmeric root, *Curcuma longa*, is believed to have anti-inflammatory properties and to aid digestion of protein. *Echinacea* before the allergy season may boost the immune system. Oil of peppermint, *Mentha x piperata*, is said to clear nasal congestion. The Ayurvedic herb *Coleus forskholii* is said to dilate the bronchi as powerfully as some prescribed drugs. *Ginkgo*, *Aloe vera*, which is said to have anti-inflammatory abilities, and khella, *Ammi visnaga*, are said to reduce bronchial constriction.
See pages 88-91.

HOMEOPATHY Homeopaths treat like with like, but at much lower levels than conventional vets do, by giving small but increasing doses of desensitizing injections. In homeopathic immunotherapy, extremely diluted preparations are made from the relevant antigen. This eliminates the risk of an allergic reaction to the homeopathic substance itself, although there is no clinical evidence that this form of therapy calms the immune system. The most common standard remedy for hay fever is *Allium 6c*. Other recommended remedies vary with the cat's personality and include *Euphrasia 6c*, *Nux vomica 6c*, *Natrum mur. 6c*, *Arsen. alb. 6c*, and *Kali iod. 6c*. *See pages 92-93.*

RELAXATION THERAPY Helping a cat to relax may improve lung function, and reduced activity diminishes oxygen requirements. *See pages 98.*

NUX VOMICA

CANCER

CANCER CELLS ARE RENEGADE cells that have avoided detection by your cat's defences. They are "parasites", in conflict with your cat's body. Feline tumours occur most commonly in the skin, blood-related organs, mouth, and bones. Slow-growing benign tumours don't spread into surrounding tissue, but malignant tumours, called cancers, invade surrounding tissue and may spread through the body.

while sarcomas arise from within deep tissues such as muscles. Lymphomas develop from lymph tissue. Benign tumours are usually harmless and lipomas, fatty tumours under the skin, are typically benign tumours in cats that rarely cause harm. To differentiate between a benign and a malignant tumour, a vet may need to examine some of the tumour under a microscope.

WARNING SIGNS

Cancers signify their presence in many ways. Act promptly if your cat develops unusual lumps or bumps that don't go away or get bigger, loses weight or appetite, smells unusual, loses stamina or interest, appears to have difficulty eating, breathing, urinating, or defecating, or is increasingly lame. These are general signs of being unwell and can have many causes other than cancer.

WHAT IS CANCER?

Cancer is a common name given to a variety of unrelated diseases with different causes and effects but with a common, dangerous ability. Cancer cells escape detection by protective DNA policing enzymes (*see pages 58-59*). They also trick the natural killer cells of the immune system into regarding the cancer cells as "self", and not attacking and destroying them. Having eluded the body's natural defences, cancer cells embark upon producing countless generations of descendant cancer cells.

Cancers are technically malignant tumours. Malignant tumours are classified according to where they originate. Carcinomas arise from the tissues that line the internal and external surfaces of a cat's skin and organs,

HOW CANCERS SPREAD

Cats, as a species, are more susceptible to carcinogenic agents than are other species. Viruses such as FIV and FIP predispose to cancer, while conditions that provoke the need for tissue repair can lead to cancer. Under certain circumstances, vaccination against rabies and also perhaps against leukaemia seems to do this. Radiation and excess sunshine can damage natural controls. Hormonal factors are also related to cancer, which is why the most common cancers affect the reproductive systems and can be reduced by early neutering (*see pages 142-143*). Some cancers evolved techniques that permit wider spread throughout the body. These malignant tumours produce chemicals that actively suppress the cat's immune system.

HIGH RISK OF CANCER
Viruses, transmitted in saliva through cat bites, play an important role in cancer risk. Feline leukaemia virus reduces a cat's natural defences, allowing another cancer-inducing virus to cause lymphoma, cancer of one or more lymph nodes. This cancer responds well to conventional chemotherapy.

CONVENTIONAL TREATMENTS

Conventional veterinary medicine uses many common diagnostic procedures, including physical examination, blood samples, x-rays, and ultrasound to make a diagnosis. A small sample of suspect tissue, a biopsy, is always necessary for an accurate diagnosis. Once a specific name is given to the cancer, the vet discusses with the owner the pros and cons of six treatment options: do nothing; palliatively control pain; surgery; radiation therapy or chemotherapy, singly or in combination; or contemplate euthanasia.

Surgery removes tumours, while x-rays and drug treatment kill as many cancer cells as possible. Because cancer is often an age-related problem, conventional vets often weigh the possible benefits and side effects of treatment against life expectancy. Surgery is the most effective treatment while radiation and chemotherapy are not as successful.

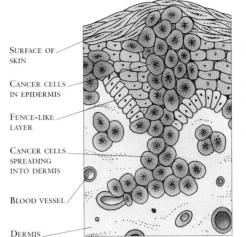

SURFACE OF SKIN

CANCER CELLS IN EPIDERMIS

FENCE-LIKE LAYER

CANCER CELLS SPREADING INTO DERMIS

BLOOD VESSEL

DERMIS

HOW CANCER SPREADS
Carcinomas develop in the epidermal cells of the skin and break through the fence-like layer at the base, gaining access to lymph or blood circulation for transport to other sites. When possible, early surgery is always the most effective way to combat a tumour. Be wary of "natural" cures.

COMPLEMENTARY TREATMENTS

No complementary therapy is a cancer cure. Many may be beneficial in reducing the risk of cancers or in slowing their development once established. Use any complementary therapy you like, as long as it does no actual harm and does not increase your cat's stress, tension, or anxiety, all known to accelerate the growth of tumours.

THERAPEUTIC MASSAGE Gentle massage relaxes dependent cats, reducing anxiety and stress and diminishing stiffness and pain. In unknown ways this may slow down tumour growth. *See pages 80-81.*

NUTRITIONAL THERAPIES There is good evidence that you should avoid feeding your cat a high-carbohydrate diet. Carbohydrates (sugars) give cancer cells extra energy. Cats with cancer benefit from high-protein diets, especially enriched with amino acids such as glutamine. High-fat diets are excellent. Fat is palatable and energy-dense, ideal for a cat that is debilitated. Dr Glenna Maudlin, Director of Nutritional Support Services at the Animal Medical Center in New York, says that, fed long term, high-fat diets may "starve" cancer cells to death because they are unable to use fats for energy. Feed a diet with 50 to 60 per cent of its energy derived from fat. Cats with cancer need more micronutrients: general vitamin and mineral supplements are excellent. Make certain your cat has ample quantities of taurine, vitamin A, and B vitamins. B vitamins may help to destroy certain carcinogens. A good balance of omega-3 and omega-6 fatty acids may reduce the severity of some cancers. Antioxidants may help to prevent cancers by keeping cells healthy, but their nourishing nature may also promote existing cancers by keeping cancer cells healthy too. Vitamins A (as beta-carotene), C, and E, and the mineral selenium are antioxidants. Use with moderation in cats with cancers. *See pages 86-87.*

HERBALISM Herbs that are claimed to have anti-cancer properties include lemon balm, *Melissa officinalis*, mistletoe leaf, *Viscum album*, barberry bark, *Berberis vulgaris*, Roman chamomile flower, *Chamaemelum nobile*, comfrey leaf, *Symphytum officinale*, Echinacea root, and fenugreek seed, *Trigonella foenum-graecum*. Recent research suggests that *Astragalus membranaceus* roots, *Ligustrum lucidum* seeds, and the TCM herbs *Oldenlandia diffusa* and *Scutellaria barbata* may be effective for preventing certain forms of human cancer. While the Chinese *Astragalus membranaceus* is non-toxic, other members of this genus are potentially dangerous. Only use herbs under supervision of a herbalist experienced with their use in cats. *See pages 88-91.*

HOMEOPATHY Homeopaths use *Hydrastis* in early stages of cancer and *Echinacea* to boost the immune system. *Viscum alb.* is often used, while *Arsen. alb.* is given to relieve pain in later stages of some cancers. Their value is unknown. *See pages 92-93.*

BACH FLOWER REMEDIES Hornbeam is given to strengthen a weakened cat, Mimulus for frightened individuals, and Olive to cats that appear to have lost the will to live. Remember, do not harm. Do not give flower remedies to the exclusion of more pragmatic ways of reducing your cat's stress. *See page 95.*

ROMAN CHAMOMILE

NATURAL DEVELOPMENT

NATURAL TRAINING

NATURAL NUTRITION

NATURAL HEALTH CARE

HEALTH DISORDERS

INFECTIOUS DISEASES

IN THE WILD, ADULT CATS had little contact with each other. In these circumstances, infectious viral diseases could not spread far. Humans have changed this, mixing together individual cats from different backgrounds. This happens primarily at cat-breeding establishments, but it also occurs, for example, in cat-rescue centres. Unwittingly, we have given infectious diseases a chance to spread.

NEW INFECTIONS

The infectious diseases that cats suffer from, and their significance in veterinary care, have changed dynamically. Panleukopenia, a cat killer when I began veterinary practice, has diminished in importance, while feline infectious peritonitis (FIP), unknown 50 years ago, is now the commonest infectious cause of cat death in some countries. Cat infections are changing because we have altered the cat's environment. New diseases emerge because we create environments they thrive in. From an evolutionary viewpoint,

NATURAL DEVELOPMENT

NATURAL TRAINING

NATURAL NUTRITION

NATURAL HEALTH CARE

HEALTH DISORDERS

VACCINE PROBLEMS

In 1991, Drs Mattie Hendrick and Michael Goldschmidt at the University of Pennsylvania's School of Veterinary Medicine reported an increase in skin tumours (fibrosarcomas) at the common injection site for vaccines. This was traced to rabies and leukaemia vaccines but none were withdrawn from the market. Professor Neils Pedersen, who discovered FIV virus, asked at a American Animal Hospital Association meeting six years later, "What would happen to a human vaccine that caused fatal tumours in 1:5,000 residents of the US?" This high incidence of vaccine-induced cancer has forced conventional vets to re-evaluate vaccine procedures.

cats have virtually no protection against some of these diseases, FIP in particular. When cats are kept in close confinement with lots of other cats, they are able to contract a variety of infectious diseases from each other. We need to understand the cat's natural defences and know what we can do to enhance them or, when they are breached, how to treat the infectious diseases.

INNATE PROTECTION

The young are most at risk from infectious disease but evolution gives them "maternal protection". (The elderly are also at risk because of their failing immune systems.) In the first milk that a kitten receives from its mother it acquires temporary protection, in the form of "maternal antibodies", against the variety of infections to which its mother has been exposed. The greater the mother's antibody response to these infections, the greater the level of maternal antibodies she passes on to her kitten. Kittens don't inherit the white blood cells that produce antibodies, just the antibodies themselves. These provide short-term protection, usually for eight to 12 weeks. A cat produces further protection when its own cells learn, and retain in their memory, the ability to produce antibodies. The cells do this when they are exposed to infectious agents such as viruses and bacteria.

FELINE INFECTIONS AND AREAS AFFECTED

This table lists the infections most commonly seen in veterinary practices around the world. Many of the diseases are relatively new and cats have virtually no evolutionary protection against them.

INFECTION	AREA OF DAMAGE
Feline calicivirus (FC)	Upper respiratory tract and gums
Feline herpesvirus (FHV)	Upper respiratory tract
Chlamydia	Eyes and upper respiratory tract
Panleukopenia (also known as feline parvo-virus, feline enteritis, and feline distemper)	Gastrointestinal tract and bone marrow
Coronavirus	Gastrointestinal tract
Feline infectious peritonitis (FIP) (a mutation of coronavirus)	White blood cells/multiple systems
Feline leukaemia virus (FeLV)	White blood cells/multiple systems
Feline immunodeficiency virus (FIV)	White blood cells/multiple systems
Microsporum felis	Skin
Rabies	Brain

PROTECTION BY VACCINATION

A vaccine stimulates an immune response that will protect a cat from a natural form of a disease. Rather than expose a cat to an infectious agent that causes unpleasant disease, vaccine manufacturers either kill micro-organisms or modify living ones so that they will not cause clinical illness. These modified microbes or parts of microbes are then introduced into the cat's system as "vaccines". Successful vaccination is the reason why feline panleukopenia is no longer the killer disease it once was.

The concept of vaccination is natural. It induces the body to manufacture its own defences. However, many cat owners and vets are concerned about possible side effects of frequent vaccination.

VACCINE CONTROVERSIES

While there is no doubt that vaccination is the safest and most effective protection against serious infectious diseases, there are valid questions about the efficacy, frequency of administration, range, and adverse side effects of some of the vaccines that are given to cats.

CARRIER STATE
Viral diseases are more problematic in cats than in other domesticated species because many of these infections can remain in a cat's body in a "carrier" state. Under stress, and sometimes even without stress, a virus from a cat that has no symptoms can be "shed", infecting other cats.

CONVENTIONAL TREATMENTS

Conventional vets routinely vaccinate against diseases that are prevalent in their localities. Because cats resent injections, vets prefer to use "multivalent" vaccines that can protect against a variety of diseases through a single inoculation. They use yearly "boosters" as an opportunity to give cats yearly examinations. When infections occur, they are treated symptomatically. Drugs are used to control symptoms. Antibiotics are prescribed even when infections are viral, to reduce risks of secondary infections.

COMPLEMENTARY TREATMENTS

Some complementary vets believe that frequent immunization with biological vaccines can damage the immune system and is a cause of the increased incidence of auto-immune conditions, allergies, and even cancer in cats. They suggest careful consideration before using multivalent vaccines, preferring "monovalent" ones that induce protection against one disease only. This involves several different injections, at different times, for different diseases. When infection occurs, they use antibiotics for acute infection and a variety of other therapies for non-life-threatening infections.

NUTRITIONAL THERAPIES Ginger, aloe vera, cinnamon, and cloves will often be recommended for their antimicrobial properties. Goldenseal and astragalus may enhance interferon production, while garlic may increase protective T-cell production.

Immune-suppressed cats with FIV or FeLV may benefit from supplements of vitamins A, B6, B12, E, and C, together with zinc and selenium. All of these may enhance the immune system. *See pages 86-87.*

HERBALISM Infusion of catmint, *Nepeta cataria*, is recommended for treating a fever, *Echinacea* to enhance the immune system, and thyme, *Thymus vulgaris*, to relax the windpipe and bronchial passages in respiratory infections. *See pages 88-91.*

HOMEOPATHY There is no evidence that homeopathic "nosodes" offer protection against infectious diseases. For respiratory infections, *Aconite 6c* is used in the early stages of a dry cough, while *Belladonna 6c* is given for repetitive coughing. *Drosera 6c* is used for coughing spasms and *Ipecac 6c* if coughing induces vomiting. *See pages 92-93.*

RELAXATION THERAPY Many viruses can remain latent in a cat's body and are then activated by stress. Any therapy that reduces stress may be beneficial. The best way to reduce stress is to avoid changes in a cat's routine. *See page 98.*

AROMA THERAPY For upper respiratory tract infections, essential oil of lavender is recommended for its soothing effect, while essential oils of rosemary and eucalyptus are thought to fight infection. All are given as a few drops diffused by a vaporizer. *See page 100.*

GINGER

NATURAL DEVELOPMENT

NATURAL TRAINING

NATURAL NUTRITION

NATURAL HEALTH CARE

HEALTH DISORDERS

THE SKIN

THE CAT'S SKIN is its first line of defence against physical dangers. Individual skin cells also play a key role in the immune system, co-ordinating defensive responses when injuries occur. The skin and hair combine as the cat's largest sensory organ, monitoring the environment and influencing not only body temperature but also, through pain sensitivity, how a cat responds to potential dangers.

WARNING

Tea tree oil has proven therapeutic value but is easily absorbed through the skin and is as toxic as turpentine. It can cause depression, weakness, lack of co-ordination, behaviour changes, and muscle tremors. Cats have died when it has been applied directly to flea bites. Only use this and other herbal products under veterinary supervision.

WHAT SKIN DOES

Skin and hair are your cat's first line of defence. A cat's skin protects against physical damage and microbial invasion. The fat underneath offers insulation. Skin is durable, elastic, and capable of excellent repair when damaged. Skin consists of an outer layer (epidermis) of sheets of flat, scaly cells. These are shed through natural wear and tear. When wear and tear is accelerated, or grooming diminishes as it does in old age, "dander" loss increases. The epidermis derives its strength from the protein keratin, which also makes up the hair and claws.

Keratin-making cells do more than just make durable keratin. They also produce cytokines, chemical regulators that are important for a healthy inflammatory response when the skin is injured. Some of the surface cells produce a pigment, melanin, that gives colour to the skin and hair.

SKIN FIRST-AID KIT

As well as the typical contents of gauze and adhesive bandages, a typical complementary first-aid kit for cats may contain nettle cream for minor burns, calendula cream for speedy healing of minor wounds, arnica cream for relieving pain from skin damage, witch hazel for soothing stings and abrasions, echinacea capsules for helping ward off infection, garlic capsules to help fight infection, and Rescue Remedy to help overcome shock.

WHAT HAIR DOES

Hair provides insulation but also physical protection for the skin. In all wild cats, "guard" hair predominates. Finer "down" hair offers insulation. Selective breeding and environmental factors modify this natural arrangement. A British shorthair, living outdoors, may have up to 900 hairs per cm² (8,100 per in²) of skin, while a Devon Rex, intentionally bred for a sparse coat, might have only 150 hairs per cm² (1,350 per in²). Our intervention means that breeds such as the rexes have poor natural insulation and diminished physical protection.

Hair growth is affected by temperature, increasing or decreasing daylight, hormones, nutrition, and genetic factors. Cats tend to drop their hair when they are stressed, which is why they leave so much of it on the vet's examining table. The state of your cat's coat is a good reflection of its general health.

HOW SKIN IS DAMAGED

A dense coat of hair is the skin's first line of defence. In any serious cat fight, hair flies but often teeth and claws do not reach the skin. Sparsely coated individuals do not have this protection. Thick skin offers a second line of defence. Male cats have naturally thickened skin, especially on the cheeks and neck, the most common sites of fight bites. Male cats neutered before puberty have skin that is easier to puncture in fights. Punctures

SKIN STRUCTURE

The outer layer of the skin (epidermis) consists of sheets of flat, scaly cells. The inner layer (dermis) consists of fibrous and elastic tissue that is infiltrated by blood vessels, hair follicles and associated sebaceous glands, and a varying density of nerves.

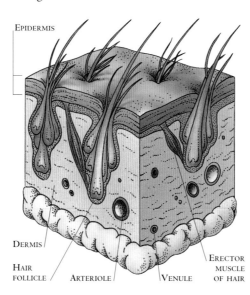

EPIDERMIS

DERMIS

HAIR FOLLICLE

ARTERIOLE

VENULE

ERECTOR MUSCLE OF HAIR

are the most common skin injuries, usually through bites from other animals. Skin has evolved a way to repair this type of damage, by forming an abscess and then discharging foreign material (*see pages 124-125*). Skin may also be torn or abraded, and has natural ways of self-repair for these injuries.

HOW CATS CARE FOR THEIR SKIN

Cats keep their hair and skin in healthy condition by grooming, dry bathing, or simply by getting accidentally wet. Saliva contains natural antiseptics. Licking and scratching are normal activities that in moderation are beneficial. Licking removes debris as well as sloughing off skin and surface parasites. Only when carried out in excess does it cause damage (*see pages 124-125*). A cat also massages its skin by rolling and rubbing, activating its sebaceous glands and removing debris from parts of the body it cannot reach with its tongue or paws.

A function of the sebaceous glands is to secrete waterproofing for the skin and hair. The skin of cats with well-lubricated coats of thick hair does not get wet when a cat is caught in rain, and dirt and debris are naturally removed by rain water.

EPIDERMIS

PUNCTURE WOUND

SEVERED BLOOD CELLS

DERMIS

PUNCTURE WOUNDS
Punctures heal quickly but the temporary breach in skin defences allows bacteria to invade, causing an abscess to develop (see pages 124-125). Because cat skin is so elastic and has a limited blood supply, visible bleeding is rare. Check for punctures by running your fingers through the fur, feeling for tiny blood-clot scabs.

CONVENTIONAL TREATMENTS

If a cat's skin defences have been breached, which most commonly happens due to a cat fight, conventional vets use antiseptics, painkillers, and sometimes antibiotics to assist repair. Skin tears are stitched when necessary, while serious skin injuries may be repaired surgically using a variety of skin grafting techniques. Protective "Elizabethan" collars, which are large cones that surround the cat's head, prevent the cat from reaching the injured area and further damaging the skin through excessive licking or chewing.

COMPLEMENTARY TREATMENTS

Complementary vets are interested in the cat's ability to self-repair. They use conventional repair methods but also question a cat's diet and state of mind.

NUTRITIONAL THERAPIES A balanced diet, high in natural antioxidants such as selenium and vitamin E, is thought to promote good healing. A general vitamin and mineral supplement is often recommended to provide new cells with micronutrients necessary for good cellular function. *See pages 86-87.*

HERBALISM Abraded skin is washed in warm, soapy water and any embedded material is gently scraped out. Warm, wet tea bags on wounds may help blood clots to form. Herbs with both antibacterial

and antihaemorrhagic properties are used. Tincture of pot marigold, *Calendula officinalis*, diluted in water can help blood clotting. Turmeric root powder, *Curcuma longa*, can be effective but it causes intense yellow staining to the skin and surrounding hair (and clothing and furniture!). Yarrow herb, *Achillea millefolium*, does not stain. It is applied topically until healing begins. It may be combined with peppermint, *Mentha x piperita*, or German chamomile flower, *Matricaria recutita*. To encourage epithelial growth from the edges of the abrasion, comfrey leaf, *Symphytum officinale*, may be used. Published studies say that new skin formation is faster when *Calendula* tincture is applied to a wound. *Hypericum* tincture by mouth is also said to accelerate wound healing. *See pages 88-91.*

HOMEOPATHY *Hypericum 6c* is used if a cat is sensitive when an abrasion is cleaned. *Arnica 6c* is recommended when bruising is present, and *Aconite 6c* if a cat is distressed. Homeopathic *Calendula* cream is often used for minor skin wounds. *See pages 92-93.*

AROMA THERAPY
Essential oil of tea tree can be toxic but it is a powerful antiseptic, antibacterial, and antifungal agent. Diluted in water, it may be beneficial for cleaning abrasions. *See page 100.*

TEA TREE OIL

SKIN DISORDERS

CAT SKIN IS PRONE TO INFECTIONS, parasites, cysts, tumours, and hypersensitivity. Hormonal upsets, metabolic disorders, even the cat's mind can affect the health of skin and hair. A cat's coat can become dull through the stress of a visit to the vet. Cats have more potential disorders of the skin than of any other body system. Many of these conditions involve inflammation, with or without itchiness.

CHECKLIST

To help determine the cause of a skin condition, ask the following questions:

- When and where did the problem first occur?

- Does it occur indoors, outdoors, or both?

- Has it occurred before in the same season?

- Are other pets in the home affected?

- Do any humans in the home have skin problems?

- Has your cat been on any drugs?

WHAT IS SKIN INFLAMMATION?

Skin inflammation is associated with infections, infestations (*see pages 126-127*), and allergic reactions. Inflammation is part of natural repair, but if it is excessive the inflammation itself causes problems. For example, cats have inflammatory cells called eosinophils that probably evolved as defence against parasitic diseases. If they are activated excessively, they cause a tumour-like problem called eosinophilic granuloma syndrome.

Within the skin, specialized cells, known as mast cells act as "gatekeepers", regulating the way in which the immune system will respond to a threat. Sometimes mast cells multiply excessively, producing a "mast cell tumour", a not uncommon feline tumour. Another population of defence cells, called memory T-cells, monitors the skin surfaces for dangerous microbes they have met before. Many inflammatory skin conditions, even flea-bite inflammation, develop secondary microbial infections.

FELINE TUMOURS

Skin tumours are benign or malignant. While mast-cell tumours and histiocytomas are common skin tumours in young cats, this basal-cell tumour (right), also called a rodent ulcer, is perhaps the most common feline tumour, usually occurring on the upper lip. These tumours spread only locally. Pale-skinned cats are more susceptible to skin cancer.

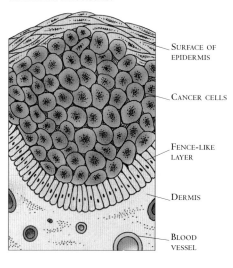

SURFACE OF EPIDERMIS

CANCER CELLS

FENCE-LIKE LAYER

DERMIS

BLOOD VESSEL

CAUSES OF ALLERGIES

The cat's environment today is very different from the one in which it evolved. In the United States, the majority of Americans spend 95 per cent of their time indoors or in transport. Houses are relatively airtight, with high humidity and temperature – ideal conditions for dust-mite breeding. The incidence of itchy skin allergies in cats has increased as we and our cats have increased the amount of time spent indoors. Cells that are involved in the immune system's allergic response produce at least 12 known chemicals, many of which are irritating and cause itchiness if they are released. In allergy, eosinophils are stimulated by environmental factors and subverted from natural parasite targets to attacking the cat's own tissues. The damage caused often leads to cellular "chemical spillage", which causes itchiness.

SKIN INFECTIONS

Minor superficial bacterial and fungal infections are relatively harmless to cats because skin is constantly being sloughed off from the surface and replaced by new healthy skin from below. Licking helps sloughing. Ringworm is the most common fungal infection in cats. Long-haired cats are more prone to ringworm because licking is less effective in their case. An abscess is a deep infection in a walled pocket of tissue just under the skin. Abscesses occur when bacteria are deposited by a tooth or claw that penetrates the skin. White blood cells attack the invaders while the body contains the battlefield to prevent the skirmish from spreading elsewhere.

CONVENTIONAL TREATMENTS

Vets treat abscesses with warm salt-water poultices to draw toxins to the surface. They lance and drain superficial abscesses, flushing the empty cavities with hydrogen peroxide or antiseptic. Deep-seated abscesses that cannot easily be drained are treated with antibiotics. Sometimes surgical opening of deep abscesses is necessary. If a puncture

CAT SKIN CARE

Cats don't make a show of skin irritation the way dogs do. While dogs are itchy exhibitionists, cats will lick and scratch in privacy. Feel your cat's coat for scabs that indicate it has been scratching an itchy skin condition. Shampoos are available for different problems: for example, bran removes grease, while oatmeal shampoo suits cats with overactive sebaceous glands. Sulphur and salicylic acid shampoos have particular uses, as do skin humectants and emollients. Use minimal restraint when wet-shampooing your cat. In the bath, use a rubber mat that it can grip with its claws.

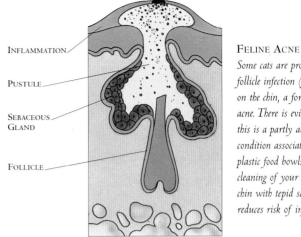

INFLAMMATION

PUSTULE

SEBACEOUS GLAND

FOLLICLE

FELINE ACNE
Some cats are prone to hair-follicle infection (folliculitis) on the chin, a form of feline acne. There is evidence that this is a partly allergic condition associated with plastic food bowls. Daily cleaning of your cat's chin with tepid salt water reduces risk of infection.

enters a joint capsule, tendon sheath, spinal canal, abdomen or chest cavity, or touches bone, antibiotics are essential. Folliculitis (feline acne) can be treated by cleaning the affected area with antiseptic cream. There are certain antibiotics, specifically erythromycin, clindamycin, and tetracycline that are thought to have anti-inflammatory properties as well as their better known antibiotic abilities.

Ringworm is not naturally present in cats' skin but in affected environments all cats carry it (some without clinical signs) and all need to be treated. Cats are shaved in the infected area and washed in povidine-iodine or two per cent chlorhexidine solution. Anti-fungal antibiotics are given orally, or less frequently as ointments or creams. At the same time, the immediate environment is treated with disinfectants that kill ringworm spores, which are capable of remaining infectious for 18 months. Carpets need to

> *"Cats don't make a show of skin irritation the way dogs do. While dogs are itchy exhibitionists, cats will lick and scratch in privacy."*

be steam-cleaned and all clothing washed, preferably with bleach. To control allergic itch, corticosteroids, antihistamines, or desensitizing injections are used.

COMPLEMENTARY TREATMENTS

Complementary vets advise cat owners to prevent problems when possible. Apply sun block (SPF 15 or higher) to the noses and ears of white cats exposed to intense sunlight.

HYDROTHERAPY Hot and cold compresses may be used to draw out pus. Epsom salts may be recommended to stimulate circulation. *See page 82.*

NUTRITIONAL THERAPIES Feeding less food starves bacteria of necessary carbohydrates. Add brewer's yeast to the diet as a vitamin supplement. Complementary vets believe feline acne is exacerbated by diet and feeding bowls. They may suggest using ceramic or stainless-steel bowls, avoiding plastic dishes and dairy products, and monitoring foods that contain natural hormone-like substances. *See pages 86-87.*

HERBALISM Slippery elm, *Ulmus rubra*, and marsh mallow, *Althaea officinalis* ointment is applied to thin-walled abscesses. The abscess usually bursts on its own without the need for lancing. Australian studies showed tea tree oil to be more effective than an antifungal drug in relieving the signs of ringworm. Tea tree oil is potentially toxic to cats so use under a vet's supervision. Other herbs said to have antifungal properties are thyme, *Thymus vulgaris*, angelica root, *Angelica archangelica*, marigold flower, *Calendula officinalis*, and rosemary leaf, *Rosmarinus officinalis*. If the herbalist believes a skin infection occurs due to toxins or a hormonal imbalance, yam, *Dioscora*, may be given to correct hormone levels, *Echinacea* to enhance the immune system, or nettle, *Urtica dioica*, solutions for its cleansing qualities. *See pages 88-91.*

ROSEMARY

PARASITE CONTROL

ALTHOUGH CATS ARE FASTIDIOUS self-groomers, many parasites have evolved to live on cat skin. Fleas and ear mites in particular are common parasites. As cats moved indoors, the cat flea thrived, becoming common to dogs and us too. Parasites transmit other parasites, such as tapeworms. With a few exceptions it is possible to control infestation without using dangerous chemicals.

CHECKLIST

There are several reasons why a treatment does not work:

- Ineffective ingredients.
- It is incorrectly applied.
- Wrong treatment times or intervals.
- Failure to treat companion animals.
- Failure to treat the immediate environment.
- Not all stages in the life cycle are destroyed.
- Reinfestation from open environment.

INTERRUPTING THE FLEA LIFE CYCLE
Fleas can be controlled by intervening at different stages of their life cycle before they reach adulthood and start feeding off cats. Using growth regulators, flea "birth control" prevents eggs from hatching or larva from maturing. If using a flea collar, make sure the collar has a safety stretch or break-away feature.

WHAT ARE SKIN PARASITES?

Skin parasites are insects that feed off, live on, or live in a cat's skin. *Cheyletiella* mites live on the surface and are very contagious. They may or may not cause itchiness. Some people are very sensitive to these mites, getting an intense 24-hour rash just from touching a cat that has them. Sarcoptic mange mites, rare in cats, cause itchiness because they burrow into the skin, damaging cells and releasing chemical irritants. Fleas and ticks feed off cats by sucking body fluids. While doing this they inject anti-coagulants into the skin. Most cats can tolerate a few flea bites, but some cats become hypersensitive to chemicals in flea bites and mount an intense generalized allergic response to a single flea.

ADAPTIVE PARASITES

Parasites, and the other parasites they carry, have evolved successful methods of transmitting themselves to cats. Ticks wait patiently in the grass for a meal to arrive.

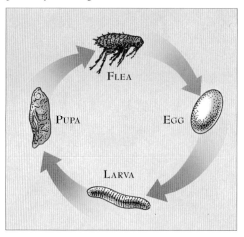

FLEA

PUPA

EGG

LARVA

They are able to sense vibration, a shadow, even minute changes in carbon-dioxide level and temperature that will indicate a cat (or human) is present. Fleas are attracted by both the body heat and the pheromones that are given off by their victims.

Most species of animals have species-specific fleas. In developed countries, the human flea, *Pulex irritans*, is now rare. So too is *Ctenocephalides canis*, the dog flea. On the other hand, *Ctenocephalides felis*, the cat flea, has been extraordinarily adaptive, moving into our homes and expanding its range of natural hosts to include dogs and us. If your dog has fleas, they are likely to be cat fleas.

CONVENTIONAL PREVENTION

Vets say that prevention is as important, if not more important, than treatment. For flea control, lay down towels wherever your cat lies and wash the towels weekly. This cleans out deposited flea eggs regularly. Having your carpets cleaned will not, on its own, get rid of fleas. Professional carpet treatments with sodium polyborate, sodium tetraborate, or sodium borate are highly effective and usually come with guarantees for a year. Don't treat your carpets with laundry-grade borax; the National Animal Poison Control Center in the United States has reported increasing cases of serious eye, respiratory, and kidney problems in cats when laundry-grade borax powder is used. Use powder that has been altered for safe pet use. Insect-growth regulators such as methoprene are used to target flea larvae specifically. It stops them from maturing, so that they cannot breed or spread.

Vets prefer new insecticides designed to be toxic only to insects, rather than older chemicals that are potentially toxic to animals too. They recommend imidacloprid (Advantage) and fipronil (Frontline). For cats that are not allergic to flea saliva, they suggest lufenuron (Program), an insect-growth regulator that is injected into cats. Fleas consume it when they have a meal from the cat. If pyrethrins are used, they

NATURAL DEVELOPMENT

NATURAL TRAINING

NATURAL NUTRITION

NATURAL HEALTH CARE

HEALTH DISORDERS

INSECT STINGS

Bee and ant stings are acidic. Irritated regions of the skin can be soothed with bicarbonate of soda solution. Wasp and hornet stings are alkali, so lemon juice or vinegar neutralize their irritation. Jellyfish stings can be rinsed with vinegar, ammonia, or alcohol. Distilled witch hazel may soothe mosquito bites, while fresh aloe vera applied to areas irritated by insect bites is soothing and non-toxic. Some herbalists suggest applying half a raw onion to an insect sting, to deactivate the poison.

CONVENTIONAL TREATMENTS

Parasites are only one cause of skin itchiness. Other culprits are certain drugs, food sensitivities, heat or cold, contact with irritants such as stinging nettles or poison ivy, internal disorders such as kidney diseases, even emotional stress. Conventional vets will try to make an accurate diagnosis of the cause of itchiness before trying to eliminate it. Itchiness can be diminished with medicated shampoos, antihistamines, corticosteroids, and omega-3 fatty acid supplements.

Parasites that already infest the cat and its environment are eliminated with effective pharmaceutical anti-parasite drugs. Any parasites in the environment are killed with insecticides or sterilized with chemicals that prevent their multiplication.

FLEA POISONS
What is toxic to a flea may also be dangerous to a cat. More cats are accidentally poisoned by parasite-control treatments than by any other poison. Never use a product designed for dogs on cats, and never use indoors a product for outdoor use.

recommend micro-encapsulated rather than natural pyrethrins, claiming fewer adverse side effects with this form of this natural insecticide. For ticks, keep grass cut low and examine your cat when it comes indoors.

COMPLEMENTARY TREATMENTS

ERADICATING PARASITES
While many complementary therapies aim to enhance immune defences as well as promote well-being, herbal therapies and environmental enhancement are primarily used to control and eliminate parasites.

HERBALISM Cider vinegar is a repellent to some insects. Because ear mites (*Otodectes cynotis*) are most active at night, treat infested ears just before your bedtime. A few drops of a solution of 50 per cent benzyl benzoate and 50 per cent water is massaged into the ear canal three times weekly for eight weeks or until there is no further discharge. Alternatively, dilute nine drops of yellow dock tincture, *Rumex crispus*, in 15 ml water and instil in affected ears every three days for six weeks. Olive oil instilled alternate days for six weeks is also recommended. Six weeks are necessary because mite eggs hatch over this period.

For fleas on cats, use a fine-toothed, metal flea comb. Place captured fleas in ammonia-laced water. Natural pyrethrin powder, especially from chrysanthemums grown in Kenya, is an effective natural insecticide. In India it is mixed with *Acorus calamus* and also used for ticks and lice.

Flea control depends upon preventing or reducing reinfestations. Sweeping, washing, and vacuuming the environment reduces adult, larval, and egg stages of fleas. Always incinerate used vacuum-cleaner bags. Some herbalists advocate leaving eucalyptus leaves under furniture and rugs or rubbing fennel foliage into your cat's coat. Nematodes are bugs that eat fleas. These are commercially available and are introduced into the yard or garden. *See pages 88-91.*

OTHER MEASURES Sticky pads that have been saturated in flea pheromone, placed under a light, are said to attract fleas to a sticky end. An ultrasonic device that emits vibrations that repel fleas can be worn on a cat's collar. *See page 100.*

CONTROLLING ITCHING
Complementary vets try to avoid using drugs to reduce parasite-induced itchiness. They feel that conventional veterinarians' use of corticosteroids, in particular, will depress the immune system at a time when it should be bolstered in its fight against parasites. Massage, relaxation techniques, and pheromones are used to diminish sensitivity to itchiness.

HYDROTHERAPY Cats with itchy skin may be sprayed or bathed in warm water containing sodium bicarbonate or oatmeal. *See page 82.*

HERBALISM Corn starch, with just enough boiled water to make a paste, may reduce itching when it is applied to irritated areas. Goldenseal, *Hydrastis canadensis*, and *Calendula* cream may also be useful. *Echinacea*, goldenseal, or *Pau d'arco* internally, may strengthen the immune system. Infusion of German chamomile flower, *Matricaria recutita*, is said to be soothing and cooling to irritated skin. Other herbs such as burdock root, *Arctium lappa*, curled dock root, *Rumex crispus*, licorice root, *Glycyrrhiza glabra*, and southernwood herb, *Artemisia abrotanum*, may reduce itchiness. *See pages 88-91.*

HOMEOPATHY *Urtica 6c*, derived from stinging nettle, may be suggested to relieve intense itching. *See pages 92-93.*

FENNEL

BONES AND JOINTS

BONE AND JOINT PROBLEMS are relatively uncommon in cats, although traumatic fractures are a risk to individuals that are allowed outdoors. Cat fights can be hazardous to bone if penetrating teeth pierce the surface and introduce infection. Sometimes we unknowingly cause bone disease by feeding our cats incorrectly; excesses or deficiencies in vitamins or minerals cause bone disorders.

CHECKLIST

If your cat breaks a bone, don't splint it yourself.

- Confine the cat to a box while you take it to the vet.
- If bone is visible, cover it with water-dampened sterile gauze or a clean, wet cloth.
- Cover this with some sort of waterproofing, such as a plastic bag.

Remember, fractures are obvious but they are often the only visible results of trauma. There may be more serious injuries that need priority attention.

WHAT BONES AND JOINTS DO

Despite appearing rigid and unchangeable, bone is living tissue, two parts mineral and one part collagen and cells, which has the ability to repair itself when it is damaged. Cats have over 240 bones, about 40 more than we do, but no clavicle attaching the forelimbs to the body, which is why they can get through small spaces. Bones facilitate movement and provide a superstructure for muscle and tendon attachments. Bones articulate by means of joints. Inside each joint is lubricating synovial fluid.

BONE AND JOINT INJURIES

Bones break in many ways and repair will depend upon the nature of the fracture. Dislocations occur when one bone separates from another. Fractures and dislocations are caused by trauma, primarily road-traffic accidents and falling from open windows. The most common bone injury in falls from windows is a dislocation of the chin. The cat's resiliently flexible body absorbs the fall but the chin hits the ground, splitting the mandible in the middle. (It looks like a fracture but technically is a dislocation.) Hip and elbow dislocations are also common.

Luxations occur when a bone slips from its anatomically normal position. Devon Rex kneecaps are prone to luxating (this is painless, the leg just can't bear weight). Infections are caused by external injuries that penetrate to the joint (osteoarthritis) or bone (osteomyelitis), or by transmission via the bloodstream. A bite is the most usual cause of painful bone infection.

OSTEOPOROSIS

An all-meat diet is high in phosphorus and low in calcium. This diet stimulates the parathyroid gland (a small gland in the cat's neck, adjacent to the thyroid) to secrete a hormone that causes calcium to be removed from storage in bones for use elsewhere.

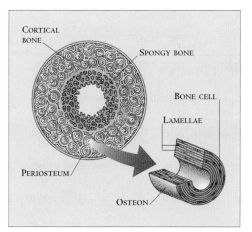

NORMAL BONE STRUCTURE

The outer membrane of a bone is called the periosteum. It encloses a hard layer of cortical bone and a softer layer of spongy bone. At the hollow core of the bone is marrow, which produces blood cells.

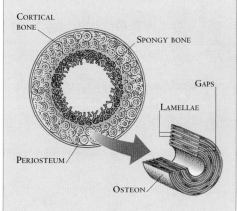

BRITTLE BONE

If a cat is fed an all-meat diet, calcium, needed for heart and muscle function, is "leached" from the lamellae of each osteon unit within the bone. Cortical bone thins, becoming porous and brittle, and prone to spontaneous fractures.

NATURAL DEVELOPMENT

NATURAL TRAINING

NATURAL NUTRITION

NATURAL HEALTH CARE

HEALTH DISORDERS

METABOLIC DISORDERS

Metabolic diseases of bones are uncommon. Osteoporosis, the thinning of bone, can be caused by an all-meat diet. Rickets, caused by a shortage of vitamin D, is now very rare. Excess vitamin A, caused by an unbalanced diet that is too high in liver, causes bony spurs to develop on the neck vertebrae. Bone cancer is rare in cats and when it occurs spreads more slowly than it does in dogs.

NATURAL WEAR AND TEAR

The cat's anatomy is less prone to wear-and-tear problems than that of other species, but, with time, production of the lubricating synovial fluid in the joints diminishes and stiffness ensues. We have also accelerated bone wear and tear in some breeds. The Munchkin, a dwarfed breed, has shortened long bones and relatively enlarged joints that are more prone to wear and tear. Some Maine Coons, larger than typical cats, suffer from hip dysplasia, a form of hip arthritis.

Despite these examples, genetic influences are usually less problematic in cats than in dogs. Most cats carry the genetic potential for excellent bone structure. The best way for a cat to avoid bone disorders is to lead a quiet indoor life and eat a well-balanced diet.

CONVENTIONAL TREATMENTS

When a fracture or dislocation has occurred, conventional vets reposition dislocated joints and fix fractures externally with splints, or internally with metal pins, plates, wires, or screws. The natural flexibility of cats makes splinting more difficult than it is in dogs. Copious bandaging is usually used, often including the trunk of the body to keep the bandage from slipping. Vets often prefer internal repairs because after-care is easier. Pins are removed about six weeks after surgery while other hardware often remains in place. Bone infection from bite wounds is treated vigorously with special antibiotics known to concentrate in bone tissue.

> **WARNING**
> You should never give paracetamol to your cat. Even a single tablet can be fatal. Be cautious with aspirin – in excess, it too can be fatal.

NATURAL DEVELOPMENT

NATURAL TRAINING

NATURAL NUTRITION

NATURAL HEALTH CARE

HEALTH DISORDERS

COMPLEMENTARY TREATMENTS

The aim of most complementary therapies is not to cure bone and joint problems, but rather to alleviate the pain and immobility associated with the various conditions and promote self-healing. When antibiotics are needed for bone infection, complementary vets augment them with live yoghurt or other beneficial bacterial supplements to offset unwanted side effects.

SHIATSU Shiatsu utilizes traditional Chinese acupresssure points that coincide with muscle trigger points. Shiatsu may be therapeutic for certain types of muscle, bone, and joint pain. *See page 75.*

TRIGGER POINT THERAPY Australian and Belgian vets report that trigger point therapy may resolve bone and joint pain that is not controlled by conventional means. They believe that muscle trigger points develop as a consequence of walking abnormally after a bone or joint injury, or surgery. *See page 76.*

CHIROPRACTIC Once bones have mended, typically after a road-traffic accident or other trauma, a chiropractor will manipulate bones and joints to ensure correct realignment. *See page 78.*

NUTRITIONAL THERAPIES Many holistic vets believe that vitamin C is beneficial in reducing viscosity of joint fluid. Antioxidants are said to reduce damage in osteoarthritic joints. A controlled calorie diet reduces weight, taking undue pressure off sensitive joints. *See pages 86-87.*

HERBALISM Choose herb treatments according to their recognized properties. Use analgesics (*see pages 112-113*) or anti-inflammatories such as angelica root, *Angelica archangelica*, greater celandine, *Chelidonium majus*, and barberry bark, *Berberis vulgaris*. Anti-rheumatics include celery seed, *Apium graveolens*, and meadowsweet, *Filipendula ulmaria*. Comfrey leaf, *Symphytum officinale*, is thought to help heal synovial membrane and joint cartilage. *See pages 88-91.*

HOMEOPATHY AND BIOCHEMIC TISSUE SALTS *Rhus tox. 6c* and *Ruta grav. 6c* are both used, as are the biochemic tissue salts *Calc. fluor.* and *Calc. phos. Arnica 6c* is commonly dispensed to help healing . *See pages 92-94.*

BACH FLOWER REMEDIES Rescue Remedy is given to calm upset cats. *See page 95.*

RELAXATION THERAPY Relaxation conditioning relaxes muscle tension and by doing so diminishes joint tension and associated pain. *See page 98.*

CHIROPRACTIC

MUSCLES, TENDONS, AND LIGAMENTS

MUSCLE DISORDERS ARE, like bone and joint problems, uncommon in cats. Most are caused by trauma. Damaged muscles are capable of speedy self-repair. If one part is destroyed by injury, remaining parts will compensate by growing larger and stronger. Muscles and their associated tendons make up the bulk of a cat's body. Loss of muscle mass is often the first indication that a cat is ill.

TENSION INCREASES MUSCLE DAMAGE

Tension, anxiety, and stress can all increase muscle damage. These emotional states stimulate production of pro-inflammatory chemicals. Relaxation turns off this chemical tap. Avoid treatments that may, even unwittingly, increase rather than decrease stress.

WHAT THE MUSCLES DO

A cat has over 500 individual muscles. Some attach directly to bones. Others taper into elastic tendons for their attachment to the skeleton. Ligaments attach one bone to another. For example, the cruciate ligaments behind the knee hold the long bones of the leg in close proximity. Tendon and ligament fibres pass through the surface of bone (periosteum) and are embedded in bone itself. A cat's muscles predominantly consist of "fast-twitch" cells that fatigue quickly. This gives the cat its explosive burst of speed but also explains its poor endurance.

MUSCLE INJURIES

A muscle strain occurs when there is moderate damage to muscle fibres with only slight bleeding and bruising. (A sprain occurs when a ligament connecting bone to bone is overstretched.) When large numbers of fibres are torn and there is consequent bleeding

VITAMINS MAY HELP

In people, vitamins B1, B6, B12, folic acid, and vitamin C are thought to be associated with myofascial pain. When treating muscular pain in cats, consider whether vitamin insufficiencies have been caused by inadequate diet, increased metabolic requirements, or increased excretion. Pregnant, lactating, and older cats may be most susceptible. So too are faddy feeders. In people, muscular irritability, tiredness, and depression have been related to low blood-folate levels.

and swelling, the injury is termed a tear. Muscle cramp is incredibly painful and occurs when muscle filaments, the components of muscle fibres, remain permanently contracted. This often occurs in cats that have suffered a saddle thrombus (*see pages 144-145*).

Muscle, tendon, and ligament injuries are often caused by a bite. Damage to a tendon may involve the tendon itself (tendinitis) or the tendon sheath (tenosynovitis). Because of their natural elasticity, tendons and ligaments tend not to repair well.

NATURAL WEAR AND TEAR

With time, muscles naturally shrink and lose their power. Metabolic disorders elsewhere in the body may also affect muscle mass. One of the best purchases I ever made for my veterinary practice was a baby-weighing scale. It enables me to detect slight changes in muscle mass, and routine weighing is in any case a good way to assess a cat's general health. Metabolic disorders and the natural wear and tear of advancing years reduce the supply of nutrients that muscles need.

Metabolic disorders produce toxins that may damage muscle fibre. Inherited muscle disease is uncommon, although two forms occur in some lines of the Devon Rex.

CONVENTIONAL TREATMENTS

Conventional veterinary medicine has been slow to accept that not only bones and joints but muscles too can be a cause of pain.

THE CLAWS

The cat's claws are controlled by digital flexor tendons. If a tendon is damaged, the claw will remain permanently retracted. When a cat is declawed, some or all of the terminal bone in the toe is also removed. This totally unnatural and mutilating practice is rare in the UK but is still common in the US.

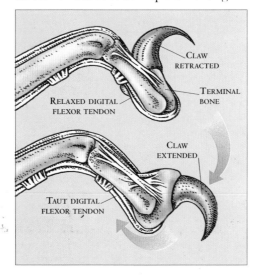

CLAW RETRACTED

TERMINAL BONE

RELAXED DIGITAL FLEXOR TENDON

CLAW EXTENDED

TAUT DIGITAL FLEXOR TENDON

Anti-inflammatory drugs are most usually recommended. Cats with saddle-thrombus muscle cramp receive carefully monitored aspirin, together with other painkilling drugs and treatment of underlying heart disease. Aspirin helps to dissolve the blood clot. Tendon tears are repaired surgically when the vet feels it is necessary. Ligament injuries are sometimes left to repair. Muscle wasting is corrected by treating the metabolic disorder at the root of the problem. New drugs that increase the lungs' ability to pick up oxygen, and the circulation's ability to transport it to muscles, are used in older cats to increase muscle strength. Anabolic steroids are sometimes used to increase muscle strength and mass in older cats.

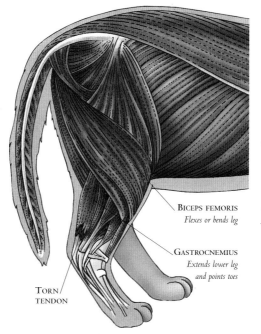

TORN TENDON
Most muscle, tendon, and ligament disorders are caused by trauma. Muscles are arranged in opposing groups with opposite actions. This cat has torn its Achilles tendon, an injury that produces little chronic pain but a noticeably flat-footed gait.

BICEPS FEMORIS
Flexes or bends leg

GASTROCNEMIUS
Extends lower leg and points toes

TORN TENDON

COMPLEMENTARY TREATMENTS

Holistic vets advise prevention of muscle damage by avoiding sudden demands on muscles. Let your cat warm up and stretch first before going outdoors in cold weather.

TRIGGER POINT THERAPY Research and clinical trials at Murdoch University's veterinary school in Perth, Australia, confirm that taut bands of muscle, which can be felt as hard, twitchy nodules, can cause tension and pain in other parts of the body, in particular around the lower spine. Unknotting trigger points is effective but the treatment can be painful and is resented by many cats. *See page 76.*

OSTEOPATHY AND CHIROPRACTIC Manipulations that focus on stretching muscles rather than manipulating joints may achieve good results. Chiropractors believe that poor muscle function in one part of the body can affect the entire system. *See pages 78-79.*

THERAPEUTIC MASSAGE Massage relaxes the cat's body while preventing the cat from overusing muscles that need to rest for effective repair. Massage stimulates blood flow and helps eliminate lactic acid built up from excess muscle use. *See pages 80-81.*

HYDROTHERAPY Ice packs or a packet of frozen peas applied immediately for 10 minutes to a strained or sprained area reduces excessive inflammation. *See page 82.*

OTHER PHYSICAL THERAPIES Patented equipment such as Transcutaneous Electrical Nerve Stimulation (TENS), Transcutaneous Spinal Electroanalgesia (TSE), and laser therapy are claimed to be effective treatments for overstretched muscles and joint pain. *See page 83.*

NUTRITIONAL THERAPIES A detoxifying diet is recommended. Muscle pain has been associated with the neurochemical serotonin. B vitamins, magnesium, and the amino acid tryptophan may be suggested because they help the body manufacture serotonin. Zinc and vitamin E supplements may be suggested too, as they are thought to reduce the intensity of muscle cramp. The amino acid taurine is recommended to maintain natural heart function. *See pages 86-87.*

HERBALISM Local treatments for sprains and strains include liniments of yarrow herb, *Achillea millefolium*, hyssop, *Hyssopus officinalis*, or sweet pepper, *Capsicum annuum*. Muscle bruising may be treated with lettuce leaf, *Lactuca virosa*, hop strobile, *Humulus lupulus*, German chamomile flower, *Matricaria recutita*, or rosemary leaf, *Rosmarinus officinalis*. Herbs used to control muscle spasm include ginger root, *Zingiber officinale*, caraway seed, *Carum carvi*, and fennel seed, *Foeniculum vulgare*. *See pages 88-91.*

HOMEOPATHY *Apis mel. 6c* is used when joints suddenly swell. *Arnica 6c* may be helpful for muscle stiffness associated with joint pain. *Ruta grav. 6c* is also frequently recommended. *Rhus tox.* is a "classic" remedy for muscle and joint conditions that worsen in cold and damp. It is also used for persistent lameness following a strain or sprain. *See pages 92-93.*

PHEROMONE AND AROMA THERAPY
Feline cheek pheromones can be sprayed in the environment to reduce anxiety. Essential oils of lavender and rosemary, in a carrier oil, are said to enhance well-being and reduce pain sensation when diffused into the atmosphere. *See page 100.*

RHUS TOX.

THE TEETH AND MOUTH

TOOTH AND GUM CONDITIONS have become the most common medical problems that cats suffer from. Some cats develop virus-induced mouth disease. Others have diet-related problems. Studies of tooth and gum disease in captive big cats suggest that those fed meat on the bone have few tooth resorption problems, while big cats fed commercially produced food get resorption "cavities".

NATURAL DEVELOPMENT

NATURAL TRAINING

NATURAL NUTRITION

NATURAL HEALTH CARE

HEALTH DISORDERS

CHECKLIST

Warning signs of advanced gum disease:

- Bad breath.
- Yellow-brown tartar.
- Weight loss.
- Enlarged neck lymph nodes.
- Mouth ulcers.
- Teeth loose or missing.
- Dribbling saliva.
- Increased irritability.
- Bleeding gums.
- Dropping food on floor.
- Subdued nature.
- Eating on one side of mouth.
- Reluctance to eat.

THE ORIGINS OF GUM DISEASE

The incidence of gum disease is now very high. A typical survey shows an incidence of 70 per cent in cats over two years of age. There is a virtual epidemic of mouth disease occurring in domestic cats. Healthy teeth and gums are essential for general good health. If teeth and gums are not regularly exercised, a deposit of plaque builds up on the surface of the tooth and lifts the gum margin away from the tooth. Diet and plaque formation are directly related, but viruses also play a role in feline mouth problems.

TEETH AND MOUTH PROBLEMS

When plaque builds up, it hardens into tartar, which enlarges the pocket between the tooth and surrounding gums, creating

SHOULD YOU GIVE BONES?

Cats evolved to eat all of their natural prey, including bones. Eating bones of rodents and small birds is nutritionally and mechanically beneficial, providing necessary minerals while at the same time keeping the teeth and gums in pristine condition. I have always introduced chicken bones into my cats' diet when they first arrive as kittens. Clinically, I rarely see gastro-intestinal problems in healthy cats caused by eating bones. Some individuals, especially Siamese that bolt their food, may be at risk from not chewing thoroughly.

a fertile environment for bacterial growth. Left untreated, bacterial waste products cause the gums to ulcerate. The supporting bone is affected and eventually nothing remains to support the teeth.

Some forms of gum inflammation are associated with virus infections. Calicivirus infection is associated with resorption of teeth, a condition akin to our cavities. Ulcers on the tongue, lips, inside the cheeks, and on the gums may be caused by infection, injury, immune deficiency, or nutritional deficiency.

THE PROGRESSION OF GUM DISEASE

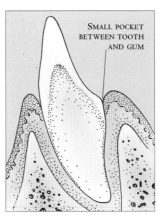

SMALL POCKET BETWEEN TOOTH AND GUM

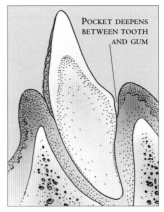

POCKET DEEPENS BETWEEN TOOTH AND GUM

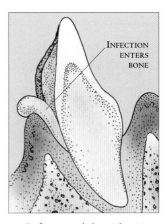

INFECTION ENTERS BONE

1 In healthy gums, the pocket between the tooth and gums is less than one millimetre. Healthy gums are maintained by natural chewing activity or brushing.

2 If plaque builds up, the pocket deepens and the gum becomes inflamed, leading to gingivitis. Removing plaque and polishing the tooth prevents further damage.

3 Left unattended, peridontitis ensues. Infection enters the bone, loosening the tooth, and enters the cat's bloodstream when it chews food, causing chronic pain.

CONVENTIONAL TREATMENTS

Vaccination against calicivirus, protection from FIV and FeLV infection, and regular dental check-ups are recommended for all cats. Resorption of tooth enamel, exposing the dentine and the pulp at the centre of the tooth to bacterial infection, is treated by tooth removal or root-canal surgery.

Painkillers, antibiotics, and antiseptics are used to control discomfort and eliminate deep infection in the support structures of the teeth. Dental home care can be a challenge. Chlorhexidine-containing agents are used as oral antiseptics. Bad breath may be caused by gingivitis, digestive disorders, and sometimes by metabolic conditions such as kidney failure. Mouth ulcers are treated according to the cause. Treatment may include antiseptics, antibiotics, painkillers, and corticosteroids for persistent ulcers associated with an overactive immune system.

CAT "CAVITIES"
Because of their low-sugar diet, non-acidic saliva, and smooth teeth, cats rarely develop cavities caused by bacteria. Instead, and for as yet unknown reasons, they suffer from enamel "resorption", which in essence is a cavity not caused by bacteria. Resorption causes chronic tooth pain.

GUM DISEASE
While viruses are probably not the direct cause of gum disease, indirectly they suppress the immune system, allowing bacteria to thrive, or they overstimulate the immune system, causing it to release inflammatory chemicals. Either way, gingivitis results. Effective treatment will depend upon identifying the cause of the gingivitis.

COMPLEMENTARY TREATMENTS

Complementary vets associate healthy digestive and immune systems with less dental plaque, tartar formation, and gum problems. They may recommend digestive herbs and advise against overfeeding. Most complementary therapies try to prevent mouth problems and, if they occur, to reduce inflammation and strengthen the body's natural defence, the immune system.

TTOUCH THERAPY Gentle massage is the most effective form of care for your cat's mouth. Massaging its gums with your fingers will prepare it for the sensation of brushing. Gum massage through gentle brushing, using a soft-bristled brush and toothpaste formulated for cats, eliminates plaque (which starts to reform six to eight hours after previous brushing). Your cat will probably resent your intrusion so associate it with a tasty reward. *See page 77.*

NUTRITIONAL THERAPIES Nutritional deficiencies are compensated for by making sure your cat has adequate levels of B vitamins and other nutrients. Supplements with natural enzymes may be recommended to reduce gum inflammation. Enzymes are essential catalysts for all metabolic processes. Enzymes found in fruit and vegetables may act as antioxidants, protecting gums from damage by free radicals. A supplement of beetroot fibre, fish oil, fish fat, microbially-produced enzymes, enzymes from uncooked fruit and vegetables, and brewer's yeast may be recommended. Meat on the bone is fed to give teeth and gums natural activity. *See pages 86-87.*

HERBALISM Gentle herbs that may help digestion include cardamom seed, *Elettaria cardamomum*, fennel seed, *Foeniculum vulgare*, and small amounts of ginger root, *Zingiber officinale*, and barberry bark, *Berberis vulgaris*. Marsh mallow root, *Althaea officinalis*, is said to help soothe sore gums. *Echinacea angustifolia* decoction may be recommended as a mouthwash. *See pages 88-91.*

HOMEOPATHY AND BIOCHEMIC TISSUE SALTS Pain associated with excessive salivation is treated with *Plantago 6c. Calc. Phos.* is recommended for early tooth and gum conditions while *Calc. Fluor.* is said to help strengthen the teeth, increasing resistance to resorption. *See pages 92-94.*

AROMA THERAPY Oil of clove, diluted two drops in one teaspoon of carrier oil, is a traditional emergency measure to reduce tooth pain. It may be mixed into a paste with baking soda to use as a homemade toothpaste, applied with a soft toothbrush. Diluted tincture of myrrh may also be recommended to relieve pain. *See page 100.*

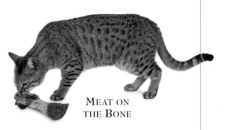

MEAT ON THE BONE

DIGESTION – THE STOMACH

ALTHOUGH CATS ARE FUSSY about what they eat, bacteria and toxins still enter the stomach. The activity of stomach acids and enzymes starts digestion, which is completed in the small intestines. Potentially dangerous substances are eliminated by vomiting. The liver helps remove fat-soluble toxins. The cat's whole digestive system can be affected by conditions both inside and outside the animal's body.

APPETITE LOSS

Loss of appetite may be a sign of disease and is potentially dangerous. After a few days without eating, the liver loses its ability to clear toxic substances. This increases the cat's nausea. Body fat reserves are broken down for energy and spill into the bloodstream. They can clog the liver and cause hepatic lipidosis. Affected cats need forced feeding, usually for one to two months, to get over this serious crisis.

WHAT THE STOMACH DOES

A cat's stomach is more than just a holding tank. It is part of an active defence system that prevents dangerous micro-organisms or poisons from upsetting homeostasis. Cat saliva kills some germs or exposes them to destruction by stomach acids and enzymes. Special receptors in the stomach detect poisons and signal a chemical recognition region (chemoreceptor trigger zone) in the brain. The brain responds with nausea, which prevents further consumption of the poison. Toxic substances that are already in the stomach are removed by vomiting.

Evolution has prepared the cat to cope with many natural poisons but not with new synthetic ones. In the stomach, hydrochloric acid helps break food down for digestion. Mucus is secreted to prevent this acid from burning the stomach wall itself. (When cats vomit back food that has been in the stomach for a short while it may be enclosed

in this protective mucus.) Bicarbonate is also secreted to neutralize acid. Stress diminishes mucus and bicarbonate manufacture. If an anxious cat eats a meal when these defences are low, a condition called "acid rebound" occurs and the cat vomits.

THE LIVER

Although vomiting is an efficient defence mechanism, poisons do get through and are absorbed into the body. When this occurs, the liver plays a defensive role. It is the cat's largest internal organ and a great chemical-processing factory, responsible for producing cholesterol and the digestive liquid called bile, both manufactured from old red blood cells that are worn out, and dietary fat. The liver is also responsible for removing toxic poisons that evaded the gastrointestinal system's first lines of defence, or converting them to safer substances.

STOMACH PROBLEMS

Concern about their cats vomiting is one of the most common reasons why people take them to the vet. It has many causes and does not necessarily mean there is a problem in the stomach itself. Inner-ear disturbances, head injuries, nervous tension, bladder infection, bowel upsets, and a variety of medications can cause nausea and vomiting. The exact cause should be known before any general treatment is undertaken.

Stomach ulcers are breaks in the protective lining of the stomach. Cats are particularly sensitive to gastric irritation caused by a number of conventional painkillers. Gastritis, which is inflammation of the stomach wall, produces signs similar to ulcers – loss of appetite, weight loss, subdued behaviour, occasionally vomiting, and, if bleeding occurs, dark tarry stools. Hairballs frequently cause vomiting, as does excessive grass eating.

Some cats, especially oriental breeds that have been weaned early, and that have a low-roughage diet and no access to natural prey, develop a "depraved" appetite, eating plastic, wool, even small, round pebbles.

STOMACH CELLS
Most cells that line the stomach secrete mucus, protecting the stomach lining from the acid produced by other cells for the purpose of breaking food down. Cats have many lipase-secreting cells, which help them to break down fat.

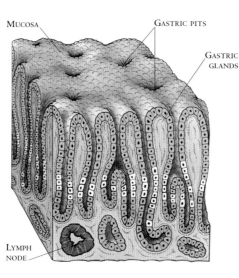

MUCOSA   GASTRIC PITS   GASTRIC GLANDS   LYMPH NODE

CONVENTIONAL TREATMENTS

The body naturally wants to rid itself of potentially toxic chemicals. This is why cats often vomit when they eat something unpleasant, but also why some drugs cause nausea and vomiting. Vets use potentially nausea-inducing drugs such as antibiotics to kill dangerous bacteria, and they may also prescribe other drugs that depress the sensitivity of the brain's chemoreceptor trigger zone. This allows the therapeutic drug to work unhindered. While nausea is controlled by influencing the brain, other drugs are given that reduce stomach-acid production, reducing clinical signs associated with gastritis and stomach ulcers. For cats with depraved appetites, tough meat is given to increase chewing activity. Food may be hidden to stimulate searches, and potential risks are removed from the environment.

REDUCING HAIRBALL VOMITING

Most hair swallowed during grooming passes untroubled through the entire gastrointestinal system, but if hair irritates the lining of the stomach it may be vomited out. Help your cat by combing out loose hair. Long-haired and elderly cats need extra attention. Don't give mineral oil. If any gets in the lungs it can cause severe damage. Use a cat laxative if hairballs are causing constipation.

POISONS

Cats are most frequently poisoned by their owners. They chew on toxic house plants. They lick off flea spray licensed for dogs but dangerous to cats. Most frequently, cat owners give their cats their own painkillers, paracetamol, aspirin, ibuprofen, and diclofenac. The veterinary poisons information service I use reports that painkillers are overwhelmingly the most common cause of cat poisoning they deal with. Never give your cat any form of medicine, either conventional or complementary, without discussing it with your vet. Keep potentially poisonous plants, including philodendrons, hibiscus, and dieffenbachia, out of reach. Standard antifreeze, ethylene glycol, is attractively sweet to cats and potentially fatal if ingested. Use less toxic propylene glycol.

COMPLEMENTARY TREATMENTS

Complementary treatments emphasize the importance of a healthy gastrointestinal system. Interfering with vomiting can prevent the body from ridding itself of toxins. Therapies aim to restore natural levels of acid and bicarbonate in the stomach. Relaxation therapies attempt to control the production of natural chemicals that in excess cause stomach inflammation.

ACUPRESSURE Repeated trials in people report that acupressure on the lower arm (acupoint Pericardium 6 in Traditional Chinese Medicine) can relieve nausea associated with motion, anaesthetics, and chemotherapy. No similar trials have been conducted with cats. See page 74.

NUTRITIONAL THERAPIES Avoid foods that irritate the lining of the stomach. Vitamin A may help prevent or treat gastritis. Vitamin E may be protective and zinc may inhibit chemicals that weaken the stomach lining. Feed cats oily fish such as sardines once a week to assist removal of hairballs. Ensure access to grass. Regular grooming prevents the build-up of loose hair. See pages 86-87.

HERBALISM According to research carried out in Pakistan, extract of plums, *Prunus domestica*, is as effective as powerful drugs for inhibiting vomiting in cats. Catmint, *Nepeta cataria*, may act as an appetite stimulant. Infusions of peppermint, *Mentha x piperita*, German chamomile, *Matricaria recutita*, and fennel, *Foeniculum vulgare*, are used to control nausea in cats. Relaxants and tonics such as ginger, *Zingiber officinale*, may relieve nausea associated with anxiety. Ginger is said to improve digestion of proteins and control nausea and motion sickness. It also affects the production of prostaglandins and by doing so may be anti-inflammatory. For hepatitis, seeds of milk thistle, *Silybum marianum*, may inhibit liver damage and promote the regeneration of liver cells. See pages 88-91.

HOMEOPATHY *Nux vomica 6c, Ipecac 6c,* and *Phosphorus* are all suggested to control vomiting. See pages 92-93.

RELAXATION THERAPY Relaxation may alter the environment in the stomach, reducing stress chemicals associated with nausea and vomiting. See page 98.

SARDINES

DIGESTION – THE INTESTINES

FELINE BOWEL DISORDERS often respond to diet changes and drugs are seldom necessary. In young cats diarrhoea is not uncommon, while later in life constipation is more likely to be a problem. Some disorders are caused by foreign bodies. Sewing thread is a particular hazard to cats. Accidentally swallowed during play, it can "saw" through the intestines, causing life-threatening injuries.

CHECKLIST

Loss of appetite can be caused by:

- Fear
- Furballs
- Diabetes
- Constipation
- Diarrhoea
- Colitis
- Overactivity
- Overweight
- Heart disease
- Urinary tract conditions
- Arthritis.

WHAT THE INTESTINES DO

Digestion takes place in the small intestines, home to more than 400 types of beneficial bacteria. Diet changes may alter the balance of bacteria, encouraging the proliferation of different varieties. With careful dietary selection, it is possible to actively promote the growth of beneficial bacteria. Diets that do this are sometimes called "prebiotic", while diets containing good bacteria such as *Lactobacillus* are called "probiotic".

The pancreas produces enzymes, secreted into the small intestine, that break down protein, fat, and carbohydrate. Kittens have enough enzyme to digest 100 grams (4 oz) of lactose daily. Once they reach adulthood, lactose-digesting enzyme activity in the small intestine will digest only about 10 grams (0.4 oz) of lactose. This is why feeding milk or cream causes diarrhoea in some cats.

The cat's small intestines are quite short, only about 1.3 m (4 ft), but are lined with longer villi than other species for greater absorption. Unlike us, or dogs, there are no peristaltic waves to push food along a cat's intestines. Instead there are migrating bursts of activity. Digestible carbohydrate plays

REFUSING FOOD

A sardine in tomato sauce dabbed on the nose may stimulate the appetite of a cat that has gone off its food through fright, furballs, or because of illness. Do not serve food straight from the fridge. At room temperature, the odour is stronger and more tempting.

SPECIAL DIETS

Feed small amounts of any special diet frequently. The ideal diet for cats with chronic small bowel-type diarrhoea (large volume, watery) is highly digestible, gluten-free, low in fat, low in lactose, with few ingredients, and excesses of potassium and vitamins. Good foods include rice flavoured with stock, fish, lean meat, and cottage cheese.

For colitis (increased frequency, small volumes, loose, mucus, blood) avoid all food additives. Provide home-prepared meals or commercial diets with protein that the cat has not eaten before, such as duck, catfish, or venison. Add fermentable fibre such as psyllium. Suggested diets are boiled skinless chicken, rice and lamb baby foods, and any other foods that are bland and fat-free.

little part in the natural diet of cats but may be beneficial in specific circumstances. Cats produce about a third of the carbohydrate-digesting amylase that equivalent-sized dogs do. Taurine in the diet is probably degraded by bacterial action. Further along, in the colon, excess fluid is removed. Water-soluble dietary fibre is fermented to short-chain fatty acids that protect the lining of the colon.

INTESTINAL PROBLEMS

Gastroenteritis is an inflammation of the lining of the stomach and intestines, usually caused by contaminated food, viruses or bacteria, allergy, or food intolerance. The cat's cecum, or appendix, seldom causes problems. This is where the small intestine joins the colon. Foreign bodies tend to block at this point and, in kittens in particular, the small intestine can telescope into the colon, causing a life-threatening blockage. Colitis is an inflammation of the colon and rectum. Constipation may be caused by the type of food consumed, or problems in the colon wall. Stress can also trigger bowel problems in certain individuals. Irritable bowel syndrome can develop after a long course of antibiotics.

CONVENTIONAL TREATMENTS

Some bowel conditions require detailed investigations with blood analysis, plain or barium x-rays, stool examinations, and endoscopic examination. Intravenous fluids may have to be given if a bowel condition has caused dehydration to occur.

Antibiotics and corticosteroids are usually prescribed to fight infection as well as to ease inflammation in some forms of inflammatory bowel disease. Exclusion diets are recommended for many forms of colitis. Fibre enhances colon activity, binds with irritating products in the intestines, and increases absorption of fluids from the gut.

Constipation tends to be a common problem in older cats. Delayed intestinal activity removes more water from the stools than normal. Eventually, the muscle wall of the colon degenerates and becomes permanently distended. This may be caused by hairballs, excess dietary fibre, lack of exercise, changes in the environment (even the litter!), pain when walking, and other serious problems.

To treat flatulence, vets recommend charcoal tablets. Constipation can be helped in several ways. Lactulose is an undigestible sugar that softens stools. The drug cisapride stimulates movement in the intestines. It also inhibits bacteria that produce toxins, inhibits ammonia production, and acidifies the colon.

Acute pancreatic inflammation is rare in cats. A variety of drugs are recommended in order to treat colitis, including metronidazole and corticosteroids.

WHAT DOES YOGHURT DO?

Typical strains of *Lactobacillus* are acid-sensitive and do not survive passage through the stomach. Acid-resistant strains have been discovered and are used in some "therapeutic" yoghurts. These friendly bacteria are believed to aid digestion in the stomach.

NATURAL DEVELOPMENT

NATURAL TRAINING

NATURAL NUTRITION

NATURAL HEALTH CARE

HEALTH DISORDERS

COMPLEMENTARY TREATMENTS

A short bout of diarrhoea is considered the natural way in which a cat's body cleanses itself of harmful material. Complementary vets allow these short episodes to run their natural course. For much longer episodes of diarrhoea, relieving stress, restoring the balance of natural bacteria in the intestines, and feeding a balanced diet are integral parts of treatment. Historically, herbs used to be an important means of keeping food safe – by killing bacteria. According to research at Cornell University in New York State, the best bacteria killers are garlic, onion, allspice, and oregano, followed by thyme, cinnamon, tarragon, and cumin, which kill 80 per cent of consumed bacteria. Complementary vets try to avoid all drugs and treat gastrointestinal disease through dietary management.

ACUPUNCTURE Some veterinarians feel that acupuncture stimulates the pancreas and its secretion of digestive enzymes. *See pages 72-73.*

THERAPEUTIC MASSAGE Massaging the abdomen of thin cats may help to stimulate bowel activity in constipated individuals. Increased physical activity is believed to reduce predisposition to constipation. *See pages 80-81.*

NUTRITIONAL THERAPIES Omega-3 fatty acids found in oily fish may ease the signs of some forms of colitis. Inflammatory bowel disease leads to excessive loss of essential nutrients. Supervised supplements may be needed. Acid-stable live yoghurt is recommended to restore beneficial intestinal bacteria. Small bowel disorders can lead to folic acid deficiency.

Psyllium husks, oatbran, and cornbran all help natural bowel elimination. Carrots and celery add bulk for regular bowel function. Linseed, senna, and cascara are natural laxatives, although the latter two make the colon more sluggish if used excessively. Lifelong dietary management is necessary to control colitis. For constipation, milk works wonders in lactose-intolerant cats. *See pages 86-87.*

HERBALISM Various herbs are used to reduce bowel inflammation. Marsh mallow root, *Althaea officinalis*, and slippery elm, *Ulmus rubra*, soothe and protect tissues. Echinacea and goldenseal, *Hydrastis canadensis*, inhibit bacteria while pokeroot, *Phytolacca americana*, heals ulceration and comfrey, *Symphytum officinale*, eases inflammation. Arrowroot, *Peuraria lobata*, in water soothes the bowels. Dandelion, *Taraxacum officinale*, is a mild laxative and B vitamin source.

Peppermint oil, *Mentha x piperita*, supplied in capsules that are specially treated to survive the acid environment of the stomach, reduces intestinal contractions and associated pain and trapped gas. Other herbs said to have similar effects include German chamomile, *Matricaria recutita*, valerian, *Valerian officinalis*, rosemary, *Rosemarinus officinalis*, and lemon balm, *Melissa officinalis*. Ayurvedic *triphala* powder may be suggested as a laxative, and light kaolin clay as a toxin absorbent and intestine protector. *See pages 88-91.*

HOMEOPATHY Homeopathic vets may recommend *Argent nit. 6c* for constipation, *Nux vomica 6c* for flatulence, *Colchicum 6c* for watery diarrhoea, and *Arsen. alb. 6c* for profuse, explosive diarrhoea. *Ipecac 6c* is used for food intolerance diarrhoea. *See pages 92-93.*

PEPPERMINT OIL

INTESTINAL PARASITES

MOST CATS ARE INFESTED at some time by intestinal parasites. Most are worm-like, but some parasites that cause diarrhoea are single-celled and invisible to the eye. One of these parasites, *Toxoplasma*, is of public health concern. Affected cats can spread infection to other cats, and us too. There is a possible relationship between the body's defences against parasites and food allergies.

CHECKLIST

- Most parasites do not cause clinical disease.
- Some parasites are potential public health concerns.
- Worm your cat preventatively according to your vet's instructions.
- Preventing your cat from hunting will reduce the risk of parasites.
- Deflea your cat routinely.
- Repeat worming after corticosteroid therapy, false or real pregnancy, or stress.

NATURAL IMMUNITY TO PARASITES

A variety of parasites spend their adult lives in the comfort of a cat's intestines. Their objective is to do no harm to the cat, but heavy infestations early in life may cause intestinal bleeding, and anaemia. Some parasites consume so many nutrients from the intestines that the cat's health suffers. In kittens a heavy parasite load can be fatal.

As cats mature, they probably develop a resistance to roundworms and hookworms, intestinal parasites with life cycles that involve migration through the cat's body. This is why roundworm infestations are common in kittens but unusual in adults. Tapeworms don't migrate so they don't stimulate an immune reaction. As a result, adult cats are often reinfested with tapeworms.

Dormant roundworm larvae in a cat's body are activated by corticosteroid treatment, or when a cat is stressed by trauma or disease. During pregnancy, dormant larvae are activated and appear in the mother's milk or cross the placenta into the foetuses.

TOXOPLASMA LIFE CYCLE

Cats acquire toxoplasma from consuming infected birds or rodents. They pass infectious oocysts in their faeces. Livestock consume passed oocysts while grazing, or by eating contaminated feed. Toxoplasma is passed on to humans either when undercooked meat is eaten, or via environmental contamination.

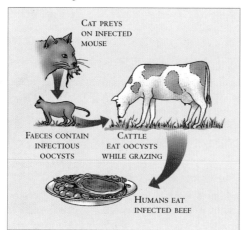

CAT PREYS ON INFECTED MOUSE

FAECES CONTAIN INFECTIOUS OOCYSTS

CATTLE EAT OOCYSTS WHILE GRAZING

HUMANS EAT INFECTED BEEF

TYPES OF PARASITES

When we think of parasites, we usually think of worms: roundworms, *Toxocara cati*, hookworms, *Ancylostoma*, and tapeworms, typically *Dipylidium caninum* from fleas but also the *Taenia* species contracted by eating infested raw meat. In addition, cats can be infested by many single-celled organisms, including *Toxoplasma*, *Coccidia*, and *Giardia*. All of these parasites are passed in faeces and can survive in the environment for months. In recent years, *Giardia*, which affects most mammals, has spread worldwide, even to lakes and rivers in previously uncontaminated regions such as New Zealand.

HUMAN HEALTH IMPLICATIONS

All feline parasites can, in theory, affect us but in practice only two are significant, *Giardia* and *Toxoplasma*. The cat contracts both by hunting and consuming natural prey, although *Toxoplasma* can also be passed in the womb from mother to kittens.

Toxoplasmosis is usually contracted by humans when we eat undercooked infected meat. Cats pass infectious eggs in their faeces for several weeks after the first occasion they eat infected prey. If their faeces gets into cattle feed, cattle pick up the parasite and transmit it in their meat. The easiest way to prevent cats from transmitting toxoplasmosis is to prevent them hunting.

Toxoplasma rarely causes clinical problems in humans. In many countries, between one third and one half the population have protective antibodies to this parasite. Danger exists for developing foetuses in pregnant mothers. Pregnant women who have never been exposed to *Toxoplasma* should wear rubber gloves when gardening or cleaning the litter tray of cats permitted outdoors.

CONVENTIONAL TREATMENTS

Rather than restricting therapy to treatment of parasite infestations, prevention is always recommended. No single drug kills all life stages of all worms. Vets use a variety of different drugs and regimens according to the local prevalence and seriousness of worm infestations. Worming should be undertaken after a cat has had immunosuppressive drugs or been "stressed". More frequent worming is necessary in warmer climates. Flea control is the best way to control tapeworms, which are transmitted when cats accidentally eat fleas while grooming. *Giardia* is treated with metronidazole. All animals that come into contact with the cat, and sometimes the owners too, are treated. Parasites are known to trigger a condition called eosinophilic colitis. Chemical by-products of defensive cells, cytokines and eicosanoids, cause damage to the colon, resulting in clinical disease.

COMPLEMENTARY TREATMENTS

Holistic vets agree that homeopathic and herbal methods of parasite control are not effective. They recommend using licensed anthelmintics from veterinarians rather than over-the-counter products from pet shops or supermarkets. These drugs are highly effective and should be given under veterinary supervision.

"LEAKY GUT SYNDROME"

Holistic vets believe there is a relationship between parasitic infestations (and other conditions) that damage the lining of the gut, and the growing incidence of immune-related disease in cats. The gastrointestinal system is a major line of defence against infection. If the gut lining becomes damaged, it becomes "leaky", allowing molecules of food that are larger than usual to leave the gut and enter the bloodstream. (The gut lining can be damaged by parasites, corticosteroids, non-steroid anti-inflammatory drugs, infections, antibiotic therapy, and other unknown factors.) The immune system is unfamiliar with these large molecules and produces antibodies against them. This unnecessary attack leads to a profusion of antigen-antibody complex which may lead to immune-mediated asthma or arthritis.

This syndrome is not recognized by conventional veterinary medicine.

TAENIA TAENIFORMIS
This tapeworm attaches itself by hooklets and suckers to the intestines of cats. Its chainlike body, up to 24 in (60 cm) long, consists of egg-carrying units that break off and pass out of the host to be consumed by a new victim.

TREATMENTS FOR "LEAKY GUT"

Holistic vets do four things simultaneously to control what they call "intestinal dysbiosis". They eliminate parasites, and small-intestine bacterial overgrowth, often with conventional anthelmintics, antimicrobials, and antifungals. They advise that food antigens (allergens) are avoided. They add digestive enzymes, beneficial bacteria (probiotics), and food substances that support the growth of beneficial bacteria (prebiotics), such as fructo-oligosaccharides (FOS). Finally, they assist repair with antioxidants such as zinc, natural anti-inflammatories such as omega-3 fatty acids in fish oil, and a supplement of the amino acid L-glutamine, said to be beneficial for healing the gut wall.

Veterinary herbalists prescribe Oregon grape, *Berberis acquafolium*, which is thought to be antiprotozoal and antifungal. *Artemesia annua* (*Qing hao*) is said to be effective against *Giardia*. Deglycyrrhizinated licorice has anti-inflammatory properties in the gut. Garlic is said to be antiparasitic but in challenge trials has not been effective against intestinal parasites. Boswellia, *Boswellia serrata*, is said to be anti-inflammatory, while *Ginkgo biloba*, *Silybum marianum*, selenium, and vitamins A, E, and C act as antioxidants.

ANAL GLANDS

When a cat keeps licking its backside excessively there may be visible rice-grain-sized segments of tapeworms in the region. However, the problem may be that the cat's scent-producing anal sacs are irritatingly full and need emptying. With advancing age, the anal sac contents become increasingly dehydrated.

GARLIC
Garlic is a well-known antioxidant and has many healing properties, but claims that it is antiparasitic have not been borne out in trials.

NATURAL DEVELOPMENT

NATURAL TRAINING

NATURAL NUTRITION

NATURAL HEALTH CARE

HEALTH DISORDERS

THE URINARY SYSTEM

URINARY PROBLEMS ARE INCREASINGLY common in cats. Lower urinary tract disease has become a significant problem in recent years and is associated with diet. Age-related kidney failure has also increased in frequency, primarily because cats now live long enough for that part of the body to decline through wear and tear. While the former can be reversed, the latter can only ever be delayed.

STRESS AND CYSTITIS
Nerve cells send messages from cell to cell using chemicals called neurotransmitters. If these chemicals are degraded or not taken-up by the next cell, they build up and are "re-taken-up", creating stronger signals that last longer. Stress, somehow, causes this to happen and in cats can lead to an emotion-induced cystitis. Drugs (re-uptake inhibitors) reduce this exaggerated neurotransmitter reaction. Non-invasive responses, such as moving a litter tray to a quieter area, can also work.

NATURAL DEFENCES
Because the urethra connects directly to the outside world, natural defences evolved to protect the urinary system from infection. Beneficial bacteria in the urethra prevent harmful bacteria from entering. In the bladder, mucus gathers together bacteria that get through, although when mixed with urinary crystals this mucus can clog the urethra in male cats, causing a painful obstruction. Antibodies are also released into the urine while urea and natural urinary acidity make bacterial multiplication difficult. In males, secretions from the prostate also act as barriers to infection. Because natural defences are so good, bacterial infections are rare.

URINARY SYSTEM PROBLEMS
Kidney problems may be genetic, acquired through injury, infection, poisoning, or diet. Because cats are now living so long, many will develop an age-related decline in kidney function, leading to chronic kidney failure.

Bladder conditions affect cats of all ages. Bacterial infection, mineral deposit, injuries, tumours, even stress can cause cystitis, an inflammation of the lining of the bladder. Bacterial infection is not a common cause of lower urinary tract disease (LUTD), but when it occurs it is more often found in females than males because their urethra, connecting to the outside world, is shorter. Mineral crystals in the bladder and urethra are common. Two types of deposit develop, struvite and calcium oxalate. Calcium oxalate uroliths are more frequent in Himalayans and Persians than in other breeds.

Cats with LUTD lick their anogenital regions as they do for worms or blocked anal glands. The typical cat with LUTD is two to six years old, overweight, disinclined to exercise, uses a litter tray, and is highly sensitive to household changes.

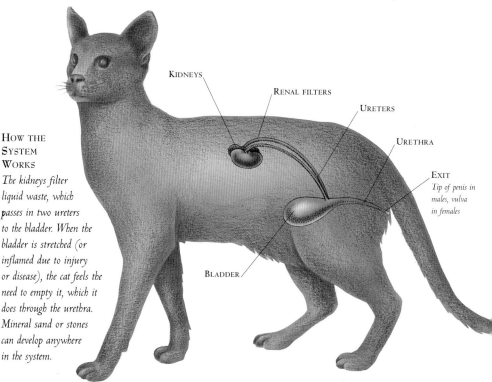

HOW THE SYSTEM WORKS
The kidneys filter liquid waste, which passes in two ureters to the bladder. When the bladder is stretched (or inflamed due to injury or disease), the cat feels the need to empty it, which it does through the urethra. Mineral sand or stones can develop anywhere in the system.

KIDNEYS

RENAL FILTERS

URETERS

URETHRA

EXIT
Tip of penis in males, vulva in females

BLADDER

NATURAL DEVELOPMENT

NATURAL TRAINING

NATURAL NUTRITION

NATURAL HEALTH CARE

HEALTH DISORDERS

WHAT CAUSES LUTD?

At one time, ash in a cat's diet was thought to cause LUTD, but this was wrong. More recently, magnesium was implicated, but this is wrong, too: magnesium does not cause LUTD. Adding magnesium oxide to the diet makes the urine alkaline, favouring struvite crystal formation. But adding magnesium chloride instead acidifies the urine, making it difficult for struvite crystals to form. A good diet keeps urine pH between 6.00 and 6.40. Over that level and a cat is more prone to struvite LUTD. Overacidified cat food pushing pH below 6.00 creates an environment for calcium oxalate crystal formation.

CONVENTIONAL TREATMENTS

There is no scientific reason to feed a low-protein diet to cats with chronic kidney failure. Uremia is managed by maintaining nitrogen balance and this is done by reducing dietary phosphorus and feeding a medium-protein diet. There is an association between too much fat (lipid) in the blood and kidney failure. Free radicals from this lipid can damage kidney cell membranes but if antioxidants are introduced into the diet they may scavenge free radicals and reduce the kidney damage.

Between one and two per cent of the cat population suffers from LUTD. These cats are significantly more likely to be fed dry food exclusively. The cornerstones of treatment for LUTD are to reduce the specific gravity of the urine to approximately 1.020, and to eliminate any urinary tract infection. Broad spectrum antibiotics are routinely used. For crystals, reduction of urine pH to between 6.0 and 6.5 is desired. Potassium chloride capsules are given twice daily with meals. Blockages are found more frequently in males than females because the tip of the urethra in a male cat's penis is only a quarter the diameter of the equivalent in a female cat. Blockages are flushed clear under anaesthetic. Large stones are surgically removed. Incontinence is controlled with drugs that improve the efficiency of the muscle at the bladder's exit.

CYSTITIS
Cats develop routine toileting habits. More frequent trips to the litter tray and prolonged time for urinating can be signs of urinary tract problems, such as cystitis.

ANTIBIOTIC SUCCESS
LUTD is rarely caused by bacterial infection, yet cats get better on antibiotics. Professor Tony Buffington suggests antibiotics have an antispasmodic action on the urethra, relieving discomfort.

COMPLEMENTARY TREATMENTS

Many cats with LUTD don't have stones, mucus plugs, or bacterial infections. They recover within a week without specific treatment. Complementary vets suggest feeding "wet" rather than dry food, and supplementing with water. They advise against scented litters, which they associate with toileting problems.

NUTRITIONAL THERAPIES Holistic vets suggest avoiding standard dry foods for cats with LUTD. Supplement tinned food with fresh cooked meat and a little cooked mashed vegetable. Always provide fresh water. To control calcium oxalate stones, feed a diet with reduced protein, calcium, and sodium and avoid excess vitamin D and ascorbic acid. Asparagus contains asparagine, said to break up oxalate crystals. Conventional and complementary vets agree on these diet recommendations for cats with chronic kidney failure. *See pages 86-87.*

HERBALISM Herbs with a reputation for preventing urinary stones include stoneroot herb, *Collinsonia canadensis,* and horsetail herb, *Equisetum arvense.* Diuretic herbs that increase urine flow are sometimes used. These include dandelion leaf, *Taraxacum officinale,* and couch grass, *Elymus repens.* Cherry stalk extract, *Prunus avium,* reduces edema. Urinary antiseptics recommended for treating bacterial cystitis include bearberry leaf, *Arctostaphylos uva-ursi,* and juniper berry, *Juniperus communis.* Herbs that soothe the urinary tract, helping the passage of small stones, include peppermint herb, *Mentha x piperita,* fennel seed, *Foeniculum vulgare,* and marsh mallow root, *Althaea officinalis.*

For kidney impairment, a cat's general well-being may be improved when any of these herbs are appropriately used: cinnamon bark, *Cinnamomum zeylanicum,* comfrey leaf, *Symphytum officinale,* and celery seed, *Apium graveolens. See pages 88-91.*

HOMEOPATHY AND BIOCHEMIC TISSUE SALTS *Cantharis* and *Equisetum* are used as remedies for cystitis. *Causticum* is used to treat incontinence. *Calc. carb.* is employed for overweight cats with uroliths. *Calc. phos.* is recommended for lean cats with the same condition. *See pages 92-94.*

BACH FLOWER REMEDIES Rescue Remedy is recommended to relieve discomfort associated with acute cystitis. *See page 95.*

RELAXATION THERAPY Some cats can develop an emotion-induced cystitis. Although the triggering events are unknown, gentle touch for highly socialized cats may be beneficial. *See page 98.*

RESCUE REMEDY

THE REPRODUCTIVE SYSTEM

NATURAL DEVELOPMENT

NATURAL TRAINING

NATURAL NUTRITION

NATURAL HEALTH CARE

HEALTH DISORDERS

FEMALE CATS OVULATE and become interested in sex as daylight increases, but males are lifelong sexual opportunists. Reproductive tract infections are more common in maiden queens. Unlike in dogs or humans, prostate problems are uncommon in older male cats. Neutering may be considered unnatural, but it is the most effective way to prevent many medical problems that affect the reproductive system.

CHECKLIST

Take the following precautions if your cat is pregnant.

- No vaccinations during the first four weeks.
- No drugs unless they are absolutely necessary.
- No insecticides unless absolutely necessary.
- No herbs unless proven safe in cats during pregnancy.
- Worming only with anthelmintics known to be safe and effective during pregnancy.
- Do not project human values on your cat. She does not need a pregnancy to feel fulfilled.

THE FEMALE REPRODUCTIVE SYSTEM

As daylight increases, the pituitary gland at the base of the brain produces follicle-stimulating hormone, which causes the ovaries to produce eggs. Repeated mating triggers a signal for the pituitary to release another hormone that stimulates the ovaries to release eggs for fertilization. Cats are "induced ovulators". As lone hunters without readily available partners they do not release eggs until they have mated.

THE MALE REPRODUCTIVE SYSTEM

Year round, the pituitary gland produces leutenising hormone, which triggers sperm and testosterone production in the testes. Sperm are manufactured in the testes and transported in a sugar-dense liquid made in the prostate gland. If the testes are removed, the testosterone level drops immediately.

IS NEUTERING NATURAL?

No it isn't, but keeping a cat as a pet isn't natural either. Think about reality when considering neutering your cat. Neutered females are healthier because of reduced medical risks. Neutered males tend to be more comfortable because they are not shunned because of odour, and they are less likely to get injured in cat fights. Neutered cats are safer from accidents because they wander over shorter distances. Neutered cats are less frustrated because they don't have to experience hormonal impulses that cannot be fulfilled because we won't let them. Neutered cats reduce the surplus unwanted cat population, making life better for other cats. Neutering does not change your cat's gender, only its production of hormones.

REPRODUCTIVE PROBLEMS

Natural cat reproduction involves frequent spring and summer pregnancies that somehow reduce the risk of genital tract infections and mammary gland problems later in life. Womb infections (metritis and endometritis or pyometra), mammary gland infections (mastitis), and mammary cancers (which make up 40 per cent of all cat tumours, most of which are malignant) are more common in older queens that have never been pregnant. (This is similar to the higher occurrence of disorders in women who started their periods early and ended late without intervening pregnancies and milk production.) Early neutering of female cats reduces the risk of mammary tumours.

Male cats have relatively few reproductive medical problems. Castrating cats does not prevent prostate cancer but does reduce risks of prostatic hyperplasia and, of course, testicular tumours, both of which are rare clinical problems.

CONVENTIONAL TREATMENTS

Neutering is usually performed to prevent unwanted kittens but it also reduces the risk of hormone-related disorders such as mammary tumours and womb infections. Neutering as early as seven weeks of age has been shown to be safe, but most vets prefer not to neuter before physical maturity.

Hormone treatments are used to enhance fertility. Mastitis is treated with antibiotics and painkillers. Caesarean section is needed if kittens are too big to pass through the birth canal. During natural birth, pressure on the vaginal walls stimulates the release of the hormone oxytocin, needed for milk letdown. Oxytocin also appears to activate a brain mechanism that helps with bonding. Mothers are less likely to reject kittens born by Caesarean if they are given oxytocin.

Over-demand for milk reduces circulating calcium and causes life-threatening eclampsia in the mother. This is treated with calcium given intravenously, sometimes corticosteroids, and milk substitute for the kittens.

A womb infection may be "flushed" by using powerful new drugs, but the most common treatment for pyometra is an emergency hysterectomy.

The male's most common reproductive problem is undescended testicles, especially in Persian cats. Selective breeding reduces the risk of this condition.

VASECTOMIES FOR CATS?

A vasectomy, removal of parts of the tubes that transport sperm from the testicles to the urethra, is an alternative to neutering. This leaves sex-hormone production unaltered. Vasectomized toms still mate and are prone to urine spraying and wandering.

Sterilization of females by removing only the Fallopian tubes and leaving the ovaries intact is never performed. Sometimes, females are sterilized by having only their ovaries removed, leaving the uterus intact. This is an easier operation to perform but it increases the risk of womb problems later in life.

KITTEN GROWTH

Testosterone accelerates muscle development and the growth of the ends of long bones. The female hormone oestrogen promotes growth of long bones by acting directly on the bone and by increasing secretion of growth hormone. Very early neutering enhances oestrogen effects. Kittens' legs grow for a longer than normal period.

TOXIC PROBLEMS

While selenium, working together with vitamin E, is an antioxidant, scavenging up free radicals, and is vital for normal sperm activity, it is toxic to cats if given in large doses. Cats are more sensitive than we are to excessive of many minerals. Do not over-supplement. Use balanced vitamin and mineral supplements prepared by reputable manufacturers.

NATURAL DEVELOPMENT

NATURAL TRAINING

NATURAL NUTRITION

NATURAL HEALTH CARE

HEALTH DISORDERS

COMPLEMENTARY TREATMENTS

Holistic vets are divided over whether or not to neuter male cats. They argue that the most common reason for neutering is what we consider to be the offensive odour of male-cat urine. Neutering does not significantly reduce the risk of medical problems because that risk is already low. Medical conditions are often treated with hormone-balancing and stress-control herbs. Optimum nutrition for breeding and pregnancy is maintained by ensuring appropriate natural nutrients in the diet.

NUTRITIONAL THERAPIES Food rich in magnesium, zinc, and vitamin B2 may help normalize hormone levels. Vitamin E and selenium enhance sperm motility. Zinc is necessary for testosterone production, although it is also claimed that zinc deficiency is related to enlarged prostate problems. Sunflower oil and pumpkin are good sources of zinc. Vitamin A deficiency results in reduced testicle size. Foods that are derived from soya are rich in natural oestrogens. *See pages 86-87.*

HERBALISM Sedative herbs such as lemon balm leaf, valerian root, *Valeriana officinalis, Melissa officinalis*, hop strobile, *Humulus lupulus*, and lettuce leaf, *Lactuca virosa*, are used by veterinary herbalists to reduce stress or anxiety in queens during mating. Catmint herb, *Nepeta cataria*, is also used to reduce stress. To enhance the performance of stud cats they may recommend zinc supplement in the diet and any of ginseng root, *Panax ginseng*, celery seed, *Apium graveolens*, for one week prior to mating, or fenugreek seed, *Trigonella foenum-graecum*, for a longer period. Sage, *Salvia officinalis*, and motherwort, *Leonurus cardiaca*, are used as natural oestrogen supplements. The "female" herbs black cohosh, *Cimicifuga racemosa*, blue cohosh, *Caulophyllum thalictroides*, and wild yam, *Dioscorea villosa*, containing high levels of plant oestrogens, are sometimes recommended to control over-sexed male cats. Dehydroepiandrosterone (DHEA), produced from wild yam, is recommended to improve sperm counts. It should be treated as a hormone, with caution. *See pages 88-91.*

HOMEOPATHY Homeopathic *Caulophyllum* is reported to reduce stillbirths in pigs. No equivalent studies have been carried out in cats. *See pages 92-93.*

BACH FLOWER REMEDIES Rescue Remedy is given for a variety of male and female reproductive disorders. *See page 95.*

EXERCISE Good muscle tone and a lean body are ideal for breeding cats. Overweight cats appear to have reduced fertility. *See page 99.*

SAGE

THE CARDIOVASCULAR SYSTEM

YOUR CAT'S CARDIOVASCULAR system circulates substances needed for good health. No cell in the body is more than five cells away from a blood vessel. Problems can develop within the system, for example in heart muscle, or outside the system in the kidneys or thyroid gland, affecting the heart and circulation. There may be a loss of the body balances necessary for a cat to function efficiently.

HIGH BLOOD PRESSURE

We suffer from high blood pressure associated with excess cholesterol diets or inhaling cigarette smoke. These are not causes of feline hypertension. Kidney disease and hyperthyroidism are the most common causes of high blood pressure in cats. These disorders need to be controlled in order to reduce dangerously high blood pressure.

WHAT THE SYSTEM DOES

The heart pumps the fluid that transports substances to and from all of the body's cells. Circulating fluid contains three types of cells: red blood cells that carry nourishing oxygen to all cells or waste carbon dioxide from them; white blood cells always on the alert to co-ordinate defences against potential threats; and platelets, the repair cells that start healing (clotting) after physical injuries.

Blood cells are manufactured in bone marrow and, to a lesser extent, the spleen. In addition to the circulation system that is directly connected to the heart, white blood cells have their own private highway, the lymphatic system, that connects all lymph nodes. Circulating fluid in the bloodstream contains sugar (glucose), minerals, hormones, and other compounds that maintain balance.

If the heart is damaged, it has the capacity to increase in size to compensate for that damage. When blood vessels are severed, the body has the ability to enlarge others to replace the damage. There are millions of

bifurcations as vessels become progressively smaller. These points of division are most vulnerable to injury. The system, including the bone marrow, is highly sophisticated and refined but it can be affected by trauma, infection, infestation, poisoning, poor diet, and physical or emotional stress.

WHAT GOES WRONG

Heart disease in cats has increased in the last 30 years. In the 1980s, taurine deficiency became a common cause of dilated cardiomyopathy, thinning of the heart walls. Because cat food manufacturers add taurine to cat food, this is now rare.

Heart and blood-vessel damage is often diagnosed but the causes, other than hyperthyroidism and kidney failure, tend to elude investigators. In cats under five years of age, the ventricles may thicken (hypertrophy). Muscle is replaced by fibrous tissue. In older individuals, damage occurs where the aorta divides into femoral arteries taking blood to the hind legs. The artery wall becomes damaged. White blood cells and platelets cling to the damage, eventually creating a clot, known as a saddle thrombus, which blocks blood supply to the hind legs (see page 145). This is excruciatingly painful to cats.

Valvular heart disease, the most common cardiovascular condition in dogs, is rare in cats. A feline heart murmur is more likely to be associated with anaemia. In anaemia, the number of red blood cells is diminished. Blood-cell parasites, injuries, virus infections such as FIV and FeLV, ulcers, poisoning, poor diet, even severe flea infestation, can cause serious, life-threatening anaemia. Sometimes the immune system attacks its own red blood cells, causing anaemia.

CONVENTIONAL TREATMENTS

Taurine supplementation and marine fish oil supplementation are given to cats that have dilated cardiomyopathy. These fatty acids also increase appetite and weight. (Don't give fish oil supplemented with added vitamins A or D.) Cats with saddle thrombus are given

THE HEART
Blood flows from the body into the upper chambers of the heart, the left and right atria, then through valves into the muscular lower chambers, the ventricles. These contract, pumping blood to the lungs and via the aorta back to the body. Healthy heart muscle and valves are necessary for cardiovascular efficiency.

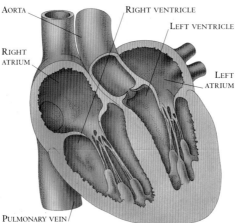

AORTA

RIGHT VENTRICLE

LEFT VENTRICLE

RIGHT ATRIUM

LEFT ATRIUM

PULMONARY VEIN

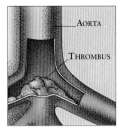

SADDLE THROMBUS
Blood is pumped from the heart down the aorta to where that vessel divides into the femoral arteries, feeding fresh blood to the hind legs. When heart disease affects blood pressure, turbulence at the point where the aorta divides into the femoral arteries damages the vessel wall, leading to a clot or "thrombus". This is an extremely dangerous and painful condition.

HEARTWORMS

It has been known since 1921 that spaghetti-like heartworms, *Dirofilaria immitis*, are a potential problem for cats. They are transmitted when a mosquito that has ingested heartworm microfilaria (the offspring of adult worms) while feeding off an infected dog, passes them while having a meal of cat blood. Because the clinical signs of feline heart disease are vague (vomiting, raspy lung sounds), the true incidence of this problem is unknown. If your cat has heartworms, be very cautious with treatment. The arsenic-based drugs used may cause a life-threatening blood clot. If your outdoor cat lives in a "hot spot" for canine heartworm disease, consider prevention with a licensed medication. A monthly meat-flavoured pill can be crumbled in food.

Vitamin C and zinc aid the absorption of iron. Blood transfusions are given according to blood type, which varies according to breed, even country of origin. In the absence of compatible blood, a "synthetic" oxygen-carrying blood replacer is licensed for use in dogs and has been successfully used on cats with anaemia due to sudden blood loss.

Corticosteroids are used to suppress an overactive immune system that destroys its own red blood cells or platelets. Specific cardiac drugs are used according to the diagnosis, which is achieved through physical examination, electrocardiograph, x-ray, ultrasound, and blood sampling.

Conventional veterinarians feel that in some circumstances a low-salt diet is good for cats with heart disease. Commercial cat foods contain added salt for palatability. Fresh food with no added salt, or commercially produced "kidney diets" that have less salt than typical foods, are often recommended for cats with heart disease.

aspirin twice weekly. Anaemia is treated by eliminating the cause and supplementing with iron, folic acid, and vitamins.

COMPLEMENTARY TREATMENTS

Holistic vets say that the recent increase in the lifespan of cats has occurred so quickly that their bodies do not naturally produce sufficient antioxidants for their old age. Consequently, they believe antioxidant supplements are beneficial for elderly cats.

ACUPUNCTURE Scandinavian studies on people showed that acupuncture (at any points, not just TCM points) can increase the heart's working capacity. *See pages 72-73.*

THERAPEUTIC MASSAGE Slow massage releases muscle tension and temporarily reduces blood pressure. Moderate, routine "walking" exercise can help to maintain circulation. *See pages 80-81.*

NUTRITIONAL THERAPIES Vitamin E and selenium are thought to be beneficial for efficient heart function. Vitamin B probably reduces levels of homocysteine, a substance that damages blood vessel cell walls. L-Carnitine is often recommended for all forms of cardiovascular disease.

Don't give D-Carnitine or D.L-Carnitine. These may actually worsen an existing heart condition. Magnesium supplementation is suggested for exaggerated arrhythmias. Coenzyme Q is recommended as a beneficial antioxidant. *See pages 86-87.*

HERBALISM Several herbs including emblic myrobalan fruit, *Phyllanthus emblica*, Ashwagandha root, *Withania somnifera*, angelica root, *Angelica archangelica*, and rehmannia root, *Rehmannia glutinosa*, may help regenerate blood cells in anaemic cats. German studies have showed that bioflavonoids found in hawthorn, *Crataegus laevigata*, dilate the coronary arteries improving the supply of oxygen to heart muscle. Motherwort, *Leonurus cardiaca*, is also recommended. Any of the above may be combined with a diuretic herb such as dandelion leaf, *Taraxacum officinale*. *See pages 88-91.*

HOMEOPATHY AND BIOCHEMIC TISSUE SALTS *Adonis* and *Digitalis* are used for congestive heart failure. *Spongia tosta 6c* is

given for rapid heart rate and ventricular hypertrophy. *Calc. sulph.* and *Nat. sulph.* are used when chronic damage has occurred. *See pages 92-94.*

RELAXATION THERAPY Training to relax leads to slower, shallower breathing and deep-muscle relaxation. This temporarily reduces both blood pressure and heart rate. *See page 98.*

MUSIC THERAPY It is possible that gentle music can relieve tension in animals. *See page 101.*

RELAXATION THERAPY

NATURAL DEVELOPMENT

NATURAL TRAINING

NATURAL NUTRITION

NATURAL HEALTH CARE

HEALTH DISORDERS

THE RESPIRATORY SYSTEM

A RESTING CAT BREATHES about 25 to 30 times a minute, twice as often as we do, taking about twice as long to breathe out as to breathe in. Any change in breathing rate is a possible cause for concern. Rapid breathing may be caused by excitement or fear but it is also a sign of pain, fever, heat prostration, and a multiplicity of illnesses nearly all of which demand immediate veterinary attention.

VACCINATION

Vaccination is the most effective way to prevent respiratory infections in cats. If a nursing cat is a carrier of FVR or FCV, her litter has a high risk of infection. This is one of the rare circumstances in which kittens should be separated from their mother.

HOW THE SYSTEM WORKS

Breathing allows oxygen from the air to be absorbed into the bloodstream to provide fuel for the cat's body to function properly. Air is filtered in the nose, then it passes through the windpipe and bronchial tubes to the lungs, and eventually into millions of thin-walled sacs where it is exchanged for waste carbon dioxide, which is breathed out.

Mucus or debris and accompanying inflammation may occur anywhere in the system. Because the system is connected to the outside world, mechanisms evolved to protect it from dangers. Coughing, sneezing, and nasal discharge are all defensive actions used to expel unwanted material.

RESPIRATORY CONDITIONS

Catarrh is the over-production of mucus in the respiratory system. It causes a nasal discharge or, more seriously, blocked sinuses. Catarrh is most often caused by respiratory inflammation, which in turn is caused by infection, pollution, or allergy.

Coughing is provoked by irritation to the trachea or bronchi. If there are repeated episodes of acute irritation (acute bronchitis), the mucous membrane becomes permanently thickened and damaged. Coughing is usually associated with lungworms (*Aelurostrongylus abstrusus*), chronic bronchitis, and asthma.

Sneezing expels foreign material such as irritating pollen from a cat's nasal passages. It is usually associated with upper respiratory tract infection, 80 to 90 per cent of which is caused by feline viral rhinotracheitis (FVR) and feline calicivirus (FCV).

A common cause of difficulty in breathing is accumulation of fluid in the chest cavity surrounding the lungs. This is often caused by infectious peritonitis (FIP) virus or feline leukemia (FeLV), but cancer, heart, and liver conditions can also have the same effect.

FELINE ASTHMA PREVENTION

Cats suffer from asthma just as we do. If you discover that your cat is asthmatic, you will need to avoid aerosols such as household cleaners and deodorizers, and use air purifiers around your home. Always keep the number of your emergency veterinary facility to hand in case of an acute attack (*see Checklist, page 147*).

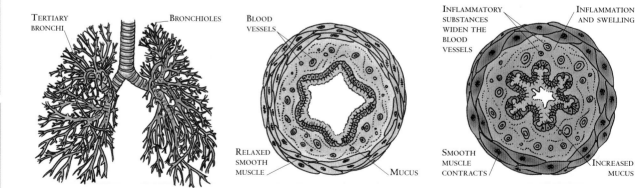

THE LUNG'S AIRWAYS
Air is breathed into the windpipe, down airways to the bronchioles, where oxygen is exchanged for waste carbon dioxide, which is then breathed out.

NORMAL AIRWAY
A normal airway is wide and covered by a fine layer of mucus, necessary for protecting the lining of the airway from damaging external substances.

DURING AN ASTHMA ATTACK
Under the influence of inflammatory chemicals, the smooth muscle of the airway contracts and excess mucus is produced, creating tight breathing.

NATURAL DEVELOPMENT

NATURAL TRAINING

NATURAL NUTRITION

NATURAL HEALTH CARE

HEALTH DISORDERS

FLU CARRIERS

A flu carrier is a cat that carries and sheds a respiratory virus although it may show no clinical signs of disease. About 80 per cent of cats that have an acute episode of feline herpesvirus (FHV) will become chronic carriers. They shed virus intermittently, usually about a week after an episode of stress. A "stress" can be a fight with another cat, going into a cattery, producing kittens, or moving home. With feline calcivirus (FCV), the other main cause of flu, about 20 to 25 per cent of cats that experienced acute bouts of illness go on to become chronic carriers. These cats may shed FCV constantly, for the rest of their lives, while showing no signs of disease.

NOSE TO NOSE

A cat's mother used to be its most likely source of upper respiratory tract infection, but nowadays cats from all sorts of backgrounds are often housed together, allowing infections to thrive. Kittens inherit only temporary protection against infections to which their mother has been exposed.

CONVENTIONAL TREATMENTS

Viruses are the most common cause of respiratory infections in cats; bacteria and yeast are secondary causes. Conventional vets use broncho-dilators, decongestants, and antibiotics to relieve clinical signs, while expectorants help loosen phlegm. If allergy is involved, and allergic bronchitis or asthma ensues, vets often use antihistamines and corticosteroids. If fluid builds up in the chest, this is drained surgically and the cat is usually hospitalized while the condition is investigated. Diagnostic techniques include physical examination, x-rays, respiratory tract swabs, blood sampling, and stool examinations for lungworm larvae or eggs.

CHECKLIST

The following measures are helpful to asthmatic cats:

- Avoid aerosols such as hair spray, household cleaners, and flea-control products.
- Avoid powdered carpet fresheners and flea powders.
- Prevent smoke from cigarettes, fireplaces, and wood stoves.
- Install an air purifier where your cat sleeps.
- Know the phone number and location of your 24-hour emergency veterinary facility in case of an acute asthmatic attack.

COMPLEMENTARY TREATMENTS

Holistic veterinarians will advise that cats with respiratory problems avoid polluted environments. Installing a room ionizer reduces potential allergens, and a humidifier keeps the air moist. Ensure that surplus weight is lost. Overweight cats have more difficulty coping with respiratory conditions.

OSTEOPATHY Soft-tissue techniques affecting chest muscles may improve the breathing capacity of cats with chronic respiratory disorders. *See page 79.*

THERAPEUTIC MASSAGE Massaging the neck and chest and gentle tapping over the lungs may help a congested cat to cough up obstructing mucus. *See pages 80-81.*

HYDROTHERAPY Steam inhalation may loosen up phlegm and relieve bronchial congestion. Placing a well-insulated hot-water bottle in the cat's bed to ensure the chest is warm may also loosen catarrh and ease congestion. *See page 82.*

HERBALISM A variety of herbs may be recommended to manage blocked sinuses and nasal congestion. These include hyssop herb, *Hyssopus officinalis,* cinnamon bark, *Cinnamomum zeylanicum,* celery seed, *Apium graveolens,* and elder flower, *Sambucus nigra.* Garlic, *Allium sativum,* and *Echinacea* may boost the immune system. *See pages 88-91.*

HOMEOPATHY *Kali bich.* is used for tenacious nasal discharge while *Pulsatilla* is recommended for a looser catarrh. *Silicea* is used to treat sinusitis. *Arsen. alb.* is commonly used for a harsh cough, *Bryonia* for a dry cough, and *Ipecac* for coughing spasms accompanied by retching. If a cough is heart-related, *Spongia* may be recommended. For cats with chlamydia conjunctivitis, *Argent nit.* is sometimes recommended for bathing the eyes. *See pages 92-93.*

AROMA THERAPY A holistic vet may recommend placing a vaporizer or diffuser in the room and using eucalyptus, tea tree, lemon, lavender, or cedarwood essential oils to relieve nasal, sinus, or windpipe congestion. *See page 100.*

ESSENTIAL OIL OF EUCALYPTUS

THE CENTRAL NERVOUS SYSTEM

THE BRAIN AND NERVOUS SYSTEM, evolution's most complex structure, require vast amounts of energy to function. The brain, for example, makes up less than a fiftieth of a cat's weight, yet at least a fifth of the entire blood supply flows directly from the heart to the brain. Protected by the skeleton, this system has evolved little capacity for self-repair; any damage is often irreparable.

CHECKLIST

If your cat has a seizure, do the following:

- Keep your hands away from the cat's mouth. Unintentionally, it might bite.

- Gently pull the cat by its scruff away from dangers such as stairways.

- Place something soft like a cushion under its head.

- If the convulsion lasts more than six minutes, take your cat immediately to the vet.

- After the seizure, comfort it if it seems anxious.

WHAT THE NERVOUS SYSTEM DOES

The brain's billions of cells communicate with every living cell in a cat's body through chemicals called neurotransmitters. The brain, through the spinal cord and nerves, co-ordinates all activities, thoughts, senses, feelings, movements, and body functions. As time progresses, nerve cells diminish in number and in their connections to other nerve cells. There is no way to halt this loss of nerve cells, but experiments show that mental and physical stimulation increase the number of interconnections between remaining nerve cells. More connections mean improved physical and mental abilities. The saying "use it or lose it" is particularly appropriate to the brain and nerves.

WHAT CAN GO WRONG

Physical injuries are the most common cause of brain and nerve damage. About 40 per cent of road-traffic accidents involve head injuries, while broken backs, with a severed spinal cord, are also not uncommon.

ARE CATS AT RISK FROM RABIES?

In regions where rabies is endemic, vaccination of dogs has reduced the incidence of clinical rabies dramatically. However, in some regions cats are not routinely vaccinated, and there the number of cats contracting rabies often exceeds the number of dogs. The only protection you can give your cat from rabies is to have it immunized by vaccination. The vet will administer the injection, the ideal site for which is located deep in the muscles of the right hind leg.

Infections such as rabies, feline infectious peritonitis (FIP), and toxoplasmosis can cross into the brain, causing convulsions, behaviour changes, or paralysis. Technically, infections cause an inflammation to the brain itself (encephalitis) or to the envelope surrounding the brain (meningitis).

Parasites such as roundworm larvae can enter the brain and cause convulsions. Other parasites, such as certain female ticks, may transmit tick-borne paralysis, which deadens the brain's control over the body.

Selective breeding has increased the incidence of lysosomal storage disease in some purebreds, a condition in which enzymes do not do their job properly, leading to a build-up of waste products. Neurological signs include seizures. Spina bifida, causing motor disability, is not uncommon in Manx cats.

Poisons against which the cat has not evolved protection can also enter the brain and cause damage. Both natural and synthetic chemicals can be dangerous. The natural pyrethrins from *Chrysanthemum cinerariifolium*, used in some insecticides, can be toxic to the nervous system. Organochlorine pesticides, formulated for use on dogs, can cause seizures if used on cats. (Never use any product on a cat unless it states specifically that it is safe for use on cats.) Ethylene glycol antifreeze, which some cats find tasty, causes kidney damage and associated seizures. Use propylene glycol antifreeze, which is less toxic.

RABIES TRANSMISSION
Evolution creates "clever" pathogens. A fox bite "injects" rabies virus into the cat. The virus travels via nerves to the brain where it causes damage. After stimulating the cat's rage centre and paralyzing its throat, the virus congregates in saliva for onward transmission through bites to another animal.

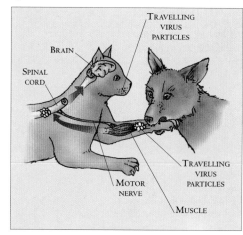

BRAIN

SPINAL CORD

TRAVELLING VIRUS PARTICLES

MOTOR NERVE

TRAVELLING VIRUS PARTICLES

MUSCLE

With the aid of new diagnostic techniques, such as MRI scans, vets now know that brain tumours are more common than was once appreciated. These are most commonly lymphomas, associated with feline leukemia virus (FeLV) infection, and meningiomas, tumours of the lining of the brain. Strokes are uncommon in cats and are usually associated with kidney deterioration or an overactive thyroid gland. Even with the best care, over time, brain and nerve function diminishes. Most cats over 16 years old experience forms of senile dementia in which brain cells progressively degenerate.

CONVENTIONAL TREATMENTS

Prevention is always easier than cure. Vets will recommend vaccination against rabies and leukaemia for cats at risk from these infections, worming to prevent parasites, and tick-control measures in regions where these are a problem. Avoidance of roads reduces the risk of trauma from traffic accidents. Trauma is treated with painkillers and corticosteroids to reduce neural inflammation. If the cause of seizures can be determined, the imbalance is corrected but this is rarely possible. Phenobarbitol is used as an anti-convulsant, but with time the liver becomes more efficient at breaking down phenobarb so increasing doses are necessary. Surgery is often successful in treating cats with neurological problems caused by meningioma brain tumours. The drug capergoline is considered effective in slowing senile dementia.

POTENTIAL DISORDER
Any Manx cat may suffer from a congenital neurological disorder called spina bifida, which interferes with normal nerve transmission. Completely tailless cats may also have malformed pelvic and caudal (tail) nerves, which can lead to incontinence.

NATURAL DEVELOPMENT

NATURAL TRAINING

NATURAL NUTRITION

NATURAL HEALTH CARE

HEALTH DISORDERS

COMPLEMENTARY TREATMENTS

Holistic vets emphasize the mind-body relationship when treating brain and nerve disorders. They look at the diet to ensure that optimum levels of nutrients are available for necessary repairs. They may suggest physical or mental therapies that stimulate or relax the nervous system.

ACUPRESSURE Under a practitioner's guidance, acupressure at an appropriate site may diminish neural pain. See page 74.

TRIGGER POINT THERAPY A specialist can locate muscle trigger points that have developed because of an abnormal gait, one that originally developed to protect the site of a nerve injury. See page 76.

CHIROPRACTIC AND OSTEOPATHY Manipulation can release a trapped nerve. These therapies may increase mobility after spinal injury by improving circulation in appropriate muscles. See pages 78-79.

THERAPEUTIC MASSAGE Touch is comforting to some cats and reduces anxiety in individuals coping with the sudden loss of motor function. Massage may be comforting to individuals recovering from seizures. It may also delay the onset of senile dementia. See pages 80-81.

HYDROTHERAPY A bag of frozen peas is an excellent ice pack, diminishing local nerve pain when applied for 10 minutes. Depending upon the type of neurological pain, this may be alternated with a hot-water bottle wrapped in a towel, also applied for 10 minutes. See page 82.

NUTRITIONAL THERAPIES Vitamin C may play an important role in treating spinal pain, possibly because it improves the quality of connective tissue. Vitamin C is also required for the synthesis of the neurotransmitters serotonin and epinephrine and for the manufacture of the body's own anti-inflammatory, cortisol. The B vitamins are important for nerve-cell functioning. Sources include pork, liver, milk, and brewer's yeast. Antioxidant vitamins, minerals such as magnesium, and fish oil may aid recovery after a neurological accident involving cell destruction. See pages 86-87.

HERBALISM For senility a veterinary herbalist may suggest ginseng root, *Panax ginseng*, myrrh resin, *Commiphora myrrha*, or Chebulic myrobalan fruit, *Terminalia chebula*. *Ginkgo biloba* is thought to boost blood flow to the brain and may delay the development of senile dementia. St. John's wort, *Hypericum perforatum*, is thought to have painkilling properties. Yarrow infusion, *Achillea millefolium*, is thought to improve circulation and lower blood pressure. See pages 88-91.

HOMEOPATHY *Aconite 6c* and *Hypericum 6c* are often considered for neurological pain. See pages 92-93.

PHEROMONE THERAPY Pheromones distract a cat from its pain and stimulate neural activity. See page 100.

ST. JOHN'S WORT

THE ENDOCRINE SYSTEM

YOUR CAT'S BODY has an amazing ability to respond to its environment. While the brain and nervous system initiate instant changes in body function, hormones are responsible for long-term balance of body activities. If hormone production does not turn on or off properly, a variety of medical conditions develop, some subtle and difficult to diagnose, others devastating and life-threatening.

STRESS AND BLOOD SUGAR

Sugar diabetes is common in cats. Some statistics show the amazingly high incidence of one in 400 individuals. This may be an inflated figure because many cats, when held while a blood sample is drawn, experience an immediate surge of blood sugar. An elevated blood sugar level on a routine blood sample does not necessarily mean diabetes. It may only be a temporary sugar response to stress.

WHAT THE SYSTEM DOES

Hormones are chemical messengers that are produced in endocrine glands throughout the body. Every single cell in the body has receptor sites for one or more hormones, which orchestrate all body processes. The pituitary gland at the base of the brain, the "master gland", produces one hormone that instructs the kidneys how much to concentrate urine, another that controls growth, and others that instruct other glands, the thyroids, adrenals, ovaries, or testes in their own hormone production.

Thyroid hormones influence growth, energy production, and energy consumption. (The tiny parathyroid glands are responsible

WHAT CAUSES HYPERTHYROIDISM?

The first cases of hyperthyroidism were reported from the east coast of America in 1979. Cases from the west coast followed shortly after. By 1980, cases were reported in Canada, throughout Europe, and from Australia and New Zealand. Although the cause of this "epidemic" remains a mystery, since that time statistics have been gathered that show that certain chemicals, and even lifestyles, increase a cat's risk of becoming hyperthyroid. Cats living indoors are four times more likely to develop this condition than outdoor cats. However, exposure to lawn herbicides, fertilizers, and pesticides increases outdoor cats' risk by 3.5. Being fed mostly canned food increases a cat's risk by 3.4, as do regular flea treatments.

for calcium metabolism.) The adrenal glands produce cortisol, the body's natural cortico-steroid, and adrenalin, both central to the "fight or flight" reaction. In clusters on the surface of the pancreas, cells produce insulin, vital for sugar metabolism.

5. MESSAGE CANCELLED
Pituitary gland receives adrenal hormone and cuts output of adrenal-stimulating hormone.

4. ADRENAL GLAND ACTS
Adrenal gland receives message and releases (i) hormones raising cat's state of alert and (ii) hormone that will return to pituitary gland acknowledging receipt of original message.

KIDNEY

1. DANGER
Unfamiliar scent reported to brain. Triggers activity in hypothalamus (region of brain in charge of pituitary gland).

3. HORMONE IN TRANSIT
Pituitary hormone is carried round the body by the bloodstream.

2. PITUITARY GLAND TAKES COMMAND
Pituitary gland is activated and releases adrenal-gland stimulating hormone.

THE "MASTER" GLAND
The brain and endocrine systems work together. Brain information is passed to the pituitary or "master" gland, which controls all other endocrine activity.

WHAT CAN GO WRONG

Sugar diabetes (*Diabetes mellitus*) is a disorder in which a cat cannot use glucose, the body's main energy source. The cat may become thirsty, lose weight, suffer fatigue, and have recurrent infections and eye and circulation problems. An increase in blood sugar in cats is usually caused by an inability of cells to use insulin properly. This feline form of diabetes is most frequently found in cats that are overweight. Stress causes the release of natural cortisol, which makes fat cells even less sensitive to insulin.

The most common hormonal problem in cats is overactive thyroid glands – known as hyperthyroidism. Although the cause of the relatively recent epidemic of this condition in cats is unknown, there is much speculation. Recently, scientists have discovered that some natural and synthetic substances can affect hormones. These so called "endocrine disrupters" are chemicals that can either mimic or block normal endocrine processes. Environmental contaminants such as PCBs and dioxins are known endocrine disrupters. Some endocrinologists believe that the cat's thyroid is a sensitive marker for changes effected by minute quantities of "thyroid disrupter" in the environment.

DISEASE AND HEREDITY
Some endocrine problems are also influenced by hereditary components. The Siamese cat is 10 times less likely to become hyperthyroid than any other breed of cat.

CONVENTIONAL TREATMENTS

Treatment of endocrine disorders is one of the great success stories of 20th-century medicine. Overweight diabetic cats are fed a controlled high-fibre diet, which helps weight loss and stabilizes blood-sugar levels. Insulin is given by injection. Underweight diabetics are fed a high-calorie diet to gain weight, then are gradually switched to a high-fibre diet. Thyroid-suppressing medication is given to hyperthyroid cats, or the offending glands are surgically removed.

COMPLEMENTARY TREATMENTS

Complementary therapies often approach endocrine problems obliquely. Rather than stimulating or suppressing endocrine glands directly, they aim to encourage the immune system to react normally and stabilize hormonal function through diet, lifestyle changes, gentle exercise, and supplements.

NUTRITIONAL THERAPIES Vitamin B6 is often recommended as it is important in the synthesis of most hormones. Nutritionists advise that cats with hyperthyroidism should not be given foods or chemicals that may stimulate thyroid activity. Canned cat foods, especially those with fish, may have widely varying amounts of iodine in their contents. Avoid high-iodine foods, or abrupt switching from low- to high-

iodine food or vice versa. Avoid thiamine supplements in hyperthyroid cats. Iron, zinc, and selenium are important in regulating thyroid metabolism. Ensure adequate but not excessive amounts in any diet. Holistic vets may sometimes recommend chromium supplementation (in brewer's yeast) for diabetic cats. Recommended diets may include high-fibre wholegrain complex carbohydrates found in wholemeal bread, rice, pasta, oatmeal, and bran. Fibre helps to promotes weight loss, slows glucose absorption from the gut, reduces post-eating fluctuations in blood glucose, and improves the cat's control of excess blood sugar. Do not give foods containing sugar. If your cat is constipated, try adding canned pumpkin to its food. *See pages 86-87.*

HERBALISM Veterinary herbalists use a variety of herbs to treat cats with overactive thyroids. These include lemon balm, *Melissa officinalis*, motherwort, *Leonurus cardiaca*, and wild thyme, *Thymus serpyllum*. They suggest following orthodox therapy for diabetes, including diet management and insulin injections, but may recommend herbs said to reduce blood sugar. These include marsh mallow root, *Althaea officinalis*, coriander seed, *Coriandrum sativum*, and nettle, *Urtica dioica. See pages 90-91.*

MARSH MALLOW

EMOTIONS AND BEHAVIOUR

ANXIETY IS NOT A DISEASE. Unpleasant emotions are a defensive response to circumstances in which a cat finds itself. During stress, adrenalin acts within seconds, while cortisol is longer-acting, backing up the stress response. There is no harm in short bouts of stress. Chronic stress stimulates a sustained release of stress chemicals that cause damage to the body, including the immune system.

CHECKLIST
Reduce the stress of a visit to the vet by doing the following:

- Use the cat carrier as a safe, secure den at home.

- See a vet who really likes cats.

- Transport your cat in its enclosed carrier.

- Talk to it quietly.

- At the vet's, prevent dogs from sniffing the carrier.

- If possible, wait in a cats-only waiting area.

- Remove your cat from its carrier yourself.

THE VALUE OF EMOTIONS
What we think of as unpleasant emotions, feelings like anxiety, worry, or stress, are defensive reactions for cats. They evolved to protect them from threats and dangers. Anxiety is like a chemical first-aid kit. The cortex of the cat's brain thinks there is a stress, communicates through the limbic system with the rest of the brain, and triggers a cascade of chemical changes that affect the entire body. These short-acting chemical changes are vital for survival. The chemicals themselves are dissipated through activity, such as escaping from danger.

In conditions of chronic stress, chemical changes occur but are not broken down. The American neurologist Robert Sapolsky says: "People with chronic depressions are those whose cortex habitually whispers sad things to the rest of the brain." This "whispering" takes place in the limbic system.

DO CATS GRIEVE?
Of course they do. The level of anxiety a cat experiences when people or other animals they are close to die, or simply move away, varies with the individual cat's personality. When an animal death occurs, whenever possible let the survivor see and scent the body of the recently deceased animal. In the following weeks, give the survivor greater attention. Increased activity with others is almost always beneficial. In rare circumstances, sedative herbs may be required.

THE ROLE OF THE LIMBIC SYSTEM
Mind and body meet in the brain's limbic system. This primitive area of the cat's brain orchestrates instincts and emotions. The nervous and hormonal systems are controlled by the limbic system through its production of chemical messengers called neurotransmitters. The role of neurotransmitters is profound. For example, serotonin is the neurotransmitter linked with mood enhancement. In people, drugs can be used to affect brain chemicals such as serotonin, but non-physical therapies such as counselling affect them too. This is also true for cats. Desensitizing, scenting pheromones, and physical activity can affect neurotransmitter levels, behaviour, and emotions.

THE CAT'S BRAIN
While there are discrete regions of the brain, such as the cerebral cortex and cerebellum, all areas are connected by the "limbic system". Limbic function may vary slightly between breeds. A recent British survey found that Siamese, Burmese, and Birmans are the breeds most often treated for behaviour problems.

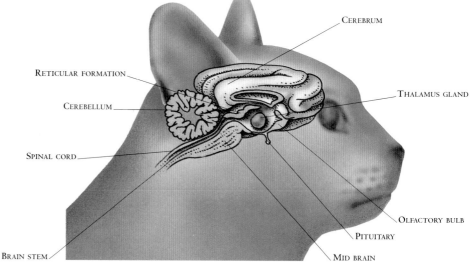

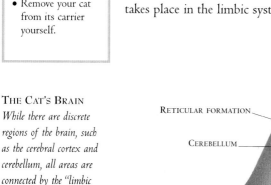

CEREBRUM

THALAMUS GLAND

RETICULAR FORMATION

CEREBELLUM

SPINAL CORD

OLFACTORY BULB

PITUITARY

BRAIN STEM

MID BRAIN

BEHAVIOUR PROBLEMS

Cats develop rational fears, of veterinary clinics for example, but also irrational fears of non-threatening sights, sounds, or situations. Anxiety, part of natural "fight or flight", is normal in many circumstances but may become excessive in situations such as being taken in a car. This may lead to panic attacks or compulsive behaviour. If your cat compulsively licks or grooms, miaows repetitively, or sucks on fabrics, it may be suffering from a physical problem or an obsessive-compulsive disorder.

An inability to relax is a form of feline anxiety common in elderly cats. Depression can be difficult to diagnose in cats. It may manifest itself in a decreased appetite, clinging behaviour, irritability, or lethargy. Grieving occurs in cats when an important member of their "family" leaves, although this too is almost impossible to define using standard veterinary medical definitions.

DISPLACED AGGRESSION
It is in the nature of cats to control their emotions, but pent-up stress needs to be released. After a stressful episode, such as a visit to the vet, a cat may lash out aggressively at an innocent victim, such as its owner or another cat.

CONVENTIONAL TREATMENTS

Increasingly, conventional vets are treating feline emotional disorders with a combination of sedative and anti-anxiety drugs, as well as counter-conditioning or desensitization training. Drugs can affect neurochemicals such as serotonin. A typical drug may raise serotonin levels. This can have a profound and not always anticipated effect on a cat's behaviour. Behavioural therapy is vital; drugs alone do not cure emotional problems.

COMPLEMENTARY TREATMENTS

Holistic vets consider diet to be central to treating emotional disorders. They recommend natural sources of the amino acid tryptophan, needed for the manufacture of serotonin and thought to help relieve depression. Mind-body therapies are commonly used, together with herbal and other treatments that reduce anxiety or increase concentration. Desensitizing a cat to its emotional problems, increased play, and improved relationships are integral to all complementary therapies.

THERAPEUTIC MASSAGE Massage, mental activity, and physical exercise are all beneficial for reducing anxiety in cats. Physical activity in particular has a "tranquillizing" effect on anxiety, reducing muscle tension and releasing mood-enhancing endorphins. *See pages 80-81.*

NUTRITIONAL THERAPIES Foods such as fish, chicken, and turkey are good sources of the amino acid tryptophan. Tryptophan is necessary for serotonin production. For

hyperactive cats, avoid any food (or drugs) with the colorant tartrazine (E102), which is especially suspect for enhancing nervous hyperactivity. Ensure adequate levels of B vitamins and zinc to control nervousness. Some holistic vets believe there may be a relationship between high-carbohydrate diets and nervous aggression. *See pages 86-87.*

HERBALISM For anxiety, herbal vets may suggest sedative herbs such as valerian root, *Valeriana officinalis*, guelder rose bark, *Viburnum opulus*, lemon balm, *Melissa officinalis*, Roman chamomile flower, *Chamaemelum nobile*, and lettuce leaf, *Lactuca virosa*. Hops, *Humulus lupulus*, may also have a sedative effect, calming nervous individuals. St. John's wort, *Hypericum perforatum*, is three times better than placebo for treating mild depression in people according to a report in the British Medical Journal in 1996. It is used with increasing frequency as "background therapy" for anxious cats undergoing desensitization training. Catmint, *Nepeta cataria*, is uplifting for cats. *See pages 88-91.*

HOMEOPATHY *Ignatia* is recommended for cats that are pining for their owners or grieving. *Pulsatilla* may be given for cats that, for emotional reasons, have become reclusive, while *Belladonna* is suggested for excitable individuals. *Nux vomica* is added for anxious cats that suffer from car sickness. *See pages 92-93.*

BACH FLOWER REMEDIES Rescue Remedy is frequently recommended to reduce anxiety while visiting the vet. *See pages 94-95.*

PHEROMONE THERAPY Extracted natural pheromones are commonly and successfully used to control a range of emotional problems in cats. *See page 100.*

HOP STROBILE

EYE AND NOSE DISORDERS

NATURAL DEVELOPMENT

NATURAL TRAINING

NATURAL NUTRITION

NATURAL HEALTH CARE

HEALTH DISORDERS

THE CAT'S SENSES, which transfer information about the environment to the brain, are well maintained. The eyes are constantly washed clean with tears laden with defensive chemicals. The nose is flushed by a natural bacteria-killing discharge. If either of these intricate structures is harmed, whether by infection, foreign bodies, or metabolic disease, the resulting medical problems can be complex.

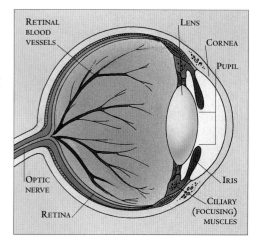

THE EYE
The cat's eyes are more sensitive than ours. The lens is much larger, capturing more light. A layer of reflective cells behind the retina bounces light back through the retina, allowing more information to be obtained even in the depth of night.

ESSENTIAL SCENTS

It is vital for cats that they can both smell and produce scent, because they recognize each other by nose-to-nose or nose-to-genital sniffing. Gland odours are produced by bacteria in the glands. Anal sacs may become populated by the wrong type of bacteria, leading to discomfort. It may be necessary to flush the sacs with antiseptic, which may temporarily interfere with odour signals.

HOW THE EYES WORK

The tough, transparent cornea protects the eye but allows light to pass through the pupil onto the lens, which focuses light onto the retina at the back. The amount of light entering is controlled by contracting or dilating muscles in the coloured iris. The nictitating membrane acts as a windscreen wiper, removing debris. This, and the rest of the conjunctival membrane lining the eyelids, is constantly bathed in a protective film of tears that ensures clear vision, prevents drying, and controls infection.

EYE PROBLEMS

Conjunctivitis is an inflammation of the eye's protective mucous membrane. It may involve redness, swelling, and a watery or mucoid discharge. If infected, the discharge generally becomes yellow-green. Chlamydia conjunctivitis produces a sticky substance that glues shut kittens' eyes. Corneal injuries may be caused by trauma or a lack of tears. A cataract develops when the transparent

proteins in the lens become cloudy. This may be hereditary, or more commonly caused by diabetes, injury, overuse of corticosteroids, even poisoning. The development of a cataract is irreversible. Glaucoma is a build-up of pressure inside the eye and may be a consequence of internal damage, such as inflammation of the muscles supporting the iris. Drainage channels become blocked.

Progressive retinal atrophy (PRA) is a rare hereditary deterioration of vision, leading to blindness, in which the blood vessels to the retina shrivel. Anatomical faults around the eyes are not uncommon in some breeds. A tear overflow occurs in flat-faced breeds such as the Persian. The natural drainage of tears into the nose becomes blocked because of the angle of the nasolacrimal duct, causing tear overflow and staining. Eye problems may also be a sign that there is a metabolic disease elsewhere in the body.

HOW SMELL AND TASTE WORK

Smell is the least understood of the cat's senses. Scent chemicals activate at least eight different types of chemoreceptors in the nose, mouth, and throat, most with direct access to the brain's limbic system. The

THE SENSE OF SMELL
Scent-sensitive cells lining the nasal cavity connect directly to the brain. These cells pick up scent chemicals, convert them to information, and feed it to the limbic system of the brain, which affects behaviours such as aggression or euphoria.

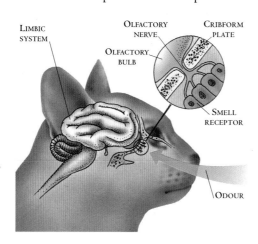

vomeronasal organ in the roof of the mouth "scents" sex-related pheromones. To get to the vomeronasal organ, these scents must be pumped from the mouth up to the scenting organ. Cats do this with a curious mouth gape. Scent is produced by body glands and is placed on objects and people. There are over 40 components to feline facial gland secretions alone. By stroking our pets we anoint them with our own scent.

SCENTING AND TASTING PROBLEMS

A flat face reduces the nasal-lining surface area for scenting. Small nostrils impede natural scenting ability. Nasal infections or foreign bodies, such as inhaled grass seeds, cause inflammation and associated loss of scenting ability. Tumours or polyps can develop in the nasal chambers.

Some respiratory tract infections damage the tongue and taste sensation. Tumours may develop on the tongue. Smell may also be impaired in hyperthyroidism and diabetes.

CONVENTIONAL TREATMENTS

Conjunctivitis is often treated with antibiotic, anti-inflammatory, or antihistamine drops, ointments, and lotions. Chlamydial eye infections in cats require weeks of antibiotic

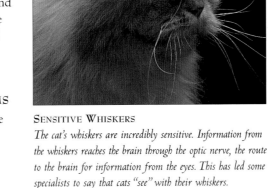

SENSITIVE WHISKERS
The cat's whiskers are incredibly sensitive. Information from the whiskers reaches the brain through the optic nerve, the route to the brain for information from the eyes. This has led some specialists to say that cats "see" with their whiskers.

treatment. A vaccine is available to control chlamydia in catteries where the condition is chronic. If cataracts develop, your vet will investigate for undiagnosed diabetes. When cataracts cause blindness and the retina still works, the offending lenses can be surgically removed. Nasal infections are treated with oral antibiotics. If possible, foreign bodies, tumours, and polyps are surgically removed. The sense of smell is vital to cats because they recognize each other by scent.

CHECKLIST

- Sight gradually deteriorates with increasing age.
- Distance vision remains acute for longer than near vision.
- Age-related "sclerosis" (hardening) of the lenses occurs in cats over 10 years old. This naturally developing cloudiness is often mistaken for a cataract.
- Scent stimulates appetite.
- Metabolic diseases, as well as upper respiratory tract infections, interfere with scenting.
- If your cat has stopped eating, try feeding foods with intense odours.

COMPLEMENTARY TREATMENTS

Many eye and nose problems are associated with allergy. Holistic vets will investigate diet and environment to determine causes of problems. They often recommend large quantities of natural antioxidants in the diet to assist both sight and scent. Some feel that systemic antibiotics may interfere with bacterial fermentation in scent glands that produce natural odours. This could lead to problems in recognition and increased fighting.

NUTRITIONAL THERAPIES Naturopaths believe that cataracts may result from free-radical damage and often recommend dietary supplementation with vitamin E and selenium to slow the development. Vitamin C and zinc are also suggested to

slow cataract formation. Antioxidants may be recommended to slow the development of PRA. Vitamin A is considered important for strengthening the layer of lutein and zeaxanthin in the retina. *See pages 86-87.*

HERBALISM To soothe sore, inflamed, "allergic" eyes or sore nostrils, a herbal vet may suggest bathing the eyes with a lightly boiled decoction of any of fennel seed, *Foeniculum vulgare*, eyebright, *Euphrasia officinalis*, or elder flower, *Sambucus nigra*. To control bacterial eye infections, decoctions of either fennel seed or Roman chamomile flower, *Chamaemelum nobile*, are used. Greater celandine, *Chelidonium majus*, infusions may also be used to bathe sore eyes. Cod-liver oil may be applied as a lubricant for cats

with a crusty nose. Infusion of mullein, *Verbascum thapsis*, may be suggested to help clear blocked sinuses. **Warning**: don't smear decongestants on a cat's coat. Some may be toxic if swallowed. *See pages 88-91.*

HOMEOPATHY *Apis mel.* may be used to bathe sore eyelids while *Arsen. alb.* is used for watery, inflamed eyes. *Arnica* is recommended if there is any bruising around the eyes or nose. *See pages 92-93.*

ARNICA FLOWER

EAR DISORDERS

156

A CAT'S EARS ARE RESPONSIBLE both for its hearing and its balance. Erect ear flaps and long ear canals capture and amplify sound. The ears are lubricated by bacteria-killing wax that prevents infection within the external ear. If the balance of protective micro-organisms in the ear is upset, infection by bacteria, yeasts, or other fungi may develop. The skin that covers the ear flaps may be prone to allergy.

CHECKLIST

- A small amount of ear wax (clear, yellow, or brown) is normal and protective.

- Cats shake their heads when they have external ear canal problems.

- Middle-ear conditions may cause a head tilt.

- Inner-ear problems affect balance and may cause rapid jerking movements of the eyes (nystagmus).

- Never use an alcohol-based solution to clean the ears.

- Never push a cotton bud in the ear. It acts like a plunger, pushing debris onto the ear drum.

- Flush out debris with warm mineral oil or olive oil.

HOW THE EARS WORK

The ear flap, called the "pinna", and the external ear canal capture sound and convey it to the middle and inner ear. Airwaves, striking the ear drum (tympanic membrane), trigger movements in tiny bones (ossicles), which in turn affect fluid-filled chambers in the inner ears. This stimulates nerve impulses that travel directly to the brain, where they are perceived as sounds. The Eustachian tubes, from the middle ears to the throat, prevent too much pressure from building up in the middle ears.

Deep within the ear are the organs of balance. These multiple-chambered structures contain fine hairs that are only visible with the greatest magnification, and which are sensitive to changes in acceleration, orientation, and movement. Together with rotational-movement receptors in the joints, these are responsible for a cat's magnificent sense of three-dimensional balance.

DO CATS HAVE A SIXTH SENSE?

How do cats seem to know you are about to come through the door? Can they predict earthquakes? Do they have a natural homing instinct?

Just as, inexplicably, cats sometimes recover from presumed fatal diseases, there are unanswered mysteries in their behaviour. Knowing you are about to come home can be explained by circadian rhythm, the cat's genetically controlled biological clock. There is now evidence that cats are sensitive to electrostatic changes in the atmosphere that precede certain types of earthquakes. This may be a function of magnetite, found in the cat's brain cells. But how a cat finds its way home over territory it has never traversed still remains a mystery.

EAR PROBLEMS

Ear flaps are prone to frostbite in winter and, in white cats, sunburn in summer. They are also tasty targets for biting insects like mosquitoes. Cats are adept at flattening their ears back for protection during fights but traumatic abscesses are still fairly common. The external ear canal is like a warm, moist incubator. Infections caused by bacteria or fungi (such as yeasts) are a not uncommon consequence of ear-mite infestation, which stimulates an over-production of earwax. Left untreated, this may cause local tumours called ceruminomas to grow on the ear canal

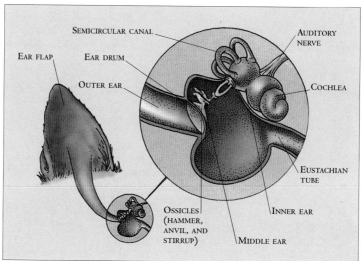

SEMICIRCULAR CANAL

AUDITORY NERVE

EAR FLAP

EAR DRUM

OUTER EAR

COCHLEA

EUSTACHIAN TUBE

OSSICLES (HAMMER, ANVIL, AND STIRRUP)

INNER EAR

MIDDLE EAR

HEARING

The outer ear receives sound and directs it to the drum, which translates it into mechanical vibrations. In the middle ear, the vibrations are transmitted by ossicles to the inner ear. Here they are translated again, this time into electrochemical impulses that travel through the nervous system to the brain.

wall, eventually obliterating it. The affected ear may be red, uncomfortable, and often sensitive to touch. Depending upon the cause there may be a brown, yellow, white, or even green discharge.

Middle- and inner-ear conditions are usually caused by spread of infection, either from the external ear, or up the Eustachian tube from the back of the throat as the result of an upper respiratory tract infection. Infected mucus may accumulate in the sinuses. An affected cat sneezes, shakes its head, and may vomit, have a loss of balance, or appear uncoordinated. Non-cancerous polyps may also develop on the wall of an inflamed ear canal.

Deafness may be acquired or, in certain blue-eyed, white-haired cats, hereditary. Some drugs are known to damage hearing.

CONVENTIONAL TREATMENTS
Veterinarians generously use antibiotic, anti-inflammatory, and anti-parasitic ear drops and lotions to control external ear infections. Middle-ear infections are usually treated with oral antibiotics and sometimes decongestants. When balance is affected, anti-emetic drugs are used. Because of the ears' long, curving

anatomy, severe or chronic external ear disease may have to be treated by syringing under deep sedation or general anaesthesia. Surgically opening the ear canal to remove one side of the funnel may be necessary to control chronic ear infections that result in constricted canals, and for individuals that have developed ceruminomas. Haematomas (blood-filled swellings) caused by excessive head shaking or injury are surgically drained.

Deafness may be caused by nerve damage or problems in conduction of sound. (It may be unilateral in white cats with one blue eye and one yellow eye.) Hearing can be tested using a technique called Brainstem Auditory Evoked Response (BAER). Conductive deafness is usually caused by inflammation, age-related nerve deterioration, foreign objects, or copious hard wax. Vets will often use Elizabethan collars to prevent a cat from scratching at an ear undergoing treatment or recovering from surgery.

A condition affecting balance on one side, called vestibular syndrome, may be mistaken for a stroke. Cats with vestibular syndrome are treated with anti-nausea medication. They can sometimes recover spontaneously over a period of several weeks.

BALANCE
The cat is renowned for its elegant righting reflex. It can rotate itself 180° in just 60 cm (2 ft). This ability depends on an efficient vestibular apparatus in the ear. Microscopic hairs in the fluid-filled semi-circular canals are sensitive to changes in orientation.

NATURAL DEVELOPMENT

NATURAL TRAINING

NATURAL NUTRITION

NATURAL HEALTH CARE

HEALTH DISORDERS

COMPLEMENTARY TREATMENTS

Holistic vets emphasize the importance of prevention. They recommend "non-allergenic" diets and effective ear-mite control. They counsel leaving the ears alone unless there is a problem, advising against preventative cleansing to remove potential wax build-up.

ACUPUNCTURE The nausea associated with vestibular syndrome and other conditions affecting balance, as well as car sickness, may be treated with appropriate acupuncture. *See pages 72-73.*

NUTRITIONAL THERAPIES Naturopathic vets feel that many ear problems are the result of immune disorders. They will ask about your cat's diet, checking for possible food intolerance. Vitamin D is often

suggested as a supplement for cats going deaf. Vitamin A is said to help the cochlea function efficiently and may be recommended together with vitamin E. *See pages 86-87.*

HERBALISM Mildly acidic decoctions kill yeast. They may be beneficial for loosening wax build-up. A vinegar/water mixture is often recommended. Olive or almond oil may help to clear residual wax after an ear infection or infestation. Damage to the ear flap from fighting may be cleaned with witch hazel. For white cats, prone to sunburn on their ear tips, aloe vera may be soothing. Marigold, *Calendula officinalis*, is used for cleaning inflamed ear canals. Ginger, *Zingiber officinale*, and *Ginkgo biloba* are said by some to reduce deafness by improving circulation to the

ear. Over-use of topical herb solutions can increase the possibility of an inflammatory sensitivity response. *See pages 88-91.*

HOMEOPATHY *Arnica* is used when there is bruising to the ear flap or if a blood blister has developed. *Kali mur.* is used to alleviate pressure in the middle or inner ear. *Aconite 6c* and *Belladonna 6c* are both used for ear infections. *See pages 92-93.*

BACH FLOWER REMEDIES Rescue Remedy may calm cats frightened by ear pain. *See page 95.*

ACONITE LEAF

INDEX

ACKNOWLEDGMENTS

Author's Acknowledgments

Researching and writing about evolutionary or "natural" veterinary care has been fascinating. And practical. It's satisfying to be able to incorporate new ideas into veterinary practice. Veterinary colleagues around the world, at universities, and in private practice contributed their observations and experience in using methods other than licenced pharmaceuticals or surgical interventions to prevent or contain a variety of medical conditions. My grateful thanks go to:

In Australia, Liz Frank and Clive Eger, Murdoch University, and Kersti Seksel; in Canada, Brenda Bonnett and Wendy Parker, University of Guelph; in England, Richard Allport, Ted Chandler, Christopher Day, Jill Hewson, Susanna Penman, Onno Wieringa, and the nutritionists Ivan Berger and Amanda Hawthorne; in France, Patrick Pageat; in Japan, Kiyoshi Kawase; in Norway, Jorunn Grondalen, Oslo University; in Scotland, John Rohrbach, (who contributed his 30 years' clinical experience in herbal veterinary medicine); in the United States, Tony Buffington, Ohio State University, Karen Overall, University of Pennsylvania, Elizabeth Lund, University of Minnesota, Lisa Freeman, Tufts University, Neils Pedersen and Benjamin Hart, University of California, James Richards, Cornell University Feline Health Center, and Jean Dodds.

Thanks too, for their creativity and flair to the Dorling Kindersley group, all of whom I've worked with before and look forward to working with again: Tracie Lee Davis, Anna Benjamin, Edward Bunting, and Sonia Charbonnier, and to Tracy Morgan for her usual photographic excellence. Finally, I really appreciate how the staff at my veterinary clinic made sure I didn't feel guilty when I took time off to write. Special thanks to everyone at the clinic: Manda Hackett, Hester Small, Tina Leake, Ashley McManus, Jenny Berry, Bas Hagreis, Grant Petrie, and Simon Tai.

Bibliography

Canine and Feline Nutrition, Linda Case, Daniel P. Carey, & Diane A. Hirakawa, Mosby, St. Louis, 1995

Consultations in Feline Internal Medicine, Editor, John R. August, W.B. Saunders, Philadelphia, 1994 and 1997

The Encyclopedia of Complementary Medicine, Anne Woodham & Dr David Peters, Dorling Kindersley, London, 1998

Evolution and Healing, the New Science of Darwinian Medicine, Randolph M. Nesse & George C. Williams, Weidenfeld & Nicolson, London, 1995

The Handbook of Alternative and Complementary Medicine, Stephen Fulder, Oxford University Press, Oxford, 1996

The Handbook of Human Stress and Immunity, Editors, Ronald Glaser & Janice Kiecolt-Glaser, Academic Press, London, 1994

The Homeopathic Treatment of Small Animals, Christopher Day, C.W. Daniel Co. Ltd., Saffron Walden, 1992

Molecules of Emotion, Why You Feel The Way You Feel, Candace Pert, Simon & Schuster, London, 1998

Myofascial Pain and Dysfunction, Janet Travell & David Simons, Williams & Wilkins, Baltimore, 1986

Textbook of Complementary and Alternative Veterinary Medicine, Editors, Alan Schoen & Susan Wynn, Mosby, London, 1998

Good general websites and starting points to other sites are:

Algy's Herb Page; AltVetMed; Animal Chiropractic and Holistic Health Forum; Herbs Research Foundation; Martindale's Health Science Guide; Virtual Library Animal Health; Virtual Library Veterinary Medicine.

Publisher's Acknowledgments

Photography: Tracy Morgan, Steve Gorton

Additional photography: Peter Anderson, Jane Burton, Peter Chadwick, Andy Crawford, Marc Henrie, Dave King, Martin Norris, Tim Ridley, Colin Walton

Artwork: Janos Marffy

Index: Margaret McCormack

Editorial assistance: Edward Bunting, Sharon Lucas

Thanks to the following practitioners: Margie Craib BSc BHSI MC MIPC; Tracy Crook MCSP SRP, Chartered Physiotherapist; Onno Wieringa BA Vet MB MRCVS lic Ac

Thanks to the following owners and their cats: Brenda Bowgen – *Smokey and Sam*; Judy Cooper – *Benji*; Fiona Kerr – *Frank and Phoebe*; Jackie Tucker – *Sefa and Lily*; Onno Wieringa – *Zilla*

Picture Credits

The publisher would like to thank the following for their kind permission to reproduce their photographs:

a=above, c=centre, b=below, l=left, r=right, t=top

Animal Photography: Sally Anne Thompson 56-57, 97 br, Sally-Anne Thompson 19; **Ardea London Ltd:** 115 t, Chris Martin Bahr 119 bl, Francois Gohier 99 br, John Daniels 22-23, 41 tr, 147 t, 151 t; **BBC Natural History Unit:** Dietmar Nill 66 drop in, Ingo Bartussek 96 b; **British Chiropractic Association: British Museum, London:** 85 tr; 78 tr; **Bruce Coleman Ltd:** Fritz Prenzel 65 tr, Hans Reinhard 4 r, 34, 101 cr, Jane Burton 47 bl, 113 t, Paul van Gaalen 8-9, Werner Layer 104-105, 108 b; **FLPA:** Gerard Lacz 1 c, 68 tr, Mark Newman 84 b, Richard Brooks 2-3; **Werner Forman Archive:** 62 bc; **Image Bank:** Janeart 24; **Network:** Hans Silvester/Rapho 38-9, 38-9, Rapho 118 b; **NHPA:** Agence Natura 156 tl, Gerard Lacz 6 bl, Stephen Dalton 43 br; **Oxford Scientific Films:** Daniel Valla 60 bl, Deni Brown 143 b, Donald Specker 115 bl, Hans Reinhard/Okapia 85 br, 97 tl; **Pharo Communications:** 127 tr; **RSPCA:** 111 tr, Angela Hampton 11 b; **Science Photo Library:** David Scharf 116 b, 117 t, Dr Kari Lounatmaa 87 tl, Eye of Science 139 t, Jim Steinberg 7 tl; **The Stock Market:** Zefa/Spichtinger 160 b; **Warren Photographic:** Jane Burton 31, 40 bl, 82 b, 121 t, 133 t, 142 t, 149 t, 154 tr; **The Wellcome Trust:** F. Croll 93 tl; **Woodfall Wild Images:** M. Biancarelli 11